सत्यमेव जयते

With the Compliments

of

The High Commissioner of India

Shri Sanjay Suri,
with best wishes,
G. Kumar

Oct 27, '21

THE
MODI
DOCTRINE

THE
MODI
DOCTRINE

New Paradigms in
India's Foreign Policy

Foreword by
Arun Jaitley

Editors

Anirban Ganguly | Vijay Chauthaiwale | Uttam Kumar Sinha

wisdom
tree

In association with

Dr. Syama Prasad Mookerjee
Research Foundation

ISBN 978-81-8328-483-7

Published by
Wisdom Tree
4779/23, Ansari Road
Darya Ganj, New Delhi-110 002
Ph.: 011-23247966/67/68
wisdomtreebooks@gmail.com

Printed in India

CONTENTS

THEMATICALLY TIED TO THE WORLD

FOREWORD

For Prime Minister Narendra Modi, foreign policy has been high priority. In a fast-changing multipolar world to which India is intricately connected, no Indian leader has shown such remarkable understanding to simplify an otherwise complex situation. By surveying, responding and where possible, moulding the international environment, Prime Minister Modi is finding answers to the questions of India's national interests.

The emphasis is clearly to be seen. In the past two years, India's proactive and pragmatic diplomatic initiatives have led to high-level engagement with unprecedented number of countries. India's global footprint is scripting the narrative about India from one of a flailing power to that of a resurgent global force; from being a balancer to becoming a leader, from following rules to making rules and setting agendas. This is nothing but transformational with tangible outcomes.

Diplomacy has got a go-getting edge. The best way to show this is through facts. Foreign investment is up 40 per cent. India jumped sixteen spots on the World Economic Forum's global competitive index and was ninth in UNCTAD investment attractiveness ranking. Indeed, India is now viewed as the most attractive investment destination. Investment and infrastructure are drivers of India's diplomacy for development. Some noted outcomes have been the India–USA Infrastructure Investment Fund with a target of US$75 billion; the French Agency for Development (AFD) providing two billion Euros credit line; India–UK Partnership Fund under National Infrastructure Investment Fund (NIIF) and India–UAE Infrastructure Fund for rapid expansion of next generation infrastructure.

Connectivity has been another defining aspect of Prime Minister Modi's foreign policy. As a natural leader reaching out and connecting to his domestic constituency, likewise, and astutely, he readily connects to other foreign leaders whether from small or big nations. There is a return value in his outreach as can be seen in fast-tracking the transport sector with collaboration and joint ventures. Japan is to build India's first bullet train and high-speed rail links; the government-backed rupee bond is to be launched in London for railway infrastructure; France and Germany are to fund Metro projects and build electric locomotive plant; partnership with the USA is underway to make transportation secure and efficient and with China plans are afoot for a railway university.

The 'Neighbourhood First' approach has revitalised South Asia as never before. Prime Minister Modi's leadership has tried to transcend the gloomy atmosphere of mistrust and hostility through bold re-engagement. By signing the Land Boundary Agreement with Bangladesh, welcoming the democratic transformation in Myanmar, nurturing an all-weather friendship with Bhutan and launching India's largest disaster relief operation abroad in Nepal, the image of India as a positive regional power has taken a new frame, reaffirming the leitmotif *Sabka Saath, Sabka Vikas*, or 'Together with all, Progress for all'.

Even small-island nations like Maldives and Mauritius become inclusive to this philosophy. The comprehensive nature of cooperation with the South Asian states is a dominant theme not a domineering one. Continued commitment towards reconstruction and development in Afghanistan, pushing the frontiers of ties with Sri Lanka by granting US$318 million LOC for railway and currency swap agreement of US$1.5 billion to help stabilise the Sri Lankan rupee define regional policies that are enduring and that bind India to the region.

At the global level, Prime Minister Modi has been successful in raising India's economic profile and calling on the diasporic community to actively participate in the reform drive for a stronger India, which the IMF MD Christine Lagarde described as a 'bright spot' on an otherwise 'cloudy global horizon'. India's development agenda is closely aligned to the Sustainable Development Goals; advocacy of climate justice, elimination of poverty and harmony with nature. The grand narrative of Prime Minister Modi is actually simply a potent reminder that democracy remains the pathway to prosperity.

The two years of the NDA government's foreign policy have been one of problem-solving and solution-driven in which engagement with the world is paramount to the development path that India has taken. India's transformation is aspirational, people-centric, non-elitist and even subaltern.

The chapters in this volume bring out the different facets of Prime Minister Modi's foreign policy since May 2014. The striking feature of the volume is the acclaimed profile of its contributors many of whom are foreign nationals or Indians settled abroad. They are not only experienced experts but express their views with candidness and without fear and favour. Some, among these, have actually been involved in strategising the Prime Minister's global outreach while some are practitioners of diplomacy. The Editors have emphasised on objective assessments and the challenges that the future presents. And rightly so, for it is important to get the pulse of the world on many of the initiatives undertaken by the government. Yet the authors remain much in unison and emphatically underline that with Modi at the helm of affairs, India is set to leverage its role and make itself a 'diplomatic superpower'.

I commend Dr Syama Prasad Mookerjee Research Foundation (SPMRF), its director Dr Anirban Ganguly and his able co-editors, Dr Vijay Chauthaiwale and Dr Uttam Kumar Sinha, for having conceived and executed this project in such a short time frame. This volume shall, I am sure, become essential reading for all those who wish to make an assessment or undertake a study of the foreign policy vision of the BJP-led NDA government under Prime Minister Modi.

—Arun Jaitley
Minister of Finance and Corporate Affairs
Government of India

MODI'S FOREIGN POLICY AS PROBLEM SOLVING

It is commonly assumed that leaders find foreign affairs easy picking, proclaiming to set the world right, if not on fire and grandiosely advancing the country's image. For Prime Minister Narendra Modi, however, global understanding is not about ridiculous assertions or claims, but a firm belief that in an age of a glocalised, polycentric world, which is uniquely tied with prosperity and vulnerability, foreign policy is closer home than ever before. In fact in many ways it begins at home. As the world's fastest growing free market and the most populous democracy, India's footprint on international affairs is a reality, as much as the truth that poverty is India's biggest challenge.

What foremost underlines the Modi government's foreign policy orientation, specifically in terms of its distinction with the past, is the ability to make it less argumentative and more problem-solving by scanning a range of alternatives and taking optimising decisions. And therefore, what makes Modi's methodology so influential is his reading of the cultural, political and economic structures at play within a global society. There is much more to the Prime Minister's foreign policy approach than just the 'charm offensive' that many seem to have been spellbound about and thus failing to go beyond the theatrics of the visits. The Modi magic or his ice-breaking style or even the freeze selfie moments are structurally conditioned wherein the strategic, economic and demographic forces frame the context of his decisions—a natural internationalist, advocating greater political and economic cooperation.

During his visit to Malaysia in November 2015, Prime Minister Modi unveiled a twelve-feet bronze statue of Swami Vivekananda, saying, 'Swami was given by God to India, I will give his statue to Malaysia'. But there is something beyond this symbolic act. Like Swami Vivekananda, a *vishwatma*—the spirit of the universe—Modi is viewing the world in terms of possibilities rather than risks. There is courage and conviction to determine the international order and positively shape relationships whether it is in the immediate neighbourhood or with the wider world. Seeking resources, technology and good practices from international partners is a spirit that drives the Prime Minister. The context cannot be missed. In his foreign policy orientation, Modi first seeks to understand and then be understood.

Modi's approach to global affairs is based on linking India's foreign policy to domestic transformation. While on the one hand, his policies seek to attract foreign capital, technology and open foreign markets for Indian products, on the other, the policies are geared towards regional stability, peace and prosperity. He has earnestly pursued the NDA government's flagship programmes like Make in India, Digital India, Smart Cities, Clean Ganga, Swachh Bharat, Skill India and Startup India. There is a development story in Modi's foreign policy.

One of Modi's remarkable accomplishments has been to energise and enthuse the Indian diaspora. The diaspora has emerged as a significant factor in domestic politics of several countries including the USA and the UK. The other notable achievement has been an emphasis towards the 'Neighbourhood First' and 'Act East' policies.

The 'Neighbourhood First' has been Modi's most significant initiative. Relations with Bangladesh have witnessed a decisive upswing with ratification by India of the Land Boundary Agreement (LBA) which had been pending since 1974. Ties with Sri Lanka have moved positively with the change in domestic leadership there. Relations with Nepal and Maldives have not been easy but Modi's policies continue to be engaging and forward looking.

Prime Minister Modi's vision and approach to foreign policy never cease to amaze. Even the most studied critics will agree that he has demonstrated a consistent, deft and sophisticated functioning. The personal rapport established with Barack Obama and with other world leaders like Shinzo Abe and Angela

Merkel have significantly enhanced India's profile and given it a confidence never seen before.

The interest that Modi has generated in China acquires even greater significance. For one, China and India are rivals, who simultaneously cooperate, contest and compete. Despite China being economically stronger, it is to Modi's credit that he has positioned India at a comparable level with China. Interestingly, if there is any country that Modi has a good account and understanding of, it is China. As the chief minister of Gujarat he visited China four times. This prior experience and knowledge has enabled Modi to economically and culturally connect with China in the wider framework of peace and development. At another level, addressing China's strategic rise is an equally important dimension of Modi's foreign policy so that India retains its influence and equally cushions itself from not becoming marginalised in the larger US–China contest.

And finally, Modi's visit to Iran, coinciding with the two years of the NDA government, embodies careful assessment and complexity management of the changing context in which Iran is now a stable and resourceful country. A non-ideological, pro-development vision to link India .o Iran and then to Central Asia and Europe through 'connectivity trade, investment and energy partnership' are purposive engagements that values Iran as it integrates with the world market.

India's participation in the development of the Chabahar Port and a tri-lateral pact to build a land transit-and-trade corridor through Afghanistan are stepping stones for bigger future involvement. As the Prime Minister of India, Modi has the right head on his shoulder, and can plan and take decisions.

Two years at the helm of affairs is a decent length of time for some earnest stock-taking especially as foreign policy has been a high priority area for the Indian government. Prime Minister Narendra Modi in his time in office has set a scorching pace of global engagement. His first visit was in June 2014 to Bhutan and thereafter he undertook visits to forty countries in five continents till April 2016.

To date in 2016, in the two years of his time thus far, Modi's policies have enhanced India's engagement globally with new thought and ideas and a believable wisdom for a stable and peaceful world.

XVIII | THE MODI DOCTRINE

Modi's world vision has been complimented by the External Affairs Ministry and Sushma Swaraj, as the first Indian woman foreign minister, has ably consolidated the Prime Minister's overseas engagement. Her political experience and dynamism has kept steady continuity in India's foreign policy and her natural ability to engage with the public has helped India to negotiate testing and emotional times, for example, the evacuation of nearly 4000 stranded Indians from war-torn Yemen in April 2015. But quite remarkable has been her humility in acknowledging the hard work of the previous UPA government when the amendment bill regarding the Land Boundary Agreement with Bangladesh was passed unanimously in the Lok Sabha in May 2015. The dynamism of both the Prime Minister and the External Affairs Minister brings in a new approach to foreign policy, one that is coordinated and consultative and equally empathetic.

The volume is divided into three sections and has contribution from twenty-three authors of which fifteen are international. The first section titled 'Modi a Global Leader but India First' captures the Prime Minister's nuanced approach, his leadership and understanding of world affairs. The second section 'Rajmandala of Bilateral and Regional Connect' has country-specific essays that build on the bilateral momentum and examine the future prospects. The third section 'Thematically Tied to the World' contextualises and examines India's pattern of engagement through the lens of development imperatives. The themes become the categories for analysis of Modi's foreign policy.

MODI: A GLOBAL LEADER BUT INDIA FIRST

The role of a global leader is extremely challenging and complex. A typical global leader has more work to do, more people to meet, has less direct authority and has to grapple with continuous flow of information. A striking aspect is that global leaders do not require prior international experience to be one. Foresight defines a leader—a clear vision for the country and its people and the ability to build a consensus to achieve the vision. The authors in this section delve into some of Modi's characteristics, conscience and charisma in the global context and evaluate its impact.

Cleo Paskal observes in her write-up, the foreign policy implementation as the 'layered, reasoned vision of Prime Minister Narendra Modi' but also feels that there is much work still to be done. In a rational assessment, Paskal informs that while Modi indeed focused on the regional countries and the major powers, he also identified and consolidated overlooked opportunities. Citing some of the Prime Minister's visits, for example to United Arab Emirates (UAE), Seychelles, Mongolia and Fiji, she writes that apart from the value of the visits themselves, at a very pragmatic level these trips have given fillip to India experts in the receiving countries, easing the way for future Indian engagement.

Ramesh Thakur views Modi as both the most internationalist Prime Minister since Jawaharlal Nehru and also the most clear-headed in articulating India's interests. He then highlights why multilateralism matters and how India will have to demonstrate ideational as well as political leadership in multilateral forums. Thakur further argues that India will need to exercise creative diplomacy in order to combine the protection of national interests with the representation of a developing country and Asian interests and feels that Modi is suitably placed to execute it.

Sreeram Chaulia in his essay examines the 'three Ds'—democracy, demography-demand and diaspora—as the fulcrum of Modi's foreign policy. Prime Minister Modi, to the author, represents a radically different India in which the diaspora or the 'extended family abroad' is a critical driver that requires to be harnessed. Modi is a true messenger, according to the author, spreading, what he describes, 'India's ethos of *Vasudhaiva Kutumbakam* (the world is one family), Vivekananda's gospel of spiritual oneness of humankind, Mahatma Gandhi's non-violence and ecological conservation and the Indian model of "live and let live" multicultural coexistence.' Chaulia very succinctly explains that there is a 're-imagination of who is Indian' and this is becoming a force to reckon before the world.

RAJMANDALA OF BILATERAL AND REGIONAL CONNECT

The major thrust of Modi's bilateral engagements has been to draw investment and technology by resuscitating stalled ties and removing hesitation and strategic confusion in dealing with strategically important countries and regions. Modi's robust engagements have led to promising investments but more will still be required. In the neighbourhood, which is India's existential space, Modi's mission has been to remove the perception of India being domineering, which creates fear and notions of interference and resentment. For that, he has approached bilateral relations in the region with a framework of connectivity and regional infrastructure development for a better quality of life to the people and a chance to prosper. Sensitivity, mutual trust and confidence and seeking solutions to outstanding issues define his bilateral engagement. In this section, foreign experts, along with some Indian analysts, express their views on aspects of the outcomes of Modi's foreign policy.

Pakistan continues to throw challenges at Modi's leadership despite his reach-out to Islamabad on more than one occasion. Balancing restraint with assertiveness is being seen as a remarkable feature of Prime Minister's foreign policy in view of the bold yet controlled action—post-Uri terrorist attacks—taken with decisiveness and an unprecedented political, diplomatic and military coordination. Yet and impressively so, the Prime Minister continues to reshape the public discourse on India-Pakistan relations and redefine the terms of victory. At the BJP national council meeting in Kozhikode in Kerala on 24 September 2016, while addressing a public rally, Modi challenged Pakistan to compete with it in a 'war on illiteracy, poverty and unemployment'.

By choosing to work diplomatically towards ensuring Pakistan's isolation and giving the army the tactical and operational autonomy to bust the terror camps across the LoC, speaks of a leadership that is measured and in control and has the courage to respond. Importantly and very clearly, past precedents are not binding on Modi's government while responding to terror attacks from Pakistan.

The terrorists attack on the army camp in Uri that killed nineteen soldiers is the backdrop for Ashok Malik's analyses of the 29 September pre-emptive strike across the LoC. The author describes it as being 'rare' and different from the past as it was publicly acknowledged by both the army and the government. Malik examines the diplomatic context which has been crafted by the Prime Minister over the last two years that made the strike impressive. Importantly to the author, it was the ability and willingness to strike, as distinct from the strike itself, that had the world watching.

In analysing India–US relations since 2014, Lisa Curtis observes that Modi's emphasis on building ties with the US demonstrates a calibrated distancing from the non-alignment patterns of Indian foreign policymaking. More specifically by pursuing enhanced defence and security ties with the US, Modi is willing to risk Chinese anger. In fact, Modi is willing to pursue a more proactive approach to coping with challenges from China. The author underlines the fact that the US will be critical in transforming India into a global power, which Modi clearly wishes.

Tariq Karim in his essay makes a cardinal point that 'good boundaries between neighbours, devoid of contention, make for good neighbourliness'. He expresses with a degree of pride that India and Bangladesh are accustomed to resolving border disputes amicably with no third-party mediation or intervention. The author appreciates the Modi government for quickly ratifying the LBA and the Maritime Boundary dispute, which has given great impetus to resolving other bilateral issues. Karim believes that strengthening cooperative bilateral relations between India and Bangladesh hold the key to making subregional cooperation feasible.

Lord Bilimoria also assesses Modi's foreign policy in the context of his visit to the UK. He picks up Modi's Wembley speech as an embodiment of his vision for India in all its elements and which clearly articulated India–UK relations as one of equals. One of Modi's greatest challenges, according to the author, is to ensure that his reforms and India's growth is inclusive and must take the challenges and needs of people living in rural areas into account. India's greatest resource is its 1.25 billion people. Lord Bilimoria is convinced that India's entrepreneurship, which was suppressed in the past, has been unleashed under Modi's stewardship.

Asanga Abeyagoonasekera observes the leadership role of Narendra Modi in South Asia and believes that Prime Minister Modi and Prime Minister Ranil Wickramasinghe are very similar in their outlook and value technology innovation to improve peoples' lives. The author states that many of Modi's domestic reforms like tackling corruption, policy transparency and consultation with provincial leaders are to be valued and incorporated by other South Asian leaders. While India and Sri Lanka are long-standing allies and commercial partners, however, they do need to seek points of closer intersection rather than detachment. Abeyagoonasekera is hopeful that Modi can give the right confidence to help create space for closer economic integration between India and Sri Lanka.

Echoing the general impression of Modi's leadership in South Asia, Hari Bansh Jha regards Modi as the first Prime Minister to realise the importance of the neighbours for India's own prosperity. He also views Modi as a statesman—having perceived that Nepal would fall into difficulties if the Constitution

XXII | THE MODI DOCTRINE

that was in the drafting process was not made inclusive. Following his own consensus-based functioning, Modi, the author writes, advised the political leaders of the country to draft consensus-based Constitution so that every section of the population could take ownership. The author is quite blunt to say that the Nepalese leadership overlooked the 'friendly suggestion' from Modi while promulgating the Constitution on 20 September 2015.

Shakti Sinha reviews India–Afghanistan relations in the backdrop of Prime Minister Modi's visit to Kabul in December 2015 to inaugurate the Parliament building, built with Indian assistance. He describes India's commitment to development partnership with Afghanistan as unwavering despite the perceived marginalisation of not having found a place in the Afghan peace process. The author firmly believes that the Modi government has been wise to fast-track India's development projects in Afghanistan and must continue to support the legitimate Afghan government's efforts to bring peace, stability and development to its people.

Shahab Khan also agrees like other neighbourhood experts, that despite strong historical and cultural consonance, bilateral relations in the region have only recently, under the leadership of Modi, practically realised the benefits. The author fears that the upward swing in India–Bangladesh relations and the sustainability of the ties will be subjected to the harsh reality of public perception in Bangladesh. Khan is, however, confident that if both the countries complement each other as economic hubs, then together they can promote growth and prosperity in South Asia. On the other hand, the more the two countries keep straining their relations, at least at the perception level, the process of intra-regional cooperation will lose momentum.

Takenori Horimoto earnestly expresses that India–Japan relations are at an all-time high. His essay describes the evolution of the two countries' engagement from the time Indira Gandhi visited Japan in 1969 and then in 1982 to the liberalisation of India's economic policy and the disintegration of the Soviet Union, to the rapid advance of China and the shift of US policy to Asia. Horimoto describes Modi's leadership with the clear strategic objective of balancing economic growth with defence capabilities or what can be described as prosperity and power. He goes on to say that for Modi, a strong economy is the foundation of his diplomacy.

'India–Germany Relationship' is co-authored by Christian Wagner and

Gaurav Sharma. The authors explore the many complementarities in the growing partnership between India and Germany. While Germany is a key provider of high-end technology and has surplus capital, India offers a growing middle class, a stable political system and is looking for more technology and capital investment. They further explore India–Germany relations through the prism of security interface, economic engagement, scientific and cultural exchange, energy cooperation and human development. The authors also suggest exploring other areas like Afghanistan and the Indian Ocean where the two countries' leadership can enhance cooperation.

P Stobdan, with a geo-philosophical interpretation, expresses Modi's foreign policy outlook as cast in India's glorious past with modern content. As a case in point he analyses Modi's visit to the five Central Asian states. India for the first time seems to have understood the deeper underpinnings of pursuing its overarching interests. The author finds Modi's reconnection to Central Asia as crucial in the strategic frame whether it is the cultural contact with Uzbekistan or the energy-rich Kazakhstan and Turkmenistan or the huge hydro-potential of Kyrgyzstan or even the historical affinity and strategic significance of Tajikistan. Stobdan, however, cautions that India should be mindful that the Central Asian countries' position on key security issues will ultimately be guided by China and Russia.

Gonchig Ganbold describes Mongolia as India's spiritual neighbour with shared cultural, religious and spiritual legacies. Modi's visit to Mongolia and gifting saplings of the Banyan tree to the main Buddhist monastery was an expression of the closeness through the teachings of Buddha. Ganbold elaborates how the principles of Buddhism have helped define Mongolia's philosophy of permanent neutrality, a core feature of its foreign policy. He recalls his meeting with Modi as inspirational and how honoured he was to be appointed as Mongolia's ambassador to India soon after. His essay also describes picturesquely the natural and cultural landscape of Mongolia encouraging Indians to visit the country that he says is the 'land of the eternal blue sky'.

THEMATICALLY TIED TO THE WORLD

The world is one of overlapping identities and interests. Modi's ability to explore universal ideas and situate it within the context of India's traditional culture is quite extraordinary. Some enduring themes like climate change, water, energy, economy and defence that connect the world with risks and opportunities have strongly scripted Modi's vision for a modern India, which according to him needs to 'refine, rebuild and transform the national character'. Understanding the Indian heritage and approaching the world in a non-doctrinaire way broadly sums up Modi's pragmatism in foreign policy.

Mukul Asher explains in his essay that Prime Minister Modi's government has unhesitatingly based its diplomacy with the explicit recognition that the country's leverage is dependent primarily on the size of the Indian economy, its growth trajectory, and the country's ability to address challenges. This, according to the author, is crucial if India is to become a US$10 trillion economy by 2032 (from US$2.05 trillion in 2014), and to create 175 million jobs by 2032. Achieving these goals will have an impact on how India is perceived externally as a partner. But, importantly, it will depend on the internal reforms and initiatives which the country undertakes.

Another crucially important theme for Modi has been rivers and the Clean Ganga programme, which Martin Grambow, Uttam Sinha and Hans-Dietrich Uhl explore. It is possibly one of the most modernising policy approaches of the government. Water is indispensable to governance, expressed as *sujalam sufalam* (water for prosperity) and Swachh Bharat Abhiyan. It is also a key instrument of regional prosperity and integration. The essay acknowledges shared experiences by highlighting some of the key situations that rivers in Germany have gone through on their way from once being heavily polluted and abused to today's good balance in water management.

Virendra Gupta picks up the theme of energy security as a key driver of India's sustained development and highlights Modi's abiding interest in the issue. The government's priority attention to relations with India's traditional as well as potential oil and gas suppliers is reflective of the government's concern for ensuring an uninterrupted supply of energy resources to fuel the economic growth. The author also highlights Modi's sensitivity for global environmental concerns and the government's push forward on renewables while importantly not abandoning the coal sector which is crucial to the new thrust for manufacturing activities.

The gloomy economic scenario of India in 2012, 2013 and early 2014 forms the backdrop of Manoj Ladwa's explanation of how Modi has turned conventional wisdom on its head when he took it upon himself to become the prime marketeer for the Indian economy. Resultantly, India was the world's top destination for Foreign Direct Investment (FDI) flows in 2015. Modi, argues the author, has not only effectively projected India as the new land of opportunity but also deftly played the saviour, by arguing the case that Make in India is not about job taking but about helping global partners become more competitive. Clearly, India now has strategic interests beyond its shores.

In exploring some of the dimensions of the Modi government's defence outreach, Nitin Gokhale expresses the view that the emphasis on using military goodwill is an important instrument in strengthening bilateral relations. He also cautions that the military role should be confined to purely professional exchanges and exercises, leaving the political dimension to the Ministry of External Affairs (MEA). The author calls for an urgent need to reset defence diplomacy given the Indian military's long tradition, professionalism, high standards of training and its much appreciated involvement in numerous United Nations (UN) Peacekeeping Missions.

In his essay, Satish Chandra strongly defends India's quest for Nuclear Suppliers Group (NSG) membership and gives a thumbs-up to India's diplomacy. Describing Modi as hands-on and prepared to stake his personal reputation when national interests so dictate, the author, is confident that such pro-active diplomacy sets in motion processes that will ultimately triumph. In any case, the question is not if but when India will become an NSG member. Chandra cites India's recent admission as a member of the Missile Technology Control Regime (MTCR) as an instance of one such success which can be attributed to the government's activist diplomacy.

In the final essay, Anirban Ganguly describes the five supporting pillars (*Panchamrit*) of India's foreign policy under Prime Minister Narendra Modi. These are *Samman*—dignity and honour; *Samvad*—greater engagement and dialogue; *Samriddhi*—shared prosperity; *Suraksha*—regional and global security; and *Sanskriti evam Sabhyata*—cultural and civilisational linkages. Ganguly feels that the foundation for this civilisational outreach and soft power engagement was initiated in August 2014 when Modi visited Japan. While trade, economy and security remain the dominant themes, the overarching symbolism of the civilisational connect is unmistakably imprinted in Modi's way of looking at the world.

CONCLUSION

The volume is an early attempt to assess the possible contours of an evolving doctrine. Yes, power does produce discourse and no leading statesman can thus escape the problem of doctrine. However, it is not final or inalterable and certainly does not take away a more nuanced conversation among foreign affairs experts and watcher of multiple perspectives leading to a higher level of public debate.

It is always important to speak truth to power, not for it and this volume precisely reflects this. The essays compiled in the volume are objectively written assessing both the foreign policy approach of Prime Minister Narendra Modi and the opportunities and challenges that the future presents. A common thread runs through the expressions and that an integrated India to the world increasingly shaped by its developmental priorities would require further steam and sharpening of foreign issues. The leitmotif of the articles is that India's approach to the world has begun to fundamentally alter, reshape and reposition.

—**Editors**

Modi: A Global Leader but India First

CHAPTER 1

THE MODI PHENOMENON: REBOOTING INDIAN FOREIGN POLICY

Cleo Paskal

An effective foreign policy has, at the very least, a guiding vision, focused execution and a consistent reassessment of tactics designed to support that vision as conditions change. Watching the implementation of the layered, reasoned vision of Prime Minister Narendra Modi's foreign policy during his first two years in power has been like getting a master class in geopolitics, while at the same time realising how much work there is still left to be done.

To understand the accomplishments of Modi's foreign policy and the challenges it faces, it helps to first examine the international context, then the broad brushstrokes of Modi's vision, the implementation, and finally assess potential future innovations.

THE WORLD IN 2014

When the BJP came to power in 2014, the world was in flux and Indian foreign policy had been, at best, paralysed.

For the previous decade, at least, China's influence had been growing across Asia, Africa and South America, in some regions and sectors displacing Western interests. Meanwhile, failed engagement in Libya facilitated a cascade of crises across the region, the Islamic State (IS) was cannibalising Syria and Iraq, the US and Iran had yet to reach a deal, China was embarking on massive marine engineering in disputed maritime zones, Japan was becoming more assertive and oil was trading at over US$100.

Given the geopolitical and geoeconomic fragmentation and uncertainty, many nations desired a closer partnership with a stronger India. Some African countries wanted a complement to Western and Chinese economic engagement—building on established pathways that had provided, for example, low cost, reliable pharmaceuticals. Japan wanted a strategic partner to balance China. China wanted more economic engagement in part for long-term strategic reasons. The US wanted an ally in the Indian Ocean and possibly beyond. Vietnam wanted an ally in the Pacific. Most countries, it seemed, wanted something from India, on their own terms.

However, it had been a long time since India was considered even an effective regional power. Delhi's impotence in the face of Maldivian upheavals was a reminder of India's contracted state. Once the election results were announced, global eyes turned to Delhi to see what would happen next.

Modi's Vision

The underpinnings of Modi's foreign policy vision could be found in the BJP election manifesto 2014:

> The vision is to fundamentally reboot and reorient the foreign policy goals, content and process, in a manner that locates India's global strategic engagement in a new paradigm and on a wider canvass, that is not just limited to political diplomacy, but also includes our economic, scientific, cultural, political and security interests, both regional and global, on the principles of equality and mutuality, so that it leads to an economically stronger India, and its voice is heard in the international fora.

From the start, Modi has demonstrated a consistent, deft and sophisticated vision. His goal of achieving 10 per cent annual growth combined with policies to provide for the needs of the 'last man in line' is contingent on reinvigorating India's economy. Reinvigorating the economy includes promoting stability and influence, and encouraging foreign investors to make in India. As a result, Modi's foreign policy, which is really just an extension and facilitator of his domestic policy, prioritises trade and investment for inclusive growth. It has been very much led from the top and has been straightforward and business-like.

Modi began by openly consolidating India's regional base. By inviting South Asian Association for Regional Cooperation (SAARC) leaders to his inauguration, Modi highlighted the neighbourhood's importance to India and India's importance to the neighbourhood. The photos of the SAARC leaders together on the dais to welcome India's new Prime Minister showed not only the region, but the world, that 'India is back' and that Modi's India was going to be very different than the one the world had seen in recent decades.

Modi then made clear his goals of stability and inclusive growth. He emphasised Make in India and encouraged entrepreneurship. On the international front, that meant doing what anyone expanding their business would do, going forth and publicising their product, in this case India. However, given the inclusive growth directive, Modi emphasised that India wasn't looking for just any partners. It was looking for the right partners. 'Red lines' were made clear, thereby avoiding the most unrealistic expectations.

Potential partners appreciated the approach. During the COP negotiations, White House spokesman Josh Earnest told reporters that Modi 'is honest and direct. He is also somebody that has a clear vision for where he wants to take his country. And that makes him not just an effective politician but an effective Prime Minister.'

Another thing that helped Modi to be effective was an adept understanding and leveraging of partners' priorities. That allowed him to secure major gains for India. One clear example of this was Modi's September 2014 visit to New York City for the General Assembly of the United Nations. This was Modi's first visit to the US as Prime Minister and media inimical to the changes in India were looking for reasons to call the visit a failure. Modi upped the ante by holding an unprecedented event at Madison Square Garden in New York for approximately 18,000, mostly Indian-American, supporters.

On stage with Modi were over three-dozen members of the US Congress, including Senate Foreign Relations Committee chair Democratic Senator Bob Menendez and the Indian-American Republican governor of South Carolina, Nikki Haley. The US politicians were there because Indian-Americans are coveted supporters. They are not permanently tied to either party and are well above the US average in education and wealth. They are potentially influential voters and donors.

Modi pulled in the Indian-Americans, the Indian-Americans pulled in the members of Congress, which couldn't help but attract the attention of the White House. In one deft move Modi showed US politicians that he held sway over a section of their own political system. No world leader had ever done anything even remotely similar on the sidelines of the General Assembly before.

Four months later, President Obama visited India and Obama and Modi declared a mutual desire to build not just a bilateral strategic relationship, but also to develop a much deeper 'global partnership'. Since then, the relationship has deepened, with the Pentagon setting up a cell specifically devoted to facilitating cooperation with India. It is the only Pentagon country-specific cell.

However, Modi didn't just focus on the regional countries and the major powers. He also identified and consolidated overlooked opportunities. Many of his trips, for example to the UAE and the Seychelles, were the first visits by an Indian Prime Minister in decades. In some cases, for example Mongolia, it was the first visit ever. Apart from the value of the visits themselves, at a very pragmatic level these trips meant India experts in the receiving countries were suddenly bumped up in importance in their own bureaucracies, easing the way for future Indian engagement.

The order of the visits was also carefully calibrated. The trip to Pakistan didn't come until after visits to most other neighbours and major powers. But there was still a visit, a visual demonstration that India is willing to try, making it more difficult for those who wanted to paint India as obstructionist.

All in all, Modi's choice, scheduling and handling of foreign visits have been close to flawless. But have they achieved the desired outcome?

IMPLEMENTATION

In 2014, India got a new government but it still had the same bureaucracy, legal system and, in many cases, information networks. There has been a quiet, concerted effort to make those systems a bit more fit for purpose. For example, in a foreign policy context, the existing Indian Foreign Service has been bolstered by a number of outside area specialists, and Twitter has been enlisted to facilitate interaction between Indians abroad and High Commissions. Additionally, under Modi, India has vastly increased the number of countries eligible for e-visas, showing long-term commitment to establishing closer relations.

However, major impediments to implementing Modi's vision remain. An instructive case in point is Modi's outreach to the fourteen Pacific Island

Countries (PICs): the Cook Islands, Federated states of Micronesia, Fiji, Kiribati, Marshall Islands, Nauru, Niue, Palau, Papua New Guinea, Samoa, Solomon Islands, Kingdom of Tonga, Tuvalu and Vanuatu.

While small in population, the PICs cover around one-sixth of the planet's surface—a vast and increasingly strategic zone between Asia and the Americas. The area includes critical trade routes, large fisheries and other resources, and the PICs are an increasingly crucial voting bloc in international forums, including for seats on the United Nations Security Council (UNSC). Traditionally West-oriented, in the last decade China has vastly increased its influence in the region, including in Fiji.

In November 2014, Modi became the first Indian Prime Minster to visit Fiji in over three decades. While there, he met with leaders from the fourteen PICs. Two days later Chinese President Xi Jinping visited Fiji as well. Underlining India's potential advantage, Xi only met leaders from eight PICs as the others have relations with Taiwan.

In August 2015, Modi sought to maintain momentum for his PICs engagement by inviting leaders from the fourteen PICs to India. There were some marquee announcement, for example a commitment to set up a space research station in Fiji, but the event also exposed some of the ground level difficulties in implementing Modi's vision.

The Indian Foreign Service is vastly understaffed and overstretched. Only two of the fourteen PICs have an Indian High Commission (China has an embassy in every PIC that it has relations with). That means depth of knowledge about the region is thin, relationships aren't being established and maintained with key people on the ground, and information flows may be less than complete. In many cases, India's local contacts are the same used by previous administrations. The result in this case was that some PICs did not even send top-level representation. It also means following through on initiatives will be difficult.

Additionally, there were missed 'easy wins'. The meeting was held in Jaipur. While beautiful and historic, Jaipur is a dry, landlocked, city with little compatibility with the primarily maritime and agricultural economies of the PICs. While the will is there on both sides and there are manifest myriad mutual benefits for deeper engagement between India and PICs, it will take more than Modi's vision alone to maintain momentum. It will also take systemic change.

FOREIGN POLICY INNOVATIONS

Modi and his government are, of course, very aware of these challenges and are actively working to innovate on foreign policy implementation. For India's partners, the first thing to acknowledge is that India is not China. While Beijing can harness its sovereign wealth fund, state media, extensive international networks and state-owned industries in direct service to its foreign policy, democratic, federated, India cannot. India's foreign policy implementation will always be more complex and diffuse. However, it will also be more stable. China may have interests, but India also has friends. It was not an accident that Modi's first foreign trip was to Bhutan, in acknowledgement of abiding bonds between the two countries. What similar country could a new Chinese leader visit? North Korea?

Another potential way for India to establish linkages would be sublateral rather than bilateral—encouraging smaller countries to have a specific state or city as a point of contact rather than the bureaucratic sprawl of Delhi. For example, had the PICs meeting been held in Kerala or Tamil Nadu, both coastal states with climates and economies similar to those in the PICs, myriad compatibilities could have been uncovered. Also, this would have allowed other sectors, such as fisheries, agriculture and education to become involved, broadening engagement beyond just the Indian Foreign Service, and encouraging multifaceted ties. This was an approach Modi himself innovated in Gujarat. During his decade as chief minister, he established sublateral ties with a range of countries including Japan and Germany—benefitting all concerned.

Another potential element in the foreign policy toolkit is India's royalty. In many countries, including the United Kingdom, Thailand, Bhutan and Japan, royal families play an informal, non-political part of foreign engagement. The policies of previous Indian governments did not encourage even informal service by the India royals to the state, in some cases seeing them as competition rather than as complementary. However, they are not competition. They operate in their own sphere. Simply put, there are some doors only royalty can walk through.

For example, during the summer of 2015, a Coronation was held for the King of Tonga in the South Pacific. India sent someone from the High Commission in Fiji. He sat in the crowd with the rest of the Diplomatic Corps. At the High Table were the Crown Prince and Princess of Japan, the Archduke of the House of Habsburgs, Baron Glenarthur from the UK and others. They come as individuals, not as state representatives, but they undoubtedly serve their nations honourably.

Had an Indian royal been in attendance, they would have been at the high table as well, reinforcing relations with the deep establishment of Tonga and the region, having a quiet chat with the future Emperor of Japan, and showing the elegance and beauty of Indian coronation wear. It would have made more of an impression and create deeper ties than a year's worth of visits by someone from the local High Commission. This is an advantage India has that few other countries share. Australia, New Zealand and Canada, for example, have no one qualified to sit at the high table, their only sovereign lives in the UK.

Were India to decide to work with selected, non-political royals as an informal, unofficial branch of foreign engagement, it would likely require the establishment of a dedicated liaison office, but it could substantially boost India's international profile and access in certain areas. Whether it is adopted as policy or not, what is certain is that India should use every advantage it has at its disposal. As Modi knows all too well, the world is in a state of flux, and India has already lost too much time. It needs to shape its own future and no longer be reactive. The options are many, but the window for interception is narrowing.

It is difficult to underestimate how many small and medium-sized countries want 'more India'. People from South America through Asia, Africa and the Pacific can dance to Bollywood numbers, spice with cardamom and curry, and feel cultural compatibilities with gently conservative, education-friendly, family-oriented India. At the same time, they are squeezed between the high prices of the West and the low quality of China, and want access to affordable, reliable, Indian education, medicine, IT and more.

As for the large countries, the US wants India as a global partner, Japan wants it as a strategic partner, Europe wants access to its markets and China wants it quietly boxed in.

Prime Minister Modi has been navigating all those expectations, against a backdrop of targeted hostility from those who don't want to see India succeed, either because they see it as an economic competitor or as an existential threat.

No other modern Indian leader has done so much in two years to shape and drive foreign policy. He did indeed 'fundamentally reboot and reorient the foreign policy goals'. The challenge now is for the foreign policy community to continue to clear away the weeds of complacency, corruption and incompetence while nourishing innovation, insight and practicality. Modi is sowing the seeds, now it will take a broad effort to allow his foreign policy to grow deep and strong roots so that India, and its real partners, can remain stable and prosper in these times of change.

CHAPTER 2

HARNESSING MULTILATERAL ORDERS TO INDIA'S INTERESTS AND PRINCIPLES

Ramesh Thakur

INTRODUCTION

Every country pursues its interests which include trying to protect national security, maximise economic welfare and promote core values. In foreign policy, this is done through an interlocking series of bilateral relationships and participation in multilateral arrangements. The point of departure for this chapter is that multilateralism matters to India and India is critical for the effectiveness and legitimacy of the existing and emerging multilateral orders. Former Prime Minister Manmohan Singh was an internationalist by instinct but a timid technocrat by temperament whose dependence on disparate coalition allies and deference to the Congress Party's family dynasty denuded the government of the necessary political space to pursue a bold foreign policy agenda. Narendra Modi by contrast is both the most internationalist Prime Minister since Jawaharlal Nehru and also more clear-eyed and hard-headed than Nehru in his definition of the country's interests, more able to stamp his own authority on cabinet and government, and more determined to cement India's place at the top global tables without being shackled with legacy shibboleths. Non-Alignment in particular is a historical anomaly with no current conceptual anchor. The sooner the anachronism is dumped, the better.

Modi is pragmatic and practical rather than dogmatic and ideological, and the one trait that will be crucial in the remaining three years of his tenure is decisiveness. Atal Bihari Vajpayee injected a healthy dose of realism into India's penchant for woolly thinking, bringing greater coherence and focus to the pursuit of national interests in the international arena. In a similar vein, instead of the vague and nebulous 'strategic autonomy' that has no operational content, Modi is likely to provide clear strategic direction and more efficient policy execution. I will end with a forensic examination of India's elusive perennial quest for permanent membership of the UN Security Council (UNSC). Before that, however, it will be useful to highlight why multilateralism matters but is grossly defective in extant manifestations; and how India gained from defecting from the global nuclear orders and is also benefitting from circumventing the institutions of global economic governance.

The Continuing Relevance and Importance of Multilateralism

Multilateralism refers to collective action by states to deal with common challenges that are best managed collaboratively to reduce costs and bring order and regularity. Many of the pressing policy challenges—climate change, pandemics, nuclear peace and safety, terrorism, food supply and water tables, fish stocks and ecosystem resources, financial meltdown—are international in origin and nature, global in scope and effects and require concerted multilateral action. In such a world, all states face mutual vulnerabilities; even the most powerful cannot achieve security or maintain prosperity through unilateral action. Yet the responsibility for making policy and the authority to mobilise the requisite resources coercively to tackle the collective threats remain vested in sovereign states. Absent a world government—global governance is explained as operating a patchwork of authority structures that produce generally adhered to norms to regulate behaviour.

The core but not the sum total of the mandated organised multilateral order is the United Nations which will remain relevant for setting international standards and norms. In an increasingly globalised, intertwined and interdependent international system, the regulatory frameworks of multilaterally articulated and policed norms reach deep into the daily business of an increasing number of nations. Great powers with skilful leaders ensure that their country is more of a rule maker than a norm taker. As India edges towards the status of a major global power, it will clamour for its rightful place at the top table for writing the rules and designing and controlling the key institutions of the multilateral order. To use its growing geopolitical heft to the optimum, India will also need to learn how to downgrade and delegitimise multilateral institutions that remain stubbornly closed to it, switching support instead to those where its voice and vote are commensurate with its rising profile, or else creating new institutions.

DEFECTIVE MULTILATERALISM

Governance for the planet is weak and multilateralism is under challenge, from arms control to climate change, international criminal justice and the use of military force overseas. The major multilateral institutions do not meet twenty-first century standards of accountability, transparency and legitimacy, which in turn damage their capacity to address contemporary challenges effectively. The existing governance institutions—rigid, risk-averse, cumbersome and unresponsive—seem no longer fit for purpose in confronting threats and actors who are daring, imaginative, nimble, agile and fluid. Global problems require multilateral solutions but the emerging multipolarity seems inclined more to confrontation than cooperation. There is an acute mismatch between the distribution of authority in existing international institutions and the distribution of military and economic power in the real world, producing a mutually undermining gap between legitimacy and efficiency. In failing to accommodate its structures, processes and agendas to the transformations sweeping the world, the UN risks atrophy and irrelevance. If it cannot be effective in constraining the international use of military force by the five permanent members (P5), of what use is it to the weak who fear aggression by the strong? If it fails to address the reality of some states fomenting cross-border terrorism on neighbours, why should victim countries have any respect for its authority?

In his speech to India's Parliament on 8 November 2010, US President Barack Obama paid tribute to India's treasured past and endorsed its long-held aspiration for UNSC permanent membership. In 2016 the same President agreed to the sale of eight F-16 fighter planes to Pakistan, knowing full well they are irrelevant against terrorists but valued as a weapon against India. Part of India's political pathology is to bask in the empty words of foreign leaders and inflate their significance, while downplaying the full import of actions by the same leaders that are gravely damaging to India's core interests.

THE NUCLEAR MULTILATERAL ORDERS

Underlying the struggle for power are ethical contestations over norms and values that define who nation-states are. Most countries have chosen nuclear abstinence because people overwhelmingly abhor the bomb as the most indiscriminately inhumane weapon ever invented. They pose an existential threat to all forms of life on planet Earth. For decades India argued that by fostering nuclear apartheid, the Nuclear Non-Proliferation Treaty (NPT) fails the test of inter-state equity. Instead India was one of the most ardent champions of complete nuclear disarmament. As its calls went unheeded, the NPT-mandated nuclear powers modernised and upgraded their nuclear arsenals, and China empowered Pakistan into becoming a de facto nuclear-armed country while Washington averted its gaze because of geopolitical compulsions, India's policy of keeping open the bomb option without exercising it became increasingly costly. The breakout in 1998 brought immediate costs but gradually over the past decade most countries have accepted India as a nuclear-armed state and several have signed civil nuclear cooperation agreements. The net security gains for India remain illusory vis-à-vis both China and Pakistan, but the deeply flawed NPT nuclear order has been irretrievably breached. The failure of the 2015 NPT Review Conference confirmed that the NPT has exhausted its normative potential in containing and eliminating the nuclear threat.

ECONOMIC MULTILATERALISM

The first global summit that Modi attended was BRICS (Brazil, Russia, India, China, South Africa) in Fortaleza, Brazil in July 2014 and later in the same year the G20 in Brisbane, Australia. The rapidly growing economies, substantial populations, military capabilities and expanding diplomatic reach of the BRICS-5 translate into rising power profiles and geopolitical clout. By 2025 the world's eight biggest economies could be the US, China, India, Japan, Germany, UK, France and Russia. The major deliverable from the 2014 BRICS summit was economic in form and content—the creation of a new development bank—but its primary motivation and significance were geopolitical. The BRICS share concerns about the US-dominated global architecture and support a rebalancing of the global trade and financial system to reflect developing-country interests. They can give voice to Southern concerns on new rules for health care, pharmaceuticals, intellectual property rights, etc. They have been more sympathetic to Russia than to Europe and the US on the Ukraine crisis and the other four abstained on the UN General Assembly resolution criticising Russia for the annexation of Crimea. Meanwhile, efforts to use US–European Union (EU) dominance of the international financial system as a lever against other major actors deepens others' perceptions of the US-centric financial order as a security threat. The West's addiction to sanctions provides a powerful incentive to the BRICS to develop long-term alternative financial institutions for parking their money and moving them internationally.

When the International Monetary Fund (IMF) and World Bank proved too resistant to change because of the built-in institutional inertia and blocking votes from those who presently control them, the BRICS set up their own bank followed by China creating the Asian Infrastructure Investment Bank (AIIB). That is, they did not defect from the existing global economic order at its failure to realign global political and economic imbalances. Instead they circumvented the existing leading institutions to create and operate their own. In a tribute to their entrepreneurship, many key Western countries defected from the US boycott and joined the AIIB as founding members.

In a world in which all politics is local but most big-ticket problems are global, the G20—more representative of the global diversity of power, wealth and values than any other group—offers the best crossover point between legitimacy (based on inclusiveness and representation), efficiency (which requires a compact executive decision-making body) and effectiveness (where those who make the decisions have the greatest ability to implement or thwart them). It brings together all countries that count—and includes none that don't count—because of economic heft, geopolitical clout and diplomatic weight. But to be rescued from drift, the G20 will need to broaden its agenda considerably from narrow economic managerialism in line with the vision of the original advocates (including this author) and architects.

To enhance global role, respect and influence, India will have to demonstrate ideational and normative as well as political leadership in multilateral forums. Moreover, it will need to exercise creative diplomacy in order to combine the protection of national interests with the representation of developing-country and Asian interests. India's global posture betrays a transitional identity as a rising power with growing economic weight that is translating into greater political clout, but a poor and underdeveloped country with a multitude of serious policy challenges: in senior scholar Navroz Dubash's words, both 'a rising power and a vulnerable nation'.

THE UNITED NATIONS

India kept its tryst with destiny two years after the United Nations was created to shape the world's destiny, yet was one of fifty-one founding UN members. The ideals of world peace and global solidarity based on sovereign equality, mutual respect and universal tolerance were immensely attractive to independent India. There have been periodic misunderstandings and disenchantments, from the early referral of Kashmir to censorious remarks in the UNSC during the Bangladesh War and after the nuclear tests in 1998. Overall, nevertheless, India took the UN seriously and was taken seriously in its halls. For example, it is hard to think of another country that had more influence in driving the campaign against the criminal apartheid regime in South Africa.

Because of the size and professionalism of its armed forces, India is among the top contributors to UN peace operations. According to the UN Peacekeeping Fact Sheet, in April 2016, 7,696 Indian soldiers and police were deployed on UN duty overseas (over 6 per cent of the total). Of course India gains some traction from this, like being elected to the inconsequential Peace-building Commission. But have Indian policymakers conducted a hard-nosed evaluation of whether the credit ledger is overshadowed by the debit? Of the 3,395 UN peacekeepers killed until 31 October 2015, 160 were Indians—more than any other nationality. Moreover, in global perceptions India is bracketed with poor countries with bloated and antiquated defence forces desperate to earn foreign money. India should contribute only if there are some industrialised countries also willing to shoulder the burden. Only then will it begin to put a distance between the professional Indian military and the image of UN operations as something fit only for impoverished and amateurish contributors who are in it for the money.

India could reassert leadership to reclaim the UN as the forum, voice and servant of the poorer and weaker majority instead of a tool of domination by the rich and powerful minority. In an age of unprecedented global connectivity, persisting pockets of debilitating poverty and deep deprivation degrade the lives of hundreds of millions, threaten social cohesion, political stability and international order and are an indictment of governments and international institutions. Developing countries have been severely buffeted by the crosswinds of globalisation and the resulting 'end of geography' in a flat world. There has been growing divergence in income levels, with widening inequality among and within nations—in effect a redistribution of wealth from the poor to the rich. The wealth of the richest 1 per cent is equal to that of the other 99 per cent. According to the 2016 Oxfam report, in 2015, just sixty-two individuals—compared to 388 five years earlier—had the same wealth as 3.6 billion people, i.e. the poorer half of humanity.

UN SECURITY COUNCIL

The most critical issue of UN structural reform is that of the UNSC. The call for reform is justified by the need for greater credibility, legitimacy, representation and effectiveness. The P5 have certain characteristics in common. They were victors in World War II and all possess nuclear weapons. They created the UN and gave themselves exalted positions at the time. Washington, anticipating a nationalist triumph against the communists, ensured China's seat at the high table as a means of having an important ally in the Pacific. This arrangement was ossified by the Cold War.

With the Cold War over and the UN espousing democratic principles, the UN needs to be reformed to reflect the changes. A static membership of the Council undermines the logic of its status, erodes the legitimacy of the Council, diminishes the authority of the organisation and breeds resentment in the claimants to the rank of the great powers. An unreconstructed UNSC will continue to suffer from a steady erosion of legitimacy and authority and gradually fade into irrelevance. It could easily become trapped in a vicious circle. Deterioration of legitimacy increases the transaction costs of compliance with its resolutions and diminishes its effectiveness, which further erodes performance legitimacy.

Countries should be permanent members based on their representational credentials and contributions of human, financial, military and other resources to attaining UN goals. On these criteria, there is surprisingly broad agreement already on India as the leading candidate. But its policy initiatives are often aspirational rather than programmatic—a slogan is no policy—and claims to status and recognition are articulated as national entitlement, not advanced as political strategy. The quest for permanent membership—an essentially political contest—can only be realised by persuading the UN community of the merits of the case, mobilising the requisite resources, adopting the most effective strategy, building winning coalitions with other potential winners and co-opting enough of the rest to neutralise their opposition.

A NON-COOPERATION MOVEMENT AT THE UN

More than a decade ago India joined Brazil, Germany and Japan in the Group of Four (G4) in a major push for UNSC restructuring. This faltered in the 2005 UN reform effort against determined opposition from some existing P5 and many regional rivals of the aspirant states. Albert Einstein famously defined insanity as doing the same thing over and over in the expectation of a different result each time.

How then might the G4 escape from the Einstein trap? First, by recalling the great success of Gandhi's non-cooperation strategy that did, after all, defeat the mighty British Empire. Similarly, India's congenital defection from the nuclear regime eventually led to its voice and interests being accommodated outside the NPT. And second, by recognising that the UNSC is the epicentre of geopolitical realism where hardball tactics rule the roost as the different powers jostle furiously and use sharp elbows liberally in pursuit of hard interests.

Combining the two, one essential criterion of permanent membership is the capacity and will to play hardball diplomacy. China, Russia and the US have demonstrated this repeatedly, for example on Taiwan, Syria and Israel. The G4 countries should engage in a deliberate and combined campaign of non-cooperation. This need not take offensive form. As Gandhi showed brilliantly, passive but polite non-cooperation is a very cost-effective strategy to force the issue against closed minds. While a concerted G4 non-cooperation movement will be more effective, there is no stopping India from acting unilaterally, just as with the NPT.

If success remains elusive, the quest for permanent membership should be quietly abandoned. Instead, the importance of the reform-proof UN that is grievously out of alignment with the changed global power structure should be downgraded, a less senior person chosen as India's permanent representative and Modi should not bother attending UN sessions. Instead India should switch to using the G20 and BRICS as credible negotiating and leveraging forums and reduce the UN to serving as a universal validating forum on the multilateral path while concentrating mainly on key bilateral relations with the US, EU, UK, France, Germany, China and Japan.

The G4 should refuse to take part in the elections to the non-permanent seats. By participating in the process and taking two-year turns as elected members, they effectively legitimise the UNSC as currently structured. Conversely, all four of them not serving on the Council for a decade or more would thoroughly delegitimise it. If we belong to a club that excludes blacks, Dalits, Muslims or women, for some time it may be worth staying on in order to try and change the admission rules. But after a few failed attempts, we have to have the courage to resign from membership of the stubbornly offensive club.

Non-participation in UNSC elections will not be enough. To drive home the conviction that the present Council is illegitimate, the G4 countries should refuse to vote for referring or citing any country for bad behaviour, such as non-compliance with nuclear non-proliferation obligations, to the Council. Again, they need not be overly aggressive about this. They do not have to support or speak up in defence of the suspect country's nuclear policies. Nor do they have to campaign against the referrals of international outlaws to the UNSC by others. But they can politely remind everyone each time that as they do not believe that the Council is fully legitimate, they would feel hypocritical in subjecting others to its compulsory coercive authority. Therefore they will abstain. In effect this is what India did by welcoming Sudan's President Omar Hassan al-Bashiras, an honoured guest, at the third India–Africa Forum Summit in October 2015 despite the International Criminal Court (ICC) indictment and a UNSC resolution to cooperate with the ICC.

Third, since all UN peacekeeping missions are authorised by the UNSC, they should refuse to contribute troops, civilian personnel or funds to UN operations until such time as the Council is reformed. Once more, they do not have to oppose the establishment of such missions. But they should let others provide the necessary personnel and, since peacekeeping operations are funded by voluntary contributions, they should refuse to volunteer any funds. Where the US has led in showing the effectiveness of purse diplomacy, the G4 should follow.

RESTRUCTURING THE INSTITUTIONAL APPARATUS OF INDIA'S FOREIGN POLICY
The above represents an agenda for a radical, progressive and forward-looking foreign policy for India in sync with Modi's style and vision. While Modi can

adopt the agenda, its implementation will require an equally radical restructuring of the Foreign Service. Individually brilliant at recruitment, India's Foreign Service officers are soon seduced into the VIP culture and captured by the collective ethos of the service. The service needs to be expanded—dramatically and rapidly—to match India's growing global profile. The recruitment should be broadened and the training modernised, and promotion by seniority ended about ten years after recruitment, being based on merit and performance thereafter. The trade bureaucracy should be absorbed into a combined ministry of foreign affairs and trade, changing it from MEA to MEAT. The foreign secretary should be appointed to five-year renewable terms and ambassadorships should be opened up to successful people from a broad cross-section of Indian society—including bringing back expatriate Indians—who can project, promote and represent India overseas. And finally, Modi should appoint a long-term foreign minister for as many terms as he is himself Prime Minister, give him/her his full confidence, delegate full authority for instituting the structural changes to the ministry and conducting the foreign policy in line with the new agenda.

BIBLIOGRAPHY

1.   Thakur, Ramesh, *The United Nations, Peace and Security: From Collective Security to the Responsibility to Protect* (Cambridge: Cambridge University Press, 2006).
2.   Cooper, Andrew F and Thakur, Ramesh, *The Group of Twenty (G20)* (London: Routledge, 2013).
3.   Thakur, Ramesh, 'How Representative Are BRICS?', *Third World Quarterly*, Vol. 35, No. 10 (2014), pp. 1791-1808.
4.   Weiss, Thomas G and Thakur, Ramesh, *Global Governance and the UN: An Unfinished Journey* (Bloomington: Indiana University Press, 2010).

CHAPTER 3

DIASPORA FACTOR
IN MODI'S DIPLOMACY

SREERAM CHAULIA

DARLING OF THE DESIS

Narendra Modi often employs the concept of 'three Ds'—democracy, demography and demand—in his spiels about India's rise and inherent strengths. But through his foreign policy prioritisation and actions, he implicitly reifies a fourth 'D' that is turning out to be no less integral to the story of India's growing influence in the world, namely, diaspora. There is a symbiotic relationship that the Indian Prime Minister has fertilised with the vast panorama of Non Resident Indians or NRIs and OCIs (Overseas Citizens of India, who include those formerly known as Persons of Indian Origin or PIOs) spread out across the world. Their adoration and fanatic fan following keeps Modi's stature as a high-flier on the international stage, and his respect and attention to them lends Indian foreign policy a comparative advantage in those corners of the world where the diaspora has planted deep roots. The diaspora is the oxygen for Modi as a world leader and Modi is the lodestar for the multitudes who departed India physically but not emotionally and culturally.

Harnessing the talents and loyalties of India's diaspora for improving the material conditions and international image of India is not Modi's creation per se, but he has walked the talk on this strategy like no other Indian Prime

Minister since Independence. From a historical evolutionary standpoint, Modi represents a very different Indian state and nation than the one which approached the diaspora warily and hesitantly since 1947.

The depth of Modi's reappraisal of India's role in the world and the corollary place of its 25 million-odd diaspora is evident from a phrase he used for the homeland in one of his many electrifying speeches before doting NRIs and OCIs in Silicon Valley, USA, in September 2015: *Bahuratna Vasundhara* or a land rich with priceless gems that can keep giving generously for the well-being of the universe. Far from the stereotype of India as a poor developing country that survives on hand-outs and financial support from rich nations and which must prevent the dreaded 'brain drain' to the Global North, he struck a chord by asserting that it has been a net giver of countless benefits, including a productive and integrated migrant workforce that is also replenishing the homeland through the reverse process of 'brain gain'[1].

To Modi, India is an unsung hero for the plethora of gifts it has showered in international affairs like the ethos of *Vasudhaiva Kutumbakam* (the world is one family), Vivekananda's gospel of spiritual oneness of humankind, Mahatma Gandhi's ideologies of non-violence and ecological conservation, and the Indian model of 'live and let live' and multicultural coexistence. In addition, he has left no stone unturned to heap praise on the Indian diaspora as keepers of the flame who have been ideal migrants in their host nations by investing sweat and blood to develop those countries. The effect of this effort has been to remind host countries that people of Indian origin are invaluable assets to them and, by inference, that the bilateral relations with the Indian state are leavened by this incomparable human resource factor.

From benign neglect to outright disowning of the rights and interests of OCIs and NRIs, the post-independence Indian state was prone to blaming them for jettisoning India due to its poverty, infrastructural deficiencies and low quality of life. Well into the 1990s, it was commonplace conversation in India that the 'brain drain' or exodus of skilled and educated Indians was a cause of the nation's underdevelopment and that the NRIs are living it up by turning their backs on their less fortunate kinsmen in India.

Nehru's policy of 'active dissociation' from the Indian diaspora owing to

---

[1] Rajghatta, Chidananda, 'Brain Drain can become Brain Gain Anytime, Modi Points in his SAP Centre Address', *The Times of India*, 28 September 2015.

concern that connecting and advocating for them would impair the sovereignty of host countries left a bitter taste for generations of Indian-origin communities abroad. His cold view of overseas Indians was encapsulated in a comment made in India's Parliament in 1957: 'If they adopt the nationality of that country we have no concern with them. Sentimental concern there is, but politically they cease to be Indian nationals'.[2] Ajay Dubey argues that post-independence India's neglect 'saw the suppression, subjugation and marginalisation of the Indian diaspora globally because...rivals and opponents of Indians found the Indian diaspora helpless and unsupported by its mother country'.[3]

One activist of the Indian diaspora from Mauritius, Anand Mulloo, writes that his community,

> Who were once told by Nehru to forget about Old India...can no longer be dismissed as a bad memory that anybody would prefer to forget. New India must lend its ears to the voices of the diaspora. The ever-expanding and strengthening diaspora prides itself of the millionaire NRIs in UK, US, Canada and Australia. And the diaspora cannot but revert from time to time to Mother India in a bid to recharge its emotional and spiritual batteries.. after years of neglect and abandon, New India wakes up and decides to remember her forgotten children overseas.[4]

Thanks to Modi, that 'New India' has materialised and it is uniting the long-lost flock to the mainland in a two-way process of rediscovery that has raised India's power projection capacity.

What Modi has done is think bolder, go farther and galvanise the diaspora like never before for comprehensive cultural, political and economic empowerment. The halting steps of previous regimes have now been accelerated to the next level by Modi through spectacular speeches backed up by long-due reforms like merging the PIO card and the Overseas Citizen of India (OCI) card, and melding the Ministry of Overseas Indian Affairs (MOIA) into the MEA.

---

[2] Nehru, Jawaharlal, 'Reply to Debate on Foreign Policy in Lok Sabha. 2 September 1957', in GOI (ed.) *India's Foreign Policy: Selected Speeches, September 1946-April 1961* (New Delhi: Government of India, 1961) p. 130.

[3] Dubey, Ajay, 'India and the Indian Diaspora', in Scott, David (ed.) *Handbook of India's International Relations* (London: Routledge, 2011) p. 258.

[4] Mulloo, Anand, *Voices of the Indian Diaspora* (New Delhi: Motilal Banarsidass, 2007) p. 26.

THE GREAT UNIFIER

Modi's diasporic support today is broad and adequately representative of India's socio-economic, ethnic and religious diversity. It is a catch-all constituency that demonstrates his own evolution from chief minister of Gujarat to Prime Minister and from right of the political spectrum to the centre. Addressing British Indians in Wembley Stadium in November 2015, he insisted that 'diversity is India's pride and its strength, and despite the country being home to many religions, over 100 languages and 1500 dialects, Indians have proved how to live together'.[5] Television coverage of Modi's mega events for the Indian diaspora often focuses on Muslims, Sikhs and other minorities with visible markers of appearance, roaring in approval from the bleachers, to reinforce the message that he is accepted across the board among NRIs and OCIs.

Since Modi is attacked by political rivals in India and a few baiters within the diaspora as a 'divisive figure' who stood for Hindu chauvinism, the approval of the vast majority of NRIs and OCIs has been critical for his reinvention as India's deliverer and rejuvenator. Simultaneously, it has made the Indian diaspora more harmonious and capable of coming together to lobby for Indian interests in their respective countries of abode.

Vijay Chauthaiwale, the BJP's architect for Modi's mobilisation of the Indian diaspora, has dwelt at length on the Modi effect in patching rivalries and divisions among NRIs and OCIs:

> The PM's persona goes beyond any community appeal, religious appeal or sectoral appeal. It also goes beyond the BJP's appeal. People are willing to come together in the name of the PM. It can happen only with Modi. When the larger goal is defined, people are willing to forget, at least temporarily, their differences. The PM's visits are becoming a great unifying force for the communities.[6]

Since the Indian diaspora is varied in its occupational and class compositions, Modi has practised full-spectrum diplomacy to encapsulate all their disparate hopes and expectations. His governance mantra of *Sabka Saath, Sabka Vikas* or take everyone along and work for everyone's welfare is mostly understood

---

[5] PTI, 'India Full of Diversity, it is our Pride and Strength: PM Narendra Modi', *The Economic Times*, 14 November 2015.

[6] Mohan, Archis, 'PM's Visits a Unifying Force for the Diaspora: Vijay Chauthaiwale', *Business Standard*, 22 August 2015.

in the context of domestic policymaking within India. But it also has a foreign counterpart, especially in Modi's diaspora component. When Modi visited the UAE in August 2015, he demonstrated a steadfast commitment to the working class diaspora and reiterated that India values them as much as the millionaires and billionaires among NRIs and OCIs. He addressed a gigantic crowd at the Dubai Cricket Stadium to buoy the spirits of Indian workers who make up more than 40 per cent of the UAE's labour force and roughly 30 per cent of the UAE's population, and contribute as much as 20 per cent of India's total inward remittances. He reminded the audience that when the West slapped economic sanctions on India after it conducted nuclear weapons' tests in 1998, Indian workers doing menial jobs in the Gulf countries made a huge contribution to fill India's coffers. In return, he announced an array of new government schemes to assist working class NRIs on consular, immigration, workplace and other contingencies, and also promised that Indian diplomatic missions would be more accessible and answerable to grievances.

But apart from new policy initiatives like the Indian Community Welfare Fund, what impressed the marginalised NRIs in the Gulf the most was Modi's passionate advocacy for them as his main priority. He said, 'This part of the world has Indians from very poor families who have come here to make ends meet. Whether I can do something for America (which has wealthy NRIs and OCIs) or not, if I fail to work for you I become restless.'[7] During his UAE travels, the Indian Prime Minister took out time to visit a labour accommodation in the industrial city of Abu Dhabi and surprised everyone by mingling with desi workers, asking them one-on-one about their working conditions and difficulties. One 'visibly moved' and excited labourer, Arshad Khan from Bihar who was employed at Al Dhafra Waste Management Company, commented that 'it was one of the most pleasant moments of his life, as his Prime Minister asked him about the problems the workers are facing'. His co-workers added that it was 'the first time such a leader has visited them' and that Modi's 'interaction with workers was a strong message to them'.[8]

Modi has also made a mark for himself in responding speedily and unconditionally to SOS calls from Indian expatriates of working class

[7] TNN, 'PM Narendra Modi's Full Speech in Dubai', *Times Now*, 17 August 2015, available at: https://www.youtube.com/watch?v=w-AhA-yjeho. Last accessed on 14 February 2016.
[8] Haider, Haseeb, 'Modi Handshake Leaves Workers Speechless', *Khaleej Times*, 17 August 2015.

backgrounds who get stranded in war zones. The remarkable alacrity and efficiency with which his government rescued thousands of helpless NRIs from Yemen, Iraq, Syria and Ukraine when they were trapped in armed conflict areas with immediate threat to their lives and liberties has no parallels in independent India's history. The BJP celebrated Modi's timely attention to the underprivileged desis in distress by asserting, 'Indians living in foreign countries now have confidence that there is a government in their country, which is concerned about them and is ready to support them when needed.'[9]

HARNESSING NRIs AND PIOs FOR INDIA'S DEVELOPMENT

Critics who mock Modi's foreign travels as high in theatrics and low in concrete takeaways ignore the extraordinary rise in inward Foreign Direct Investment (FDI) that India has enjoyed since he took office as well as intangible gains of creating a circle of mutual inspiration between the diaspora and aspirational Indians in the mainland. In Silicon Valley, Modi fused the American dream with the Indian one at the people-to-people level. 'Inderica'—a confluence of talent and originality between India and America—is on the anvil thanks to the Prime Minister's active encouragement. This convergence is represented through formations like the Indian Investment Initiative (III), a vehicle to channel Indian-American funds into small and medium enterprises in India with the support of the government of the USA.

Modi is well aware that calls to patriotism and self-belief whipped up through speeches are not enough to turn around the dismal image of India in the eyes of its own extended family abroad or to extract the most from them for India's nation-building projects. Modi's diaspora policy aims *inter alia* at maximising FDI from the Indian diaspora to motor India's economic growth. His adrenalin-pumping and chest-thumping speeches in New York, Sydney, London, Toronto et al are appetisers to translate goodwill into larger volumes of inward FDI from the diaspora. As he told over 18,000 desis in Singapore in November 2015, 'FDI is not only Foreign Direct Investment but also First Develop India.'[10]

Towards this end, the Modi government has undertaken policy reforms such as treating non-repatriable investments by NRIs and OCIs as equivalent

---

[9] PTI, 'BJP Lauds PM Modi on Evacuation of Indians from Yemen', *The Indian Express*, 5 April 2015.

[10] PTI, 'FDI is First Develop India, Narendra Modi tells Indian Diaspora in Singapore', *Deccan Chronicle*, 25 November 2015.

to domestic investment so that they will not be subject to restrictions related to FDI.[11] The PIO and OCI card schemes have been merged since January 2015 by amending the Citizenship Act, giving the former enhanced work, residence and property rights in India and ending byzantine reporting rules. This is the closest India has come to granting dual citizenship to the diaspora and has energised NRI and OCI participation in the Indian economy. NRIs have been permitted to invest in India's National Pension Scheme, delivering relief to low-wage émigrés who lack social security in their countries of work. Physical connectivity between nodal hubs of Indian diaspora concentration and different cities of India has also been fast forwarded to ease travel. The British Indian industrialist Swraj Paul, who was prevented from investing in India by protectionist local capitalists in the 1980s, has argued that thanks to Modi's penchant for simplification and easing of bureaucratic hurdles, 'it was for the first time in three decades that the Indian diaspora is feeling that their contribution to the country has been recognised'.[12]

STRENGTHENING THE NRI LOBBY

Apart from economic and cultural leverage, Modi is explicit in seeking to reap political advantages for Indian foreign policy via the lobbying energy of a rejuvenated and reconnected diaspora. Ram Madhav, BJP General Secretary, has commented that 'we are changing the contours of diplomacy and looking at new ways of strengthening India's interests abroad. They can be India's voice even while being loyal citizens in those countries. That is the long-term goal behind the diaspora diplomacy. It is like the way the Jewish community looks out for Israel's interests in the United States.'[13]

Vijay Chauthaiwale has also spelt out how the Indian diaspora can act as cheerleaders for India by reaching out to local media, legislators and citizens in their countries of residence: 'They can tell them about the good changes taking place in India and remove the image of India as an inefficient place to visit and invest in.'[14] The Indian-American academic Ronak Desai has likewise

---

[11] PTI, 'Government Relaxes FDI Norms for NRIs, OCIs and OCI', *The Economic Times*, 22 May 2015.

[12] PTI, 'Narendra Modi's New Policies for NRIs a Welcome Step, Indian Diaspora will Respond: Lord Swraj Paul', *The Indian Express*, 29 September 2014.

[13] Lakshmi, Rama, 'India wants to turn 25 Million in the Diaspora into Global Ambassadors', *The Washington Post*, 18 February 2015.

[14] Ibid.

argued that Modi is looking to expatriates to 'provide him with powerful constituencies of support abroad, capable of influencing the policies of their adopted countries'.[15]

Parallel to Modi and the official apparatus of the Government of India that is promoting political activism of the Indian diaspora in the USA, the BJP as a party has also come up with an action plan to reorient its overseas branches from cultural events and professional networking to lobbying and formation of 'pressure groups'. They have been tasked with targeting 'local lawmakers, Parliamentarians, media and other leading figures and create awareness about our country', and to also 'join hands with the Indian Embassies and hold independent programmes to showcase India's contribution to the world'.[16] What drives the current generation of Indian lobbyists is a devotion to Modi's brand of leadership, 'an emerging version of deeply nationalist India; (not) much interested in appearing on the international stage as Nehruvian, Anglophile or Westernised. Instead, they want India to represent itself as a global economic and political power, having long shed its colonial trappings'.[17]

By the time Modi took over the task of India's global renaissance in 2014, attitudes within the country towards desis had already been morphing for the better. Modi's notion of 'brain gain' through a give-and-take between the homeland and the diaspora had been circulating for years in India. But by passionately implementing the diaspora portion of his foreign policy in the far corners of the globe, Modi has essentially put the desi on a pedestal as a hero who is India's pride and an extension of the mind and body of the Indian nation. As he told one mass of NRIs and OCIs in Malaysia while multitudes back in India watched on television, 'India is not confined to its territory. India exists in every Indian in every part of the world.'[18] The re-imagination of who is 'Indian' is happening not just among the diaspora but within India, thanks to Modi's strategy of conjoining all the scattered pieces of Indian-ness and presenting a formidable force before the world.

---

[15] Desai, Ronak, 'Modi's NRI, NRI's Modi', *The Indian Express*, 2 December 2014.

[16] Sharma, Pratul, 'BJP Bid to Turn NRI Friends into Lobbyists', *The New Indian Express*, 25 January 2015.

[17] Sathian, Sanjena, 'Narendra Modi's Secret Weapon', *Ozy*, 2015, available at: http://www.ozy.com/provocateurs/narendra-modis-secret-weapon/41339. Last accessed on 15 February 2016.

[18] IANS, 'Modi Lauds Malay Indians, Announces $1 Million for Students', *The New Indian Express*, 22 November 2015.

Rajmandala of
Bilateral and
Regional Connect

CHAPTER 4

REINVENTING STRATEGIC RESTRAINT: MODI'S PAKISTAN SHIFT

Ashok Malik

Early on the morning of 29 September 2016, Indian Special Forces returned from a daring predawn raid across the Line of Control (LoC), the mission accomplished to a nicety. Seven or eight—'the number is in the high single digits', said a senior official at a high-level briefing that followed—launch pads across a 200 km expanse and each roughly one to three km into Pakistan-occupied Kashmir had been attacked simultaneously. The intelligence about them had been precise and so was the execution. A number of terrorists and Pakistani army soldiers, helping them as auxiliaries, had been killed.

The casualties could only be estimated. In the weeks preceding the 'surgical strike', as the raid came to be described, terrorists had crossed the LoC in units of four. As such, going by that template, it was guessed that about thirty terrorists, waiting to cross into Indian territory—the launch pad is the final and temporary shelter before any attempted infiltration—had been killed. Yet, this was speculation and in any case the numbers didn't matter; the message did.

Cross-LoC strikes and incursions have not been unknown in the twenty-five years of the bloody proxy war Pakistan has engaged in Jammu & Kashmir. In the time of the first NDA government (1998-2004) and in the decade of the UPA government that followed, there were unconfirmed reports of skirmishes that had taken Indian troops across the LoC in reprisal actions and pursuit of terrorists. Some of these were confirmed in the aftermath of 29 September, by retired army officers and former ministers.

Yet, what happened on 29 September was different from those previous episodes, whatever their individual specificities. This was the first (or rare) pre-emptive strike India had conducted after receiving geographically and tactically exact intelligence on a group of terrorists about to cross into Indian territory and seeking to trigger acts of violence and terrorism. It was also the first such strike to be publicly acknowledged and owned up to by the army and the government. In a sense, the Rubicon was crossed.

This strike came ten days after the attack on an Indian army camp in Uri, in which nineteen soldiers died. Inevitably, the early commentary linked the two episodes and in the public imagination this was retribution for Uri. Strictly speaking that was not true. The cross-LoC operation did not represent punishing the perpetrators of Uri but signalled a new resolve to go further—cross red lines as it were—to anticipate and pre-empt future attacks and future Uris. It was a milestone in the evolution of the Pakistan policy and counterterrorism approach of the government of Prime Minister Narendra Modi.

While the military and intelligence backdrop and execution of the cross-LoC strike was impressive, it came in a certain diplomatic context. That context had been painstakingly constructed and crafted by the Modi government, led by the Prime Minister himself, over two years. It is that context that requires careful assessment and appreciation. Not all elements of that context were created by the Modi government, but it accentuated the advantages, prised open opportunities where these existed and, when it perceived a diplomatic and strategic lever, sought to grab it rather than dither. That ability and willingness to strike, as distinct from the strike itself, was what had the world watching.

There were three aspects to the Modi government's preparation and build-up to 29 September: These related to the domestic mood and concerns; to winning the approbation of as well as assuaging global powers and the broader world community; and the signal being sent to Pakistan. It is crucial to look at each of these independently.

Let us begin with the domestic constituency that Modi had to address. Terrorism in Jammu & Kashmir and in the Indian mainland outside the Kashmir valley is a twenty-five-year tragedy. While India's ability to completely liquidate the terror infrastructure in Pakistan is recognised as insufficient—it would be insufficient for any external power, even the United States—its capacity to deter attacks while these are being planned and to impose costs on those who seek to or actually inflict damage on India and Indians has been disappointing and has led to a fair degree of public anguish.

When he came to office in May 2014, Prime Minister Modi had a mandate and an obligation to reorder the prevailing norm. In his election campaign and his political identity and persona, he product-differentiated himself from immediate predecessors as being less tolerant of terrorist incursions from across the LoC and across the international border and more willing to build and use capacities that would punish or injure those seeking to terrorise India.

After a sufficient period in his term—and certainly at the end of five years—the inevitable questions would be asked. Had capacity to deter and punish terror attacks improved since May 2014? Had there been practical demonstration of this enhanced capacity and if not, why not? Frankly, after Uri the murmurs had begun and being a grass roots, down-to-earth political leader, Modi was conscious of this mood and of the overall anger in the country.

That the summer of 2016 had been turbulent only added to the impatience. The Kashmir valley had faced its most volatile pan-Islamist uprising since the early 1990s, not as bad as that perhaps but worse than anything since. Pakistan had exploited the atmosphere following the killing of terrorist Burhan Wani by Indian security forces. In the first nine months of 2016, there had been thirty-five infiltration attempts across the LoC. Twenty were intercepted; fifteen proved successful in some manner or the other, an indication of the logistical difficulty if not impossibility of 'sealing the LoC'.

Pakistani army commanders remained in denial about the infiltration even as their leaders sought to provoke India and test Modi. In India, the limits to strategic restraint had been reached and emotions both in the public and in the army—for which Uri constituted one of its biggest set of peacetime casualties—needed an outlet.

Prime Minister Modi had embraced enormous political risk in visiting Pakistan and the heartland of Punjab—Lahore and Raiwind—in December 2015. The answer to this had been the attack on the Pathankot air force base by a Jaish-e-Mohammad unit, backed by sections of the Pakistan army, in January 2016. Nevertheless the Modi government responded with measure and reason and gave Islamabad the benefit of doubt. A Pakistani investigative team, including an officer of the Inter-Services Intelligence, was even given permission to visit Pathankot and carry out its own inquiry, with the understanding that reciprocal facilitation and access would be provided to Indian investigators who wanted to question Pakistan-based suspects.

Pakistan, of course, did nothing at its end. It continued to remain in obstinate denial about the masterminds of Pathankot, as it had about those who had planned and carried out previous terrorist attacks. The experience after Pathankot meant Modi's room for a similar response after Uri was constricted if not absent. The public would not be as generous this time; the mood was that much more unforgiving.

Ironically, the diplomatic room for Modi had expanded for precisely these reasons. He had freedom to do that much more after Uri. For the past decade-and-a-half, after the attack on Parliament in December 2001 and then after the Mumbai terror outrage of September 2008, the world had mentally prepared for an Indian 'counter-action' of some nature and at some stage. By 2016, following the Abbottabad raid, where Osama bin Laden was found hidden in a Pakistani cantonment town, and after the Pakistani military had all but sabotaged the government of Ashraf Ghani, an Afghan president virtually handpicked by the Americans, Western impatience with Pakistan was in any case at a high. Consequently, the West's (and the United States') intentions and instrumentalities when it came to holding back India were lower than in earlier years.

Even so, India's behaviour could not be reckless or impetuous or driven solely by media headlines. It had to be calibrated and thought through and had to come with the sense that it was being forced upon India after all other options had been exhausted. In this, Pakistan's cussedness after Pathankot, its lack of appreciation of the risks Prime Minister Modi took when he visited Prime Minister Nawaz Sharif's home town, and its continued facilitation of infiltration through the spring and summer of 2016 built a perfect platform for the Modi government's diplomacy.

After Uri and before 29 September, all this was deftly used to build a case with the United States, with the Chinese—who advocated talks but could not fundamentally deny Pakistan's arming of and providing of sanctuary to terrorists—with the other permanent members of the Security Council, with key Sunni Arab powers such as Saudi Arabia, the United Arab Emirates and Qatar, and with a broad arc of the Muslim world, from Turkey (grudgingly receptive to India's entreaties, but not entirely unreceptive either) to Iran to Malaysia.

Ambassadors from these countries, as well as other major powers, were also briefed within hours of the cross-LoC operations. India was pointed and careful in stressing that 29 September did not represent a military operation targeting Pakistani troops—it was a counterterrorism strike motivated by absolutely reliable intelligence and aimed at anticipating and pre-empting an attack within India and upon Indians. The collateral killing of Pakistani soldiers, and what they were doing in close proximity to so-called 'non-state actors' and jihadists, was for the Pakistani authorities to explain.

The reaction from the global community—voices of support for India's pre-emptive counterterrorism operation, summary dismissal of Pakistan's alternative scenarios, and in many instances a non-reaction as if it were business as usual—validated the substance of the Indian government's diplomatic endeavour. It established international powers and partners had faith and trust in Prime Minister Modi and in what the media quickly nicknamed the 'Modi doctrine'.

Finally, what bearing did 29 September have on the India-Pakistan equation? It is nobody's argument that this has resolved the terrorism challenge for all times to come. Rather, the desire of the terrorist militia and their state benefactors to strike (and 'take vengeance') was underscored by India putting its domestic security apparatus on even higher alert than usual. However, the Modi government was mature in not unduly provoking Pakistan and in allowing its government and army wriggle room. It did not publicly and needlessly contest the Pakistani insistence that this was just usual cross-LoC firing and nothing out of the ordinary.

The nature of the cross-LoC operations and why these were unprecedented was conveyed to important diplomatic partners, stakeholder institutions and the domestic constituency in India. It was absorbed and believed. While some political groups in India insisted that the visual and photographic evidence collected at the destroyed launch pads be shared with the public, the Modi government was cautious in understanding the ramifications of such a move. It would leave Pakistan with little space for denial at home and deprive its government of a face-saver. It would force the Pakistani military into escalation, if only to fight off local pressure.

The Indian government did not want to instigate such an expansion of the conflict or embarrass the Pakistani military and government. This was always, it maintained, a limited counterterrorism operation. This nuance and maturity to the Modi government's Pakistan diplomacy was widely appreciated. It behoved a responsible power.

The more serious message for Pakistan was that the Modi government and its strategic brains trust believed the 'escalation threshold'—the threshold beyond which a conventional skirmish would escalate into a full-blown conflict with potentially nuclear implications—was higher than had been previously thought and feared. The 'low escalation threshold' theory had been adroitly used by Pakistan and by Pakistani sympathisers in the administration and the think-tank community in Washington, DC—particularly the so-called 'nuclear ayatollahs'—to hem in India and prevent it from any meaningful response to a terrorist attack emanating from Pakistan or from Pakistani-controlled territory.

After 29 September, if the escalation frontier had been tested once, for an immaculately conceived and narrow-focused counterterrorism exercise, it could and would be done again. Indeed, the frontier would be explored further as Indian confidence and capacities grew.

Has then the Modi government set a standard operating procedure—whereby when actionable intelligence is available, India will not hesitate to launch a pre-emptive strike across the LoC? Will this doctrine stop at pre-emption or will it extend to post facto imposition of costs? Will it expand to other geographies, territories and domains, beyond the limited confines of the LoC? It is these questions that today trouble Pakistan and it is that strategic ambiguity that has been added to India's military, diplomatic and external-policy quiver. In times to come, it could be recognised as one of Prime Minister Modi's most important contributions.

CHAPTER 5

STEADY PROGRESS ON INDIA– US SECURITY TIES UNDER MODI GOVERNMENT

LISA CURTIS

Indian Prime Minister Narendra Modi has energised Indian diplomacy and pursued a bolder and more innovative foreign policy than his predecessor, Manmohan Singh. As part of his enterprising foreign policy, Prime Minister Modi has focused specifically on strengthening Indian–American economic, political and security ties and visited the US thrice in less than two years. Washington has been receptive to his outreach and has also sent a steady stream of high-level US visitors to New Delhi, who have repeatedly emphasised the increasingly important role India will play on the global stage. The result has been a qualitative improvement in India–US relations since 2014.

The recent hiccup in the relationship over US F-16 sales to Pakistan notwithstanding, the US and India are poised to make additional progress on defence and security cooperation in the remaining months of the Obama administration. The bipartisan support in Washington for closer India–US ties and the two sides' ever-converging security interests mean continued strengthening of their strategic bond is practically assured.

PUTTING INDIA ON GLOBAL POWER PATH

Prime Minister Modi's invitation to SAARC leaders, including Pakistani Prime

Minister Nawaz Sharif, to his swearing-in ceremony on 26 May 2014, gave the first indication that he intended to pursue bold foreign policy initiatives. He spent nearly thirty days of his first six months in office abroad, visiting major Asian powers like Japan and Australia and paying a high profile visit to Washington, DC following the UN General Assembly in September 2014.

By all accounts, Modi is living up to the BJP Election Manifesto to '…fundamentally reboot and reorient the foreign policy goals…so that it leads to an economically stronger India, and its voice is heard in the international fora.'[1] Modi has brought the same kind of drive and initiative to his goal of turning India into a global power as he did to unleashing the economic potential of Gujarat, when he served as the state's chief minister. According to well-renowned India expert Ashley Tellis, 'Clearly, Modi seeks to transform India from being merely an influential entity into one whose weight and preferences are defining for international politics.'[2]

Modi's emphasis on building relations with the US, including his unprecedented invitation to US President Barack Obama to serve as chief guest at the 2015 Indian Republic Day celebration, demonstrates his interest in distancing his government from the traditional non-alignment patterns of Indian foreign policymaking. His willingness to move closer to Washington is partly motivated by his belief that turning India into a global power requires international recognition and access to technology that the US must take the lead in delivering.

Modi and his advisors also seem to recognise that the most effective way to hedge against China's rise is to develop close strategic partnerships (not alliances) with democratic powers, like the US, Japan and Australia, which are equally wary of Beijing's rise.

This policy orientation differs considerably from that laid out in a 2012 study by prominent Indian academics titled, *NonAlignment 2.0: A Foreign and Strategic Policy for India in the Twenty First Century*. In that study, which seemed initially to enjoy tacit support from the former Congress-led government, the authors highlighted the need to distance New Delhi from Washington to placate

---

[1] 'BJP Election Manifesto 2014', available at: http://bjpelectionmanifesto.com/pdf/manifesto2014.pdf.

[2] Tellis, Ashley J, 'India as a Leading Power', *Carnegie Endowment for International Peace Paper*, April 2016, available at: http://carnegieendowment.org/files/CP_268_Tellis_India_final1.pdf.

Beijing since India finds itself currently outmatched by China with regard to military and technological capabilities. The authors argued that it would be risky for India to rely too heavily on the US since an India–US strategic partnership 'could become a casualty of any tactical upswing in Sino-American ties.' They further noted that the American alliance system is on the decline and that it is uncertain 'how the US would respond if China posed a threat to India's interests.'[3]

So while US officials emphasised their desire to see India play a larger role in East Asia as part of the US Asia rebalance strategy, the previous Manmohan Singh government reacted cautiously to the US public overtures and appeared conflicted about a strategy to deal with rising China.

By contrast, the Modi government is more willing to risk Chinese ire by pursuing enhanced security and defence ties with the US, even as it seeks stronger economic and business ties with China. One example of this more forward-leaning posture was the January 2015 signing of the 'Joint Strategic Vision for the Asia-Pacific and Indian Ocean', committing the US and India to cooperation outside of South Asia. The statement specifically mentioned 'ensuring freedom of navigation and over flight' in the South China Sea, confirming their mutual commitment to maritime security and to curbing China's maritime and territorial ambitions.

India's willingness to elevate the US–India–Japan trilateral talks to the ministerial level and to allow Japanese participation in the Malabar naval exercise on a permanent basis further shows Modi's interest in pursuing a more proactive approach to coping with challenges from China.

DEFENCE TIES: CORNERSTONE OF ENHANCED PARTNERSHIP

At the heart of improved India–US relations over the last couple of years has been progress on the Defense Trade and Technology Initiative (DTTI) that was launched in 2012 with the goal of breaking down bureaucratic barriers and other obstacles in order to enhance defence trade between the two countries. During President Obama's January 2015 visit to India, the two sides announced

---

[3] Khilnani, Sunil; Kumar, Rajiv; Mehta, Pratap Bhanu; Menon, Prakash Lt Gen (Ret); Nilekani, Nandan; Raghavan, Srinath; Saran, Shyam and Varadarajan, Siddharth, 'NonAlignment 2.0: A Foreign and Strategic Policy for India in the Twenty First Century', 2012, available at: http://www.cprindia.org/sites/default/files/NonAlignment%202.0_1.pdf.

the establishment of working groups to explore co-development of jet engine technology and aircraft carrier systems and co-production of unmanned aerial vehicles (UAVs) and specialised equipment for military transport aircraft.

Marking their progress on maritime security cooperation, Indian Minister of Defence, Manohar Parrikar in December 2015 made the first-ever visit by an Indian defence minister to US Pacific Command. During that same trip, US Secretary of Defense Ash Carter and Minister Parrikar flew together on a V22 Osprey to the deck of the USS Eisenhower to discuss and assess advanced carrier cooperation.[4] By similar token, Secretary Carter was the first US Defense Secretary to visit an Indian operational military command when he went to the Eastern Naval Command in Vizag in June 2015. Yet another concrete example of the positive trajectory of the defence relationship was the finalisation in September 2015 of the US$3.3 billion deal for India to buy Boeing Apache and Chinook helicopters.

A potentially significant step in improving India–US strategic ties—perhaps the greatest since the passage of the 2006 Hyde Act in support of US–India civil nuclear cooperation—was the introduction in late March 2016 of the US–India Defense Technology and Partnership Act. Introduced by Representative George Holding (R, NC), it lays out specific steps for enhancing defence ties between the two countries. These steps include, among other things, designating a point person to coordinate the interagency policy process regarding defence trade and technology transfer with India; facilitating the transfer of advanced technology for combined military planning with the Indian military on humanitarian assistance and disaster relief, counter piracy and maritime domain awareness; coordinating with India on contingency planning on mutual security threats; and amending the Arms Export Control Act to streamline the export control and arms notification process for India, putting it on par with NATO countries and other key US military allies.[5]

Some US strategists may be sceptical of the idea of treating India the same as a NATO partner or treaty ally, primarily because of India's continuing

---

[4] Verma, Richard Ambassador, 'US–India Relations: A Conversation with US Ambassador to India Richard Verma', The Brookings Institution, 11 December 2015, available at: http://www.brookings.edu/events/2015/12/11-verma-us-india-relations.

[5] HR 4825 – US–India Defence Technology and Partnership Act, 22 March 2016, available at: https://www.congress.gov/bill/114th-congress/house-bill/4825/text.

close military links with Russia and concerns about technology control. But Washington must also factor in the evolving security situation with regard to China and the need for countries like India to play a key role in helping to maintain the balance of power in Asia and to ensure freedom of the seaways. To fulfil its role in helping to stabilise and secure the Indo-Pacific region, India needs adequate defence capabilities and access to advanced military technology. While it can obtain some of these technologies from countries like France and Israel, it is in the US interest to be a key supplier for Indian defence needs to solidify strategic ties and draw the two militaries closer.

If India signs foundational defence agreements with the US, such as the Logistics Supply Agreement (LSA), the Communications Interoperability and Security Memorandum of Agreement (CISMOA) and the Basic Exchange and Cooperation Agreement (BECA), it would certainly ease technology control concerns and enhance the case for implementing the Holding Act. In the past, Indians have raised concern that these agreements would somehow sacrifice their military independence and provide the US with too much information on their operational abilities and practices. These concerns are magnified by America's continued close relationship with Pakistan. There is some concern that the Obama administration's announcement to provide Pakistan with eight additional F-16 aircrafts just weeks after the 2 January attack on India's Pathankot airbase could set back tangible progress on India–US defence cooperation.

Another check on increasing India–US defence collaboration has been the lack of private sector friendly policies, despite the Modi government's interest in catalysing India–US defence industrial partnerships. The government has talked about developing India's indigenous defence industry to reduce its reliance on importing defence equipment and technology but actual progress on the ground has been slow. The government has increased the foreign investment cap for defence projects to 49 per cent (up from 26 per cent) and stipulated that foreign investments exceeding 49 per cent will be approved on a case-by-case basis.

But defence industry experts have pointed out that until India increases the FDI cap to 74 per cent, international firms are likely to remain wary of risking major investments in the Indian defence market.[6] India needs to ease

---

[6] Sriram, Jayant, 'A cannon yet to fire – not a single big ticket proposal', *The Hindu*, 13 December 2015, at http://www.thehindu.com/business/Economy/defence-manufacturing-in-india-after-relaxing-fdi-norms/article7983617.ece.

regulations on private business and give up procurement policies that continue to favour public sector enterprises. International companies generally favour reaching their own agreements with Indian private sector firms, but current defence procurement policies make that difficult.

HOMELAND AND CYBER SECURITY COOPERATION

The continuing global and regional terrorist threats demand that New Delhi and Washington build a better foundation of trust when it comes to homeland security cooperation and intelligence sharing. India and the US stand to mutually benefit by expanding their counterterrorism cooperation in terms of sharing best practices for preventing terrorist attacks, countering the ideology that drives terrorism, disrupting terrorist recruitment via social media and working together on the diplomatic front to delegitimise terrorism. The September 2015 US–India Joint Declaration, which resulted from the Strategic and Commercial Dialogue, noted their efforts to finalise a bilateral agreement to expand intelligence sharing, terrorist watch-list information and mutual legal assistance.

While India faces its most severe terrorist threats from Pakistan-based groups, there is some concern that the ideology of the ISIS could find resonance among individual or small groups of Indian Muslims, creating a greater home-grown terrorist threat.[7] In the light of India's arrest of two dozen ISIS sympathisers, in January 2016 including some from southern states like Tamil Nadu and Karnataka, it may be prudent for New Delhi to broaden its counterterrorism focus beyond the India–Pakistan dispute and work more closely with the US on ISIS-related threats.

Another area ripe for cooperation is cyber security. The Strategic and Commercial Dialogue held in September 2015 resulted in the two sides agreeing to a Track 1.5 program to further discussions on Internet and cyber issues. The two sides recognised that cyber security and information sharing were integral elements to the joint fight against terrorism. With the third largest population of online users, India faces increasing vulnerabilities to cyber threats.

[7] Narain, Akanksha and Rajakumar, Vikram, 'Revamping India's Counter-Terrorism Approach', RSIS Commentary No. 071/2016, 4 April 2016, available at: http://www.worldaffairsjournal.org/content/analysis-revamping-india%E2%80%99s-counter-terrorism-approach.

India's decision in July 2015 to support a multi-stakeholder approach (that involves civil society and industry) regarding governance of the Internet opens the way for increased consultations between Washington and New Delhi on developing a framework for regulating the cyber domain.

IRRITANTS

Amidst the good news and bonhomie on the India–US front, the announcement of the US F-16 sale to Pakistan shortly after Pakistan-based terrorists attacked an Indian airbase came as a jolt to the relationship. Immediately following the US announcement, the Indian Foreign Secretary summoned the US Ambassador to register Indian objections. The Indian government is concerned that the F-16s could be used in the event of a conflict with India and thus the sale impacts the overall strategic stability of the region. The Obama administration, however, argues that Pakistan uses the F-16s in its counterterrorism operations in the tribal border areas and that America's control over the training and spare parts necessary to operate the aircraft provides the US a degree of leverage in how they are employed.

While the US arguments may be valid, the timing of the announcement of the sale was highly unfortunate. It came a little over a month after the Pathankot attack and before it was clear that Pakistan would take action against the group responsible for the attack, the Jaish-e-Mohammad (JeM). While Pakistan has arrested some members of the JeM, including the leader of the group Masood Azhar, no charges have been filed. And there are serious doubts whether Azhar will remain in custody, given that Pakistan frequently releases from jail terrorists that target India, like the Lashkar-e-Taiba (LeT) leader Zakiur Rehman Lakhvi, who was set free on bail in April 2015. If the F-16 sale had been announced at a time when India–Pakistan relations were on a more positive trajectory, India may not have objected so strenuously.

Another irritant has been the US stance towards China's role in South Asia. Indian officials are frustrated that the US is warmly welcoming China's role in Afghanistan reconciliation talks and the Chinese plans to vastly increase infrastructure investment and development in Pakistan through the so-called China Pakistan Economic Corridor (CPEC). Indian observers believe that China will collaborate with Pakistan in Afghanistan to the detriment of

India's interest. They argue that if the US wants India to play a larger role in the Asia-Pacific, it must also help protect New Delhi's security interests along its western border, including by denying China a larger foothold in the region.

Meanwhile, US observers believe an enhanced Chinese role in Afghanistan and Pakistan could help stabilise the region. They say China's interest in curbing the influence of Islamist extremists in the AfPak region and preventing them from spreading their influence in western China is driving the Chinese to pressure Pakistan to crack down on terrorists. They believe China's role in an Afghan peace process is essential to moving Pakistan in the right direction with regard to influencing the Taliban.[8]

MOVING FORWARD

The US should take advantage of the opportunity to deepen ties with India by focusing on building Indian defence capabilities and expanding its access to advanced naval technologies, so that India will maintain its edge in dominating the Indian Ocean Region (IOR). The US should also strengthen trilateral US–India–Japan cooperation and look for opportunities to include Australia in such endeavours.

The recent announcement by the US Pacific Commander, Admiral Harry Harris, that the US, India and Japan will conduct joint naval exercises in the north Philippine Sea this summer and his calls for greater quadrilateral naval cooperation among the US, India, Japan and Australia, are signs that the US will focus more attention on multinational efforts to maintain free and open seaways. Increased naval cooperation among the quad countries could include sharing intelligence and conducting joint surveillance and reconnaissance operations or simply looking for ways to coordinate Humanitarian Assistance and Disaster Relief (HADR) operations.

While the Modi government has shown more boldness in its willingness to cooperate closely with the US, Japan and Australia on mutual maritime goals, Washington must also keep its expectations of India realistic. Washington should recognise that Indian strategists understand that they are still behind

---

[8] Rubin, Barnett, 'Afghanistan and the Taliban Need Pakistan for Peace Talks', *Al Jazeera*, 16 January 2016, available at: http://www.aljazeera.com/indepth/opinion/2016/01/afghanistan-taliban-pakistan-peace-160110055820128.html.

China with regard to military capabilities and economic strength. Thus they will balance their desire to show Beijing that they have strategic maritime security options with their need to maintain peaceful relations with China and avoid military hostilities along their disputed land borders.

With regard to US policy towards Pakistan, the US will need to demonstrate that it can pursue relationships with both countries simultaneously but without harming India's core national security interests. With Pakistan, the US requires counterterrorism cooperation, Pakistan's involvement in stabilising Afghanistan and for Pakistan's nuclear weapons to remain safe and secure and out of the reach of terrorists. With India, the US has broader security interests in seeing the country play a more robust role in providing stability in the Indo-Pacific region.

The US must firmly acknowledge that support for terrorism will not be tolerated and continue to work closely with India to target South Asia-based terrorist groups including the LeT, JeM and others. Washington must also be clear that it will determine the future of its relationship with New Delhi based on India's global role and will not be constrained by the Pakistani military's perceptions of regional security, which tend to be skewed in favour of maintaining hostile India–Pakistan relations.

Reinvigorating the India–US homeland security dialogue will also help bolster overall security ties. The Indian Home Minister, Rajnath Singh, and his US counterpart Homeland Security Secretary, Jeh Johnson, are scheduled to meet later in 2016 for the third iteration of the Dialogue. The last Secretary-level meeting took place nearly three years ago under the previous UPA government. The US has been remiss in not scheduling this important dialogue sooner.

Prime Minister Modi further advanced India–US ties during his fourth visit to the US in early June 2016. During the visit, Modi held his seventh meeting with President Obama and received a warm reception from Congressional Members on both sides of the aisle when he addressed a joint session of the US Congress. The most significant take-away from Modi's visit was the designation of India as a 'Major Defense Partner', which will facilitate technology-sharing and put India on par with America's closest allies and partners when it comes to defence licensing. The US Ambassador to India Richard Verma described the new designation as representing the US vision of India 'as a leading power that can uphold international norms and support what Defense Secretary Carter called…a "principled security network" in Asia.'[9]

The visit also brought progress on nuclear and non-proliferation issues. The two sides announced the start of preparatory work on a site for six civilian nuclear reactors to be built by Westinghouse in the Indian state of Andhra Pradesh. The announcement helps remove an irritant in the relationship stemming from India's passage of a strict nuclear liability law in 2010 that holds suppliers liable for damages in the event of a nuclear accident. The Joint Statement also noted that India will become a member of MTCR, marking a step forward in India's quest for full-fledged membership in the global nuclear non-proliferation regime.

CONCLUSION

During his first two years in office, Prime Minister Modi has taken great pains to strengthen strategic ties with Washington, raise India's international profile and signal his country's readiness to help keep the broader Asia-Pacific region stable, secure and open. With these priorities set in New Delhi, it appears that cooperation with the US—particularly on security issues—is sure to stay on an upward trajectory.

---

[9] 'Modi effect: US calls PM's Indo-US vision as "Modi Doctrine",' *Indianexpress.com*, 10 June 2016, at: http://indianexpress.com/article/india/india-news-india/modi-effect-us-calls-pms-indo-us-vision-as-modi-doctrine-2845032/.

CHAPTER 6

INDIA'S LAND BOUNDARY AGREEMENT WITH BANGLADESH: ITS IMPORTANCE AND IMPLICATIONS

TARIQ A KARIM

At the midnight hour on 15 August 1947, the single geopolitical configuration that had been known historically and universally for millennia as the Indian subcontinent was reconfigured by the partition of India at independence from colonial rule.[1] India's tryst with destiny on that fateful midnight foisted upon it two huge boundary lines with two truncated newly-created states, West Pakistan and East Pakistan (later, since 1971, Bangladesh). Notably, post-colonial India's largest border was with Bangladesh (4,096 km).[2] Also notably, the India–Bangladesh border is, globally, the fifth largest among single borders shared between two countries.[3]

In a sense, the border with Bangladesh was perhaps the most difficult to manage because of the very permeable nature of the geographic terrain. The difficulties were exacerbated by the fact that both states had inherited enclaves

---

[1] Chronologically, the process of colonisation of the subcontinent by Europeans commenced by Portuguese inroads in 1502, followed by French, Dutch and finally British

[2] Followed by its border with the People's Republic of China (3,488 km), Pakistan (3,323 km), Nepal (1,751 km), Myanmar (1,643 km), Bhutan (699 km), and at least notionally with Afghanistan (106 km—in disputed area).

[3] After US–Canada (8,891 km), Kazakhstan–Russia (6,846 km), Argentine–Chile (5,300 km) and PR China–Mongolia (4,677 km).

inside each other's respective territory (fifty-five Bangladeshi enclaves with an area of 7,110 acres inside Indian territory and 111 Indian enclaves with an area of 17,160 acres inside Bangladesh territory) and also inherited Adversely Possessed Lands (APLs). These enclaves were a legacy of gambling debts over games of chess indulged in between the Rajas of Cooch Bihar and Rangpur in the eighteenth century. Parcels of land owned by each were used as stakes. Following post-partition independence, when these princely states acceded to and merged with India and Pakistan respectively, these parcels of land became effectively converted into enclaves. The tortuous complexity of the enclaves was further compounded by some of them possessing enclaves within enclaves (or exclaves). Over time, the human rights situation of the growing population inhabiting these enclaves increasingly overshadowed the territorial dispute between the two countries. These enclaves were home to a total population between them of around 53,000 inhabitants,[4] who found themselves being relegated to becoming virtually stateless. The state to which they notionally belonged as citizens could not access them because they were ensconced within the territory of the other. The state in which these unfortunate people found themselves thus isolated would not access them because they were 'citizens' of the other. Over the last six decades these enclaves also became the safe sanctuaries for various unsavoury mafia-like dons, whose thriving business embraced all sorts of nefarious activities, ranging from ordinary commodity smuggling to drug and narcotics peddling, arms smuggling and, worst of all human trafficking.

In addition to these enclaves, the Radcliffe Award for partitioning the subcontinent also left the two newly independent nation-states saddled with adverse possession: thirty-eight patches of Indian land (in possession by Bangladesh) measuring 3,000 acres and fifty patches of Bangladeshi land measuring 3,345 acres (in possession by India).

These issues had remained festering since the Partition, adversely impacting relations between the two new states in various ways, a legacy inherited by Bangladesh that emerged from the ashes of war-ravaged East Pakistan in 1971.

---

[4] A joint census carried out in July 2011 revealed that there were 14,215 people residing in Bangladeshi enclaves in India and 37,269 people residing in Indian enclaves in Bangladesh. Both sides agreed that the peoples in these enclaves would be allowed to choose their nationality prior to the exchange, and both countries would cooperate in ensuring smooth transition.

An agreement in principle had been reached between Prime Minister Nehru and his then Pakistani counterpart, Malik Firoze Khan Noon in 1958 to exchange these territories. Attempt to exchange three of these by transfer, namely, South Berubari (to India) and Dahagram and Angarpota (to Bangladesh) was effectively stymied and held in abeyance for long, by the Indian Supreme Court's injunction following a PIL that any transfer of territories required a Constitutional amendment. That injunction also stopped further attempts to operationalise the agreement, which itself became hostage of the deteriorating relations between India and Pakistan, as did the Teen Bigha corridor between these two sets of enclaves meant for allowing people from the respective sovereign mainlands to travel to these enclaves.

After the birth of Bangladesh in 1971, serious negotiations were resumed and the bonhomie that marked relations between the peoples and leaders resulted in the signing on 16 May 1974 of the Land Boundary Agreement (popularly known as the Indira-Mujib Pact) by India's Prime Minister Indira Gandhi and Bangladesh's Prime Minister Sheikh Mujibur Rahman. That Agreement should have resulted in completing the joint demarcation of the borders and the exchange of enclaves and adversely possessed lands by the two. However, before significant progress could be achieved in undertaking the demanding ground work required (joint surveys and agreed identification of border pillars demarcating the territories of the two), Sheikh Mujibur Rahman and almost his entire family was brutally killed in a military putsch on 15 August 1975. A military-backed junta replaced his government and shortly thereafter the four senior-most leaders of the deposed Awami League government were also killed at the behest of the new junta while in prison, effectively decapitating the Awami League and ensuring its prolonged exclusion from the political arena. Following this, relations between India and Bangladesh plunged into a nadir from which it never really re-emerged to their original moorings established in the early seventies, until the return of the Awami League to power in June 1996, after over 21 years in the political wilderness.

A testimony to the rancour, that for the greater part defined the bilateral relations post-August 1975, was that while border demarcation work continued, albeit at slow pace all the time in the intervening period, only two letters were exchanged between the two governments on the subject, on 7 October 1982 and 26 March 1992, and thousands of strip maps that had been agreed upon and signed by the respective Surveyors-General, that would have given them legal status, were never countersigned by the designated plenipotentiaries of the two countries. In other words, if any one side had any mala fide intentions towards the other, any one of the over 10,000 strip maps could have been reopened for contention (as indeed the author was witness to personally in 1995 but was able to forestall).[5]

When Sheikh Hasina was elected to power, in June 1996 (somewhat unexpectedly as per the ruling dispensation's calculations at that time), a little over 60 km of the 4,096-long km still remained undemarcated. Although she was able to sign the historic Treaty on Sharing of the Ganga/Ganges Waters at Farakka within six months of assuming office, on 12 December 1996, and resolve amicably the long festering insurgency problem in the Chittagong Hill Tracts that required India's active support and assistance, and although she took the first effective measures to address India's security concerns as a precursor to arriving at these agreements, only small headway was made on the boundary issues, whether land or maritime.

India and Bangladesh jointly prepared a list of enclaves in 1997, and also set up two Joint Working groups to work out the details of the enclaves in 2001. Testimony to this glacial movement was the fact that when she was swept to power by a landslide victory in December 2008 with an overwhelming mandate for change, there still remained undemarcated 6.4 km of land borders. Resolution of the land boundary and maritime boundary disputes became a priority agenda of the new government, which understood that its own ambitious development goals could best be achieved by ensuring good and strong relations with its immediate neighbours, particularly India. Without this, any efforts towards larger subregional/regional cooperation efforts would remain a chimera.

What makes this particular border of great significance is that this largest of the three bitterly disputed post-colonial borders that India inherited was resolved remarkably amicably, through bilateral negotiations between the contesting states, with no third-party mediation or intervention. This was

---

[5] Some 11,000 strip maps were all finally signed, in quadruplicate, by the author, as High Commissioner to India and his counterpart Rajeet Mitter in Dhaka in August 2011, prior to and as a prerequisite for the LBA and Protocol signed in September 2011.

only possible because the leadership on both sides manifested visionary statesmanship and ensured translation of their political will to their respective bureaucracies tasked with finalisation of the mutually agreed deal, eschewing narrower considerations of local politics and breaking free of the post-Partition syndrome that had held their attitudes to each other needlessly hostage for over six decades.

The signing of the Additional Protocol for operationalising the 1974 Land Boundary Agreement, by the two Foreign Ministers in the presence of the Prime Ministers of the two countries in Dhaka on 6 May 2011 finally brought the long and tortuous process of negotiations to a closure. However, the LBA and its Additional Protocol needed to be ratified first by the respective Parliaments and could only come into force on the dates of exchange of the instruments of ratification. The UPA government of Prime Minister Manmohan Singh tabled the agreement in the form of the 119th Constitutional Amendment Bill in the Rajya Sabha in December 2013, but unfortunately the choppy dynamics of electoral politics intervened, and this final act of closure was only achieved after the new Parliament and government in India led by Prime Minister Narendra Modi was elected to power in May 2014.

Within less than a year of assuming office, the Rajya Sabha ratified the Bill unanimously on 6 May 2015 followed by unanimous ratification by the Lok Sabha on 7 May 2015. A new history of resolving bilaterally contentious issues was created for the region. A month later, Prime Minister Modi undertook his first official visit to Bangladesh and after the Foreign Secretaries of the two countries had signed the instruments of ratification, he exchanged the same with his Bangladeshi counterpart. For Prime Minister Sheikh Hasina, it must have been a particularly gratifying and emotionally charged moment—she had succeeded in bringing to an amicable closure a process that had been started by her illustrious father in 1974. The journey of togetherness as mutually cooperative and developmentally reinforcing neighbours envisioned by the father then but tragically interrupted by his assassination in 1975, was left to his daughter to resume almost forty years later. Significantly, the Maritime Boundary dispute, which had also served to vitiate bilateral relations between the two countries, was also resolved amicably through the good offices of the Permanent Court of Arbitration in July 2014. Both sides accepted gracefully the final verdict of the award in the larger interest of friendly relations and cooperation for development.[6]

Good boundaries between neighbours, devoid of contention, make for good neighbourliness. In a region that had projected an image of singular lack of bonhomie and established a negative record globally for its inability to get its regional cooperation act together in any meaningful manner in over six decades, putting the most thorny of boundary issues behind them by Bangladesh and India was a game-changing development. Prime Minister Narendra Modi, in an interview on the eve of his visit to Bangladesh in June 2015 had likened the unanimous ratification of the LBA and its Protocol by the Indian Rajya Sabha and Lok Sabha to the fall of the Berlin Wall. How relevant was this analogy?

In an article that this author had written for the *Daily Star* newspaper of Dhaka, which was published by that paper as a curtain-raiser on the day of his arrival in Dhaka on 7 June 2015, the author had asserted as follows:

> If one takes into account that the partition of the historical Indian-subcontinent on the eve of its independence from British Colonial rule on August 14, 1947 was also through the drawing of a line across a map that had hitherto represented a single geopolitical landmass for millennia, and that post-Partition the strident divisive jingoism actually fortified the walls that were built within the mindsets of the new nations so created (which were far stronger and more impermeable than the lines on the ground), the analogy drawn by Mr Modi is not at all as far-fetched as sceptics would wish it to be. When many in India, Bangladesh and elsewhere in the subcontinent had come to believe that border issues spawned by the Radcliffe Award that marked the Partition could never be resolved, the ability of negotiators not only to arrive at the final agreement, and of Parliaments in both countries actually managing to get it ratified, with disparate voices from right to left of the political divide coming on the same platform and voicing support, is a monumental shattering of a glass ceiling of sort. It demolishes

---

[6] Despite some internal pressures for resolving the matter through bilateral negotiations, Bangladesh, wisely opted for seeking arbitration under the relevant provisions of the United Nations Convention on Law of the Seas, thereby insulating itself from political dissent on whatever deal it would have been able to arrive at via the bilateral process. Bangladesh Foreign Minister AH Mahmood Ali hailed the Arbitration Court's award as 'a victory of friendship between Bangladesh and India'.

a tenaciously held myth by many that problems between India and its partitioned neighbours could never be resolved. The mindset that this event demolishes is perhaps far more important than the barbed-wire fencing that has been put on the ground reflecting the sheer difficulties on the ground in managing a vastly porous border whose lines were fuzzy and unclear to many on both sides. I view this as prizing apart the hitherto very narrowly defined space of mutual comfort and trust through fragmentation of the mindset of yore that had bedevilled bilateral relations between the two neighbours, as also the beginning of a process that may, yet, ultimately make the fence irrelevant.[7]

OPENING NEW VISTAS OF CONNECTIVITY

The resolution of land and maritime boundary disputes has directly translated into a significant and increasing confluence of visions and interests as well in both the countries, particularly in the sectors of water and energy cooperation: in respect of how waterbodies should be holistically and better managed bearing in mind the heavy environmental and ecological price that all have paid by ignoring the growing water crisis; and how an architecture for long-term energy security can be put in place to fuel their developmental ambitions.

With this most thorny and challenging dispute resolved, Bangladesh was enabled to resolutely advance towards assuming fully its strategic role as hub of connectivity, by river, rail, road and air for which it is uniquely positioned, not only between the Indian mainland and the latter's North East states, but between the whole of India (and indeed South Asia) and East Asia. While it would be an easier task to reconnect land and rail-links that had been laid during the colonial times but rendered asunder following the Partition in 1947, the bigger challenge would be to restore the riverine connectivity that had existed historically in the region. While much has been written about the North East Indian states, as well as Bhutan and Nepal, being landlocked, people over two generations have forgotten that these entities had been historically always water-linked with greater Bengal and the Indian mainland. Prior to Partition, men and goods used to be transported along and by these vast stretches of

---

[7] Karim, Tariq, 'Indian PM Modi's visit to Bangladesh: The Importance of Seizing the Moment', *Daily Star*, 7 June 2017.

waters, the Ganga and the Brahmaputra, from Allahabad (Uttar Pradesh) and Guwahati (Assam) to river ports of Narayangane and Kolkata in Bengal. There were feeder links from Bhutan and Nepal to these rivers as well. It was only after the 1965 India–Pakistan War that the latter effectively dropped an 'iron curtain' fortifying the Radcliffe line in the eastern part of Partitioned India, snapping the river connection and triggering the progressive atrophying of navigable channels, riverbeds becoming silted up, riverbanks shifting whichever way the torrential force of the waters meandered, and the rivers devouring over the decades tens of thousands of hectares of arable and habitable land. In my opinion, the neglecting of these water stretches also cumulatively resulted in the massive pollution accruing to these pristine waters, a challenge that all countries concerned are now struggling to overcome.

As a result, upstream and downstream industries that had nurtured a flourishing river economy declined and eventually disappeared, public attention shifted elsewhere, and the life and civilisation-sustaining rivers became polluted and problematic waters, bearers of man-made and industrial effluents and toxic waste that wreaked havoc on the river ecology. In one of her earliest pronouncements after being elected to power in December 2008, Prime Minister Sheikh Hasina had asserted that she 'wanted her rivers and waterways back'. This, I believe, was not merely a sentimental declaration aimed only at cleaning up badly polluted rivers, but a recognition that by ignoring our rivers and concentrating only on roads and highways (very difficult to maintain during the best of climatic conditions), Bangladeshi and Indian planners had ignored and gone against the very geo-morphology of the terrain that defined this subregion, and indeed the lives of its peoples.

India's Prime Minister Modi also believes, just as passionately as Prime Minister Sheikh Hasina does, that our rivers have to be rejuvenated and restored. Modi has already directed that India must develop in earnest national waterways as assiduously if not more than it had to date been pouring in resources for developing national highways. Restoring the waterways would enable far more goods and human traffic to be transported across them, far cheaper and for much longer distances per unit fuel or money; restoration of the waterways would also revive in the process upstream and downstream activities that had described the way of life historically for the peoples inhabiting its many river basins, as well as significantly reducing the carbon footprint of the country.

Bangladesh and India can both work towards linking up their respective national waterways and expanding the same to assume subregional arterial dimensions, by facilitating directly or by developing nearby hubs thus also freeing Bhutan and Nepal from their land-locked situations. Opening up the rivers to better and more optimised used of river transportation in turn will open up new service sectors and industries. Peoples of the rivers would once again reconnect with, and resume ownership of, these vast waterbodies that had nurtured their way of life for millennia. Dying rivers would be revived and the ecology resuscitated. The generation of hydroelectricity would also serve the purpose of rendering surplus hydrocarbon resources for intra-regional use or export abroad. They would also dramatically reduce the current rate of deforestation (for fuel as well as for illegal logging). The regeneration of forestry and increasing forest coverage would create new, and enhance existing, carbon-sequestration zones. All these activities and measures could be used as trade-offs, in our negotiations on climate change dialogues, in terms of the existing provisions of the Kyoto Protocol. Additional important spin-offs from these exercises would be sharply cutting down on or eliminating soil erosion that generates new poverty (because every year in devastating floods, the rivers literally devour thousands of acres of land that leave people homeless and cashless); and progressive siltation of riverbeds would be reduced.

Both would need to develop communication infrastructure in harmony with each other and always keeping in mind the larger goal of connectivity regionally for economic development of all. Both should also seek to break out from remaining hostage to Benapole-Petrapole (at West Bengal–Bangladesh border near Jessore) and Agartala–Akhaura (at Tripura–Comilla border) being, for almost a half century, the two principal gateways for trade. While a third gateway at Dawki–Tamabil (at Meghalaya–Sylhet border) is in the process of upgradation, some more points facilitating more direct north-south movement (like the present grossly inadequate Changrabandha–Burimari, Banglabandha–Fulbari and Nakugaon–Dalu points) should be made user-friendly and more meaningfully operational. All these additional gateways would immensely benefit Bhutan and Nepal as well.

Energy security is required to fuel the South Asian industrial revolution to lift its teeming millions (40 per cent or more of its total population) out of the morass of poverty. In this sphere as well, Bangladesh and India have succeeded in doing something that had been summarily dismissed by many as being in the realm of fantasy. Bangladesh is not only purchasing 500MW of power from India (in 2012), after linking Bheramara, a point in its western grid with India's eastern grid point at Berhampur (in West Bengal). With non-denominational electrons flowing across borders, there has been a surge of appetite for more and more power being obtained from across hitherto impermeable borders. The Bheramara-Berhampur transborder grid line is being expanded now to augment flow capacity to 1000MW and ultimately 2000MW. This increasing cooperation in the energy and power sector is an area that offers numerous win-win scenarios. Bangladesh has just started importing another 100MW, to begin with, from the Palatana Power Project in Tripura (that was enabled, in the first place, with Bangladesh's assistance) by linking Bangladesh's grid at its eastern border in Comilla with the Indian grid in Tripura. Additionally, work on the India–Bangladesh Friendship Power Company, a joint venture thermal power plant that will generate 1320MW of electricity (the largest such bilateral joint venture to date) is reportedly progressing fast the plant and will become fully operational within the next couple of years.

The most exciting prospect lies ahead, by the two countries linking up their respective north-eastern grids that could be transformed to become the gateway and conduit for India to finally invest in harvesting hydropower up to 60,000-80,000MW. Bangladesh could enter into joint or sole investments, in hydro and other modes of power generation and also offer evacuation through Bangladesh in return for a sizeable quantum of that power being dropped in Bangladesh.

In return, Bangladesh needs Indian approval for evacuation of hydropower (10,000MW at least, should we so desire, from Bhutan alone) from Bhutan and Nepal. Talks are underway for PPP in the energy-power sector between India, Bangladesh, Bhutan and Nepal. In the foreseeable future the power grids of Bangladesh, Bhutan, India and Nepal (BBIN) being connected with each other is no longer in the realm of fantasy. One can envision the ultimate linking of all these presently separate bilateral power grids into a subregional mesh of interlinking grids of symbiotic interdependence in the energy sector, forming the architecture of long-term energy security for this subregion.

Strong cooperative bilateral relations between India and Bangladesh hold the key not only to making subregional cooperation feasible, but also to helping India meaningfully operationalise its Act East Policy. Both these goals are two sides of the same coin. Ultimately, one has the audacity to hope that the template of this new bilateral relationship may even serve as a model worth emulating by the rest of the SAARC countries that continue to be prisoners of their historical inheritance from the traumatic Partition of 1947. India and Bangladesh continuing to working closely together will be the key to any meaningful transformation of the larger regional relations for the better.

The sound bases for subregional cooperation and development are therefore now firmly in place. India and Bangladesh can now work together on the larger and more far-reaching agenda that they both need desperately to address, for economic development and uplift of the quality of lives of their peoples, so many of whom happen to be concentrated in the eastern subregion of SAARC. Security is no longer a single dimensional phenomenon, limited to conventional security of the state and its citizens. Non-traditional security issues, like water security, energy security and ecological and environmental security have in recent times become far more consequentially important and all-encompassing, subsuming traditional security concerns. All these issues are in a sense, holistically interrelated and feed into each other. Addressing these will directly translate into governments also being enabled to address concerns of ensuring for their citizens food and employment security. But not addressing these meaningfully will, in all likelihood, have a deleterious multiplier force effect of further aggravating existing conventional security threats.

Whether, and to what extent, progress can, or will be made is dependent on one single factor that looms large over everything else—deeply entrenched mindsets, perhaps more now in the smaller neighbours than in India that is today a far more self-confident nation than it was say a decade or two earlier. The baggage that we have is our unfortunate legacy from the cataclysmic Partition of 1947, and of that post-colonial aberrational phenomenon called the Cold War which subsumed so many of the world's discourses in the last half century and whose spectre still casts a dark shadow on many present-day discourses, keeping alive still the spirit of discord and malevolence in bits and parts. To overcome this, history has to be perceived as a narrative to draw lessons from, not to imprison ourselves in a time warp.

While it becomes imperative for the strong and large to be more generous, and sometimes even to appear to be self-effacing, to give the smaller and weaker the sense of secure space and trusting comfort, it is equally incumbent on the latter to lower their guards that are frozen in perpetual belligerence of self-defence and more often than not loathe to recognise the moment when a good offer is being made and accept the hand offering that. Such a moment is now upon us, which bodes well for our bilateral relations as well for regional economic integration—at least in the eastern BBIN (Bangladesh–Bhutan–India and Nepal) subregion of SAARC. Let us seize it. Let us demonstrate, to ourselves and the rest of the region, that there is nothing to fear but fear itself, and nothing succeeds like success!

CHAPTER 7

NARENDRA MODI:
THE LEADER WITH CLEAR VISION

KARAN BILIMORIA

I remember meeting Prime Minister Narendra Modi for the first time when he was the chief minister of Gujarat and I was attending a Pravasi Bharatiya Divas event. I have attended and spoken at this event from day one in 2003. Even in those days all eyes were on him as one of the high profile chief ministers in India, who was making great strides in economic development in his state.

It was, without doubt, a surprise when Narendra Modi and the BJP won an outright majority in the 2014 Lok Sabha elections. Prime Minister Modi's 2014 election campaign was groundbreaking in its use of technology, social media and holograms, with Modi addressing giant crowds which we could not dream of in the UK. With this said, it came as a complete surprise to the world when he won an outright majority in the politically-fragmented landscape in India—it is a country with so many parties, many viable and existing only in their own state. It was therefore a challenge and a feat for a single party to win an outright majority on the national stage—Narendra Modi defied the odds and achieved this conclusively in 2014.

The Prime Minister was very clear in his vision for India and equally clear in articulating it. The invitation he extended to leaders of neighbouring countries to attend his inauguration at the Rashtrapati Bhavan was a magnanimous gesture—a clear indication that his would not be an ordinary tenure; it would be unique from day one.

Narendra Modi has travelled extensively, more than any other world leader that I can think of. I remember watching in awe as the Prime Minister spoke at Madison Square Garden on his first visit to the United States after he took office. The arena was packed with almost 20,000 people in attendance and the reception he received was phenomenal. I remember thinking, how, when he visits England, could we ever match this?

Eventually, Modi did visit the UK in November 2015 and I was privileged to play a part in helping to organise the trip. He was the first serving Indian Prime Minister to address both Houses of Parliament in Westminster, and that too in the Royal Gallery, an honour normally reserved for visiting heads of state, with Narendra Modi preceded by President Xi Jinping of China just a few weeks prior. During his visit to the UK, the Prime Minister made a huge impact. His speech in Parliament was that of a global statesman—it touched on a wide variety of areas and emphasised the length and breadth of the India–UK relationship—one steeped in 400 years of history. His speech to the business community hosted by the Lord Mayor at the Guildhall in the City of London was spot on—it reassured the business community that India was a country on the move and open for the UK to invest in and partner with. The icing on the cake and the pièce de résistance was his speech at Wembley Stadium to the Indian community. He was welcomed by Prime Minister David Cameron, who made a short speech, and then Prime Minister Modi spoke for almost one-and-a-half hours without notes and there was applause virtually every minute! He proved that, speaking in Hindi, he is the finest orator in the world by far. I remember saying to myself then, 'Madison Square Garden: eat your heart out!'

Narendra Modi's Wembley speech was a summary of his vision for India in all its elements: Skill India—improving people's education and capabilities; Make in India—reinforcing the importance of manufacturing, creating jobs and strengthening the economy; Clean India—a cleanliness drive including cleaning the river Ganga; the Smart Cities initiative—which is addressing the issues associated with India's huge urbanisation that has taken place over the past few decades (India now has over 40 cities with a population of over one million people each); Digital India—which aims to improve digital infrastructure and promotes digital literacy. His speech also clearly articulated that the relationship between the UK and India is one of equals.

On the one hand, India is a country with a population of over 1.25 billion people, whilst Britain has a population of just over 60 million people. The UK is one-twentieth the size of India, yet it is the fifth largest economy in the world and is the most successful economy in Europe. Britain is still a global power, which is reflected by its permanent seat on the UNSC and its influential voice as a member of the G7, G8 and G20, as well as, of course, the EU.

Britain is a tiny country, but it still has world-class capabilities in every field, such as the finest universities in the world, alongside the United States. London is the number one financial capital in the world and the UK continues to be a world leader in a number of fields, including accountancy, manufacturing, architecture, design, creative industries and law.

The UK and India are ideal partners with many areas of synergy and mutual benefit. They also share a strong emotional bond. I have always said that the UK has a special relationship with two countries: the United States and India.

The world has been watching India closely and the consistency of the economic reforms emanating from the country has been a source of great encouragement. The steady trickle of reforms, which include increasing the threshold for foreign investment in insurance; allowing foreign investment in the defence sector; creating an Independent Monetary Policy Committee, allowing interest rates to be set proactively and reactively on an independent basis; allowing foreign investment in food processing for the first time; and, most importantly, the Prime Minister is trying to implement the Goods and Services Tax (GST) throughout the country—which has been touted as having the potential to increase India's GDP by almost 2 per cent. All this has been excellent in helping to attract investment to India. Apart from the Prime Minister, champions of these reforms, notably Arun Jaitley, should also be praised. However, when it comes to reforms, more needs to be done—for example, the Higher Education sector in India remains closed. As Chancellor of the University of Birmingham, I know that a number of foreign universities want the sector to open up and are looking forward to the opportunity of being able to operate in India. Some universities would even like to open more than one campus in India. All this would greatly benefit Indian students and the country's economy.

The BJP and Prime Minister Narendra Modi face a number of obstacles in introducing new legislation. One hindrance is that the party does not have a majority in the Rajya Sabha and so is forced to compromise on certain policies. The most difficult obstacle for implementing reforms in India is its federalised structure. Federalisation gives states an enormous amount of autonomy and independence, often a great strength in such a multicultural country, however it poses a challenge in the implementation of many necessary reforms that the Central government wants to introduce, but which are not supported by individual states.

Narendra Modi should continue with his focused, clear vision for India's growth path and, if he can work with the states and convince them to proceed on his journey alongside him, there will be no stopping India's growth path under his leadership.

It is clear that economic growth is not enough. Looking back to the election of 2004, the BJP-led government under Prime Minister Atal Bihari Vajpayee—known as the 'India Shining' government, consistently achieved growth rates of close to 10 per cent. This did little to stop the BJP from being defeated in the 2004 election as the growth was not seen as inclusive. One of Narendra Modi's greatest challenges is to ensure that his reforms and India's growth, which has recently overtaken China's, is inclusive. Growth needs to not only lift millions of people out of poverty and into the middle class—which will soon be size of the EU's population—it must also take the challenges and needs of people living in rural areas into account.

India is by far the most secular, pluralist, multicultural and diverse country in the world. Its greatest resource is the 1.25 billion people living in the country. Since economic liberalisation in 1991, India's entrepreneurship, which was suppressed in the past, has been unleashed. India is now a country of aspiration and opportunity, where anyone can get to the top from anywhere. There is no better demonstration of this than Narendra Modi. The Prime Minister's humble beginnings saw him selling tea at railway stations as a boy and now he is the leader of the largest democracy on the planet and is one of the most powerful and inspirational leaders on the world stage. If Modi, with his brilliant communication and oratory skills, can pursue his clear vision for India with the energy, focus and conviction that he has been showing, and if he can implement and execute policies in an inclusive way, India will rise from an emerging global economic superpower to a global economic superpower.

CHAPTER 8

INDIA AND SRI LANKA: RIGHT LEADERSHIP AT THE RIGHT TIME

ASANGA ABEYAGOONASEKERA

If they answer not to thy call, walk alone!

Rabindranath Tagore

INTRODUCTION

Narendra Modi did walk alone. His success in transforming Gujarat was evidence to the entire world. The vision was set and he paved his own path. Eventually, many Indians believed he could transform the world's biggest democracy. The India he took over was still one where many lived in poverty, with the underprivileged living in both urban and rural pockets across India. Modi was a commoner who made it to the top of the political ladder, keeping with the beat of the common man. India holds proud its rich democratic institution. The embodiment of this pride lies in the success of elevating a common man to the highest level.

As the new Prime Minister stepped into Parliament for the first time, he bowed, with his forehead touching the stairs—a sign of highest respect for the 'Temple of Democracy', which he called the Parliament after his victory. Modi proudly said, a common man like him and his political rise to the highest position is a clear indication of the democratic wheels of the nation turning. 'A new hope has arisen in the common man, at the end of the day for whom is the government? It is for the poor.'

With a focus on the poor, he initiated certain remarkable programmes for the less privileged which reminds me of the late President Ranasinghe Premadasa of Sri Lanka, who worked tirelessly to rebuild the country for the common man. Premadasa initiated gigantic development programmes such as 200 textile factories, houses for the underprivileged and the 'Jana Saviya' programme to fund rural community. Premadasa was also a common man who was elevated to the highest position at a time when the country was in turmoil with the Southern insurrection and the Northern War with the Liberation Tigers of Tamil Eelam (LTTE) in 1989.

Modi, identifying that some 680 million lack means to meet their basic needs, questioned, 'How can we be successful in eradicating poverty?' Around 65 per cent of India's 1.2 billion people live in villages and the majority of rural residents still have no access to the formal banking systems. Modi wanted to get rid of financial untouchability to help the poor and reduce their exposure to 'moneylenders who charge extremely high interest rates for loans'. India is one of the world's biggest economies but of the estimated 247 million households in the country, only about 145 million had access to a bank account.

Modi vowed to change this situation by calling out for a bank account for everyone and making this a national priority. Jan Dhan Yojana, the national mission on financial inclusion was launched on 26 January 2015, giving low income groups and rural households access to the Indian banking system. The scheme has displayed great results and has encouraged many otherwise excluded common people to park their savings in banks, rather than using gold bullion, jewellery and various informal investment schemes. Modi wishes to double the farmer's income by 2020 by improving the health of the soil across agricultural areas in India. He states, 'I am not an economist but I have worked with farmers.' Unlike the former Indian Prime Minister, Dr Manmohan Singh, Modi is not an economist but he knows how to work towards value addition of the agro-products.

REGIONALISM AND SOVEREIGNTY: THE DILEMMA OF THE SOUTH ASIAN REGION

In another significant remark, Prime Minister Modi announced a common satellite for South Asian nations at the Eighteenth SAARC Summit in Kathmandu in November 2014. This points towards a direction of favouring commonality over isolation. These efforts have the potential to bring South Asian nations closer, a priority which requires much sustained progress. For South Asia to work as one common region is a great challenge given the historically rooted political tensions, especially between India and Pakistan. A paradigm shift in thinking is required and Modi has the leadership capability to make South Asian nations better and prosperous by connecting them to the Make in India hub. This gigantic initiative was launched on 25 September 2014 to bolster job creation and skill enhancement in twenty-five sectors of the economy. The campaign designed by Wieden+Kennedy to transform India, was visible everywhere, even during my visit to the foothills of Davos.

India lies at 130 (2016) on the World Bank's 'doing business index', a slight improvement of four places compared to 2015. This position needs improvement as many Southeast Asian and other nations such as China (ranked at number eighty-four) are in a better position than India. The underlying idea behind the Make in India policy focuses on improving businesses and combines incentives with easy handling and faster machinery with least hindrances. The biggest untapped resource is the country's unemployed youth population which needs development and relevant training in certain key areas. Modi is on the right track when focusing the policy to involve youth in the twenty-five key industries of the nation.

Modi has aggressively marketed his government's programmes like Make in India, Clean Ganga, Swachh Bharat, Digital India, Smart Cities and Skill India to the global investors aimed at making India an industrial hub by urging them to set up industries in India instead of just FDI. The idea is to make India a destination for production of goods and exporting the same to the rest of the world. Getting rid of the red tape and creating a conducive business environment with 100 smart cities will help in achieving the target of affordable housing by making the investors partners in the plan. This is another massive task Modi has promised.

This entire economic plan will benefit the common people of India. However, South Asia made several plans in the past which delivered less due to various reasons. India may have 100 smart cities and Sri Lanka may have 100 day reform programmes, but the common man should not conclude that such programmes are merely political slogans. Regionally there is much commonality in most

South Asian countries that could be collectively examined. We tend to ignore the regionalist approach and confine efforts to our own national borders—the rhetoric of protecting of our own, including the nation's sovereignty.

Improvement in accountability and the quality of political culture are areas which need attention. With high corruption in most South Asian nations, the Corruption Perception Index by Transparency International clearly establishes deep-rooted malaise of corruption as the biggest challenge to growth and development in South Asia, with not much having changed during the last decade. High political corruption needs effective tackling. India under the Modi government has set about the task to curb corruption through efficacious governance and administrative reforms. The government has supported and strengthened new anti-corruption websites such as ipaidabribe.com, which is a testimony to digital technology enabling the quantification and identification of areas of corruption. The Right to Information (RTI) Act is a noteworthy achievement in India through which an ordinary person can question politicians and government authority, a feature other South Asian countries can adopt. Sri Lanka is still struggling to get the RTI passed.

Under the Modi administration, Indian foreign policy has improved dramatically with many small and large nations, most notably, the USA. The visit of President Obama as chief guest for the 2015 Republic Day, the first US President to visit India twice in a tenure, is a clear indication of this. Modi, with his successful foreign policy connect visited thirty-seven countries till March 2016 and welcomed leaders from twelve countries, including the US, Germany, Sri Lanka, Afghanistan and Bhutan. The centrepiece of his foreign policy is the 'Neighbourhood First' strategy to improve relationships with India's neighbouring countries. After more than thirty years, an Indian Prime Minister visited Sri Lanka in March 2015, a significant moment for India–Sri Lanka relationship with the new regime of President Maithripala Sirisena. This is seen as resetting the relationship as the former regime of President Mahinda Rajapaksa was tilted more towards China.

During Modi's visit to Sri Lanka, he announced that Indian and Sri Lankan companies would work together to develop oil tank facilities that could refuel visiting ships in Trincomalee, a desire to help the northern city become 'a regional petroleum hub'. India is planning to undertake a major investment in Sri Lanka's maritime infrastructure. Modi's 'Sagar Mala', a development plan initiative to improve the domestic maritime infrastructure and to build ten coastal economic regions within its 7,000-km coastline could have a huge impact on Sri Lankan ports. In fact, the entire maritime South Asia should be developed eventually and India and other nations' stake should be considered.

To shift the strategic relationship with China especially with regard to massive loans borrowed during the Rajapaksa regime is something the Sri Lankan government will find challenging to move away. The Chinese project such as the Colombo Port City is a clear indication of this circumstance. China is a significant global actor and its strategic reach is a reality that Sri Lanka cannot ignore or sidestep. Prime Minister Wickramasinghe's visit to China in April 2016 has bolstered further China–Sri Lanka relations, which the joint statement described as 'all-weather friendship'. The Prime Minister has already announced a 10,000 acre development zone to China in Hambanthota.

The much-debated and controversial Comprehensive Economic Partnership Agreement (CEPA) for which former President Rajapaksa's government held negotiations with India from 2005-8, ended as a non-starter and was shelved due to much opposition. Now a new framework, the Economic and Technology Cooperation Agreement (ETCA) is under discussion, to be finalised by the close of 2016. Again we see certain social groups as well as the former President opposing the agreement.

A study of the sixteen years of FTA between India and Sri Lanka showed that in 1999 the value of Sri Lankan exports to India was US$49 million. This has gone up to US$645 million in 2015. There is certainly more scope to improve trade between the two nations and hopefully the ETCA could add value to this existing commercial relationship. Most of the fear is centred on the India–Lanka Accord, which was not adequately discussed and was done at a speed which the public did not much appreciate. PM Wickramasinghe has clearly stated public participation and discussion before implementation of the ETCA. A protest was held in Colombo against opening up of certain sectors such as IT and IT-enabled shipbuilding fields with the fear that such a step would lead to the domination of Indian employees leaving locals disadvantaged.

Of the pressing issues which trigger regularly is the India–Sri Lanka fishing boundary. Sri Lankan fishermen accuse their Indian counterparts of poaching in their waters in the Northern seas and using destructive practices such as bottom trawling. The Sri Lankan authorities have banned destructive methods that deplete the marine life and destroy the seabed.

Finding solutions for this is a priority. The Sri Lankan opposition group leader Dinesh Gunawardena recently accused the government in the Parliament of not finding solutions to resolve the fishing problem and questioned the credibility of the government to solve other issues. The proximity of maritime borders between India and Sri Lanka prove a challenge to demarcate fishing boundaries. However, both nations need to find a way forward before they can move to larger projects such as building a physical bridge between the two nations as proposed by the Sri Lankan Prime Minister.

With the leaderships of both the Prime Ministers, India and Sri Lanka can create space for closer economic integration. Modi and Wickramasinghe are very similar in their outlook and value technology innovation to improve peoples' lives.

SOUTH ASIA AND ITS ASPIRING YOUTH

The South Asia Bridge Initiative, a platform set up by the South Asian Young Global Leaders of the World Economic Forum, was held in Colombo in February 2016 with an interaction session with Prime Minister Wickramasinghe. The platform discussed the importance of regional integration and the critical role the youth can play. Following this, an advisory council has been set up to assist the Prime Minister. More importantly, the receptiveness of the Prime Minister to such an initiative shows a positive character of a leader searching for solutions that can bring prosperity to a region that has a high poverty rate. In Sri Lanka, according to the 2016 World Bank report, more than 40 per cent of the population lives on less than LKR 225 a day. In India more than 400 million people continue living in poverty and a similar state of poverty prevails in other South Asian countries. Clearly all political leaders in South Asia need to implement policy reforms to move towards development so as to alleviate poverty.

The improvement of the quality of life by providing the best possible education, healthcare, housing and safety especially for women and children are basic necessities in the region. According to the Global Competitiveness Index (GCI) 2014-15, almost all South Asian countries fall in the Transition Driven

(Stage 1) category. In contrast, most East Asian nations are in an Efficiency Driven (Stage 2) or Transition to Innovation Driven (Stage 3) category. Sri Lanka has moved to Stage 2 in 2016, an improvement in many areas of society, especially the human development index. South Asian nations need to realise their potential demographic dividend especially the youth bulge and bring in policy reforms and economic sustainability for the transition of the youth into the labour market. Prime Minister Modi, with his statecraft of bringing foreign investment and modernising India's domestic economy could transform the entire region into a zone of prosperity. His leadership is a refreshing change for the entire region. The present Sri Lankan Prime Minister with more than three decades of experience in Parliament and Prime Minister Modi with his vision could work towards this transition and join hands rather than walk alone. Never has there been an opportunity for the two nations to strengthen relationship and make individual lives better. The lives of millions of people both in India and Sri Lanka living with a nominal amount will change by seizing this historical opportunity.

India and Sri Lanka, as long-standing allies and commercial partners and most significantly neighbours, need to seek points of closer intersection rather than detachment whilst protecting the sovereignty of nations big and small.

CHAPTER 9

MODI'S MODERNISING EFFECT: A PERSPECTIVE FROM NEPAL

HARI BANSH JHA

INTRODUCTION

Narendra Modi completed two years of his tenure as Prime Minister of India in 2016. During this period, India's image at the international level quadrupled; while at the domestic front the country exhibited all round development. By inviting the heads of state/government of all the South Asian countries to his swearing-in ceremony as per his 'Neighbourhood First' policy, he exhibited rare capability of statesmanship. Such a move is intended to create harmonious relations between India and the neighbours. In addition, the SAARC got a new lease of life for which credit largely goes to Modi. Today, SAARC is treated as a regional block that delivers. Before his participation in the Eighteenth SAARC Summit in Kathmandu in November 2015, this regional organisation was regarded merely as a talking place. It has now become evident that no Indian Prime Minister ever since India's independence in 1947 made as much effort for the promotion of democracy, economic development and betterment of relations with foreign countries in such a small period of time as done by Prime Minister Modi. By virtue of this fact, today he stands as the tallest figure among the Indian politicians and frontrunner among the world politicians.

NEIGHBOURHOOD FIRST POLICY: A CASE OF NEPAL

Narendra Modi is the first Prime Minister of India who realised the importance of the neighbours for India's own prosperity. Participation of the heads of state/ government of South Asian countries in his swearing-in ceremony opened a new chapter in India's relations with the neighbours. Subsequently, his visit to Afghanistan, Bangladesh, Bhutan, Nepal, Sri Lanka and Pakistan further cemented India's ties with those countries. He is the first Indian Prime Minister to visit Sri Lanka after a gap of twenty-eight years. During his visit to Bangladesh, he made a historical agreement with the country to settle the most contentious Land Boundary issue. The only country in South Asia where he could not go is Maldives, due to the political upheavals there.

In view of his 'Neighbourhood First' policy, Modi first chose Bhutan, the tiny Himalayan nation, as his first foreign destination. He put this country in an 'ultra-special' category and provided substantial support in building infrastructural facilities.

Prime Minister Modi's next visit was to Nepal where no Indian Prime Minister had visited for seventeen long years. Through this visit, he proved that a country like Nepal which is so close due to the open border system and also due to the traditional relations on all fronts cannot remain that far in India's neighbourhood. Therefore, at interval of a few months he visited this country twice and in doing so left a far-reaching impact on the mind of the Nepalese. During his historical speech at Nepal's Constituent Assembly/Parliament in August 2014, he pledged to provide US$1 billion support to Nepal for various development activities. His soft corner towards the Nepalese people was also reflected when he went out of the way to support the victims of the deadly earthquake of 25 April 2015 in which around 9,000 people were killed and hundreds of thousands of people were injured.

Estimates are that Nepal incurred economic losses worth US$7.4 billion due to the earthquake. India reached the victims even before Nepal's own state machinery could approach them. India's generosity towards the Nepalese people was internationally recognised when the Indian rescue teams reached Kathmandu within six hours after the earthquake. Indian rescue teams also helped nationals of other countries to reduce their sufferings on humanitarian ground. India also made a commitment to provide US$1 billion for the reconstruction of structures that were destroyed during the earthquake.

As a statesman, Modi perceived that Nepal would fall into difficulties if the Constitution that was in the process of being drafted was not made inclusive. Therefore, in the Nepalese Constituent Assembly he advised the political leaders of the country to draft a consensus-based Constitution so that each and every section of the population could take ownership in it. Unfortunately though, the Nepalese leadership overlooked this friendly suggestion while promulgating the Constitution on 20 September 2015.

Consequently, the Madhesis, one of the dominant ethnic communities in Nepal living in regions bordering Indian states of Bengal, Bihar and Uttar Pradesh, started an agitation against the Constitution. They found the new Constitution to be more regressive than any of the six Constitutions promulgated in the country since the 1950s.

During the Madhesi uprising in 2015, fifty-five protesters along with two Indian nationals were killed. Besides, thousands of people were injured and many more people from the region were compelled to seek asylum in India. Blockade of the border by the Madhesi agitators created severe shortage of goods, including essentials like oil, LPG and medicines. Besides, most of the industries, educational institutions, transport services and other economic activities in Nepal in general and Terai in particular were closed. There was a colossal loss to the economy worth US$2 billion a month due to the Madhesi movement.

Realising the plight of the common people in Nepal, India used its goodwill in Nepal to end the 135-day economic blockade imposed by the Madhesis at the Birgunj-Raxaul border. With this development, trade and economic relations between Nepal and India became normal. During his visit to India in February 2016, Nepalese Prime Minister KP Sharma Oli acknowledged that all Nepal's misunderstandings with India were removed. Expectations are that Nepalese leaders would make the Constitution inclusive so as to accommodate the concerns of the Madhesis, Tharus and other Janajati groups of Nepal. Somehow, it was mainly on account of indirect mediation by Modi's government under its 'Neighbourhood First' policy that helped Nepal address its internal problem and restore peace, which in itself is a great achievement.

CONTRIBUTION IN SOUTH ASIAN REGIONAL AND SUBREGIONAL AFFAIRS

In the wake of the SAARC Summit when Modi visited Nepal, the second time, in November 2014, he put forward the idea of SAARC Motor Vehicles

Agreement (MVA). When Pakistan signed the agreement on Energy Cooperation and ignored two other equally important SAARC MVA and SAARC Regional Railways Agreement, he promoted the idea of subregional cooperation among four SAARC member countries, including BBIN. Accordingly, the transport ministers of BBIN signed the MVA in Thimpu, Bhutan in June 2015.

The MVA is expected to have far-reaching implications on the economy of the subregion as it would contribute significantly in reducing travel time and cost of transportation of goods from one country to the other. The prospect is high for an increase in intra-state and inter-state trade among the countries of the region. A country like Nepal might be immensely benefitted from this agreement for its increased access to India, Bangladesh and Bhutan.

In addition, the MVA will also help the member countries in harnessing their natural resources. There exists 190 billion cubic million metre (cbm) of natural gas reserves, 900 million tons of coal reserves, 75,000 MW of hydro-power, 513 million tons of oil reserves and 4.4 billion tons of limestone reserves in the subregion. Also, 25 per cent of the region is under forest cover.

Expectations are that the growing links among the countries of this subregion due to the MVA would tend to reduce domestic conflicts and contribute towards peace, prosperity and stability of the region. Modi's vision for the development of the BBIN region was well reflected when Bangladeshi Transport Minister Obaidul Quader said during the signing ceremony of MVA, 'Let our borders no longer be treated as separators but connectors.'

COMMON GOOD FOR GLOBAL COMMUNITY

Being fully aware of India's rich culture, Prime Minister Narendra Modi gave a call in the General Assembly of the United Nations, New York in 2014 to observe Yoga Day each year. As is well known, yoga, which is part of the rich tradition of Hindu culture, is the science and art of keeping a person fit physically, mentally and spiritually. In view of the importance of this proposal, it was endorsed by the global community—irrespective of religious, racial or other bases. Accordingly, on June 2015, International Yoga Day was observed by the United Nations in which most of the countries of the world participated. More than increasing India's pride at the international level, this event is expected to create a better world for the generations of tomorrow.

In addition, Modi played a key role in the formation of New Development

Bank of BRICS and also for the formation of AIIB of twenty-one Asian countries. Such activities are intended not for India's benefit alone, but more so for the collective interest of the developing countries. In several ways, these new institutions are likely to emerge as an alternative to existing international financial institutions like the World Bank, the IMF and the Asian Development Bank.

PROMOTING BILATERAL RELATIONS

Modi is internationally recognised as a person who thinks out-of-the-box in dealing with issues related to foreign affairs. During the short span of time of merely two years, he took India's relations with foreign countries to new heights. For this, he toured Seychelles, a country which no Indian Prime Minister had visited for thirty-four years. His visit was again the first Prime Ministerial-level visit to Australia after a gap of twenty-eight years, to Fiji after a gap of thirty-three years and to Canada after a gap of forty-two long years.

Soon after assuming office, Prime Minister Modi gave a new twist to India's Look East Policy by changing it to the Act East Policy. Towards this end, he gave utmost priority to strengthening relations with the Association of Southeast Asian Nations (ASEAN) member countries and also with Japan which holds a strategically important place in global affairs. Also, taking full advantage of India's secular image, he improved the country's relations with West Asia. Accordingly, a landmark agreement was signed with Iran to make Chabahar Port operational. This deal was crucial for India as it would help the country to develop links with Afghanistan and promote trade with inner Asia. His tour to the United Arab Emirates (UAE) subsequently helped India to have an agreement with it for making deposits of oil. Oil thus deposited by UAE in India could be used for meeting emergency needs of the country and also for its sale by UAE to other countries. His visits to countries like the US, Russia, Germany, Brazil, Mongolia, China, South Korea and Japan generated a lot of goodwill towards India.

Returns from the visits by Prime Minister Modi have already started trickling in, particularly in the foreign investment sector. FDI increased by 29 per cent to US$40 billion during April 2015-March 2016. The US–India Business Council has already invested US$28 billion in India since September 2014 and another US$45 billion is in the pipeline; while Japan made commitment for the investment of US$35 billion. China committed to invest US$22 billion in India in renewable energy, power, infrastructure, steel, small and medium sector industries. On top of all this, the UAE has also pledged to invest in India in the infrastructure sector to the tune of US$75 billion.

Recognising India's important role in shaping the international economic order, Barack Obama became the Chief Guest at India's Republic Day parade on 26 January 2015. Later, French President Francois Hollande officiated as Chief Guest on this occasion in 2016. With the growing relations between India and China and also due to the genuine efforts made by Prime Minister Modi to strengthen defence sector, India's border with China is safer than at any time during the last few decades.

MODI'S CHARISMA ON THE HOME FRONT

Even at the home front Modi's effort to revamp the socio-economic and scientific development of the country cannot be overlooked. As part of the economic reforms policy, India's Planning Commission which was based on the Soviet Union's centralised planning approach was replaced by the more dynamic government think-tank known as National Institution for Transforming India (NITI) Aayog. An effort has been made to accelerate the growth of different sectors of the economy, including the industrial, agricultural and service sectors, for which purpose massive focus has been given for the development of infrastructural facilities.

India plans to register the total population of 1.25 billion by using its Aadhaar digital ID. This would largely promote the inclusion of disadvantaged sections in the welfare schemes. On this basis, now cash will be provided to the poor as substitute for cheaper rations in kind. According to an estimate made by the World Bank, the Aadhaar digital identification system will help India save nearly US$1 billion a year through reduction of corruption and leakages for the Indian government.

Under the Pradhan Mantri Jan Dhan Yojana, millions of bank accounts have been opened for the poor to enable them to get due benefits from social security schemes. The Swachh Bharat Abhiyan (Clean India Campaign) has been introduced to maintain hygiene and sanitation throughout the country. In the absence of hygiene, each Indian citizen has to spend a significant portion of their income on the treatment of diseases.

Under the National Skill Development Mission, an effort is being made to provide vocational training to 500 million people till the end of 2022. Unorganised Workers Identification Number (U-WIN) Smart Card has been introduced for the first time in the country for the benefit of 400 million workers in the unorganised sector.

As per the slogan *Jai Jawan Jai Kisan* (Hail the Soldier, Hail the Farmer) given to India by the Indian Prime Minister Lal Bahadur Shastri in 1965, Prime Minister Narendra Modi has introduced Pradhan Mantri Fasal Bima Yojana and Soil Health Card Scheme for the benefit of Indian farmers. In addition, farmers would benefit from the supply of neem-coated urea (fertilizer) and also from the Deendayal Upadhyaya Gram Jyoti Yojana that promotes electrification in rural areas. Due attention has been given to Indianise the education sector under the 'Educate in India' initiative.

The manufacturing sector is likely to benefit from the Make in India programme. Startup India, Standup India campaign is likely to create jobs. In view of the fact that 10 million youth enter the Indian job market each year, a new thinking has developed under this campaign 'not to be job-seekers, but be job-givers'.

In the scientific sector, India in its first attempt was able to send its satellite to Mars, which is a record in itself. Greater focus is given for the digitalisation of the country in all possible sectors. Considering the importance of the railways in the national economy, substantial efforts have been made for its modernisation. For this, all the basic restrictions on foreign investment in the railways have been removed. In another major development, provision has been made to allow foreign investment in defence and insurance sectors from 26 per cent to 49 per cent.

In order to give greater autonomy to the states, the share of the states in the central tax revenue has been increased to 42 per cent from 32 per cent. As per his vision to transform India into a modern nation, Modi is set to celebrate the seventy-fifth anniversary of Indian independence as India's century. For this, all necessary preparation is being made to build at least 30 km of road each day as part of the strategy to develop the infrastructure sector. The government plans to construct about 50,000 km of road in the next five to six years at an estimated cost of US$250 billion. Plans are afoot to construct 100 million toilets till 2019. By the year 2020, 100 new smart cities will be built, which has the potential to create millions of jobs.

India's rate of economic growth which had dropped to 5.4 per cent in 2014 has picked up to 7.5 per cent. The inflation level of below 5 per cent is an all-time low giving a great respite to the people. Because of the expanding economic activities, India is now aspiring to raise its share in world trade to 3.5 per cent by 2020, up from 2 per cent.

CONCLUSION

During the last two years, Prime Minister Narendra Modi has tried his best to achieve his goal to transform India into a modern, prosperous and peaceful nation. The policies and programmes of his government are geared to achieve this goal. For this, the administrative system is sought to be revamped and made pro-people to ensure proper delivery of service. To cope with people's growing expectations, the Modi government has been acting fast to give due delivery to them both on the domestic and foreign fronts.

On the completion of one year in office in 2015, *The Times of India* had carried the Ipos poll in order to evaluate the Modi government's performance. Interestingly, in this survey his government was given distinction with 77.5 per cent score. In 2016 his government has performed better. Under the dynamic leadership of Modi, India has emerged as world's fastest growing economy, even surpassing China. At a time when most of the countries of the world are going downward in terms of economic growth, India is moving ahead showing signs of prosperity.

CHAPTER 10

INDIA–AFGHANISTAN RELATIONS: A REVIEW

Shakti Sinha

Prime Minister Narendra Modi was in Kabul on 25 December 2015 to jointly inaugurate with the Afghan President Ashraf Ghani the Parliament building, built by the Indian government. Modi's visit was a big hit in the Afghan media, especially on social media. The government of Afghanistan decided to name one of the blocks of the building after former Indian Prime Minister Atal Bihari Vajpayee, who had offered to build this powerful symbol of democracy as a sign of India–Afghanistan friendship and partnership. It was in Vajpayee's time that India re-engaged with Afghanistan in the aftermath of the US intervention that dislodged the Taliban in late 2001. The pace of engagement accelerated almost immediately and despite fatal attacks on Indian targets including diplomats, development staff and projects and the start-stop peace process, has largely maintained its momentum.

That India has emerged as a major development partner, arguably the fifth-largest bilateral donor over the fourteen-year period to Afghanistan should not have come as a surprise to analysts who have worked in Afghanistan on the ground. India's development partnership with Afghanistan goes back to the 1950s, and till transit trade through Pakistan was not an issue, India was Afghanistan's largest export market for dry fruits. The civil war (1992-6) and subsequent Taliban rule caused a break, though India did extend humanitarian assistance through UN agencies.

India's total commitment for the reconstruction of Afghanistan is US$2 billion with more than half disbursed. It has funded/co-funded three very important infrastructure projects: the construction of the 218-km road from Delaram to Zaranj which gives Afghanistan access to an alternate port, Chabahar in Iran; it has reconstructed and expanded the Salma Dam which would produce 42 MW of power and irrigate 75,000 hectares of land when fully commissioned by mid-2016 and it has co-funded and built transmission towers over the Hindu Kush as part of the Northern Electric Power System (NEPS) that has brought electricity to Kabul and other areas. Some of the key Indian projects are the following:

- Food assistance to primary school children and construction and rehabilitation of Schools (US$321 million disbursed)
- Supply of 250,000 tonnes of wheat
- Construction of a power line from Pul-i-Khumri to Kabul (US$120 million)
- Annual scholarships to study in India—higher education (initially 500 per year, increased to 675 and then to 1000)
- Construction of Delaram-Zaranj road ($150 million)
- Construction of the Salma Dam Power Project (US$200 million)
- Construction of the Parliament building (US$27 million disbursed; budget US$178 million)
- Small development projects, initially in the South East, and then extended all over the country (the final budget would be over US$130 million).

This is just a sample of India's development partnership with the Afghan people and government. And yet, when the Afghan peace process was initiated, and later resumed at Islamabad, besides Afghanistan, the other three nations involved were Pakistan, the US and China. Predictably, many Indian observers are upset that this Quad has been created instead of a Pentagon to include India. Others may even fantasise a Quad with India but minus Pakistan. The question that arises is—has India lost the plot in Afghanistan? Has the commitment of US$2 billion in development assistance and actual expenditure of a little less than US$1.5 billion been a waste? Has the Modi government been totally outmanoeuvred by Pakistan insofar as Afghanistan is concerned?

The answer is an unequivocal 'no' and there is no need for Indians to get disheartened by the developments on the Afghan front. Both India and Afghanistan are victims of Pakistan's state-sponsored terrorism, which while manageable in India's case, is an existential threat to Afghanistan. An unintended fall-out of the Soviet occupation of Afghanistan was to allow Pakistan to become the key arbiter in Afghan affairs. The US actively supported by Saudi Arabia and China armed different Afghan jihadi groups to take on the Russians; they also accepted Pakistan's condition that all arms and support would flow to its Inter-Services Intelligence Directorate (ISI) who would decide on what to give to the different groups. Post-Soviet withdrawal, Pakistan was unable to install its favourite, the Hizb-ul-Islami leader Gulbuddin Hekmatyar as Afghanistan's pre-eminent leader. It then shifted its substantial support to the rising jihadi group from Kandahar, the Taliban. The ouster of the Taliban in 2001 was a huge setback for Pakistan's plans in the region, but it was able to convince the Americans about its utility in the war on terrorism and in the bargain it recreated the Taliban on its soil and went about destabilising Afghanistan.

There are three more aspects that must be factored in to better understand the objective circumstances of India's Afghan policy. Pashtuns are Afghanistan's biggest ethnic group, around 40 per cent of the population, but there are more Pashtuns in Pakistan than in Afghanistan, with strong cross-border social and economic links joining them; Afghanistan has not recognised the Durand Line as border between the two countries since, according to them, the Pashtun areas of British India (now Pakistan) should have come back to them once the British left the subcontinent.[1] Two, millions of Afghans, predominantly Pashtuns, took refuge in Pakistan during the Soviet invasion and the civil war, and while most have returned, millions have stayed back. This further blurs national boundaries and sovereignty. Three, Afghanistan is a landlocked country and the two countries not only share a long border, but Pakistan in effect is Afghanistan's gateway to the world (this makes operationalising Chabahar Port

---

[1] The Treaty of Gandamak (1893) which was forced upon the Afghans led to these areas becoming part of British India, for a period of 100 years. At independence, the Afghans demanded that these areas should be returned to them since one of the parties (Britain) had withdrawn. Consequently, the Afghans voted against and held up Pakistan's admission to the United Nations. And historically, the Pashtuns have treated this border as a legal fiction.

at the earliest an Indian priority). These historical, social, cultural, economic and geographical factors limit India's ability to work with the Afghan state as it seeks to stabilise and develop Afghanistan.

It is also useful to appreciate the local political situation in Afghanistan and how it is evolving. President Ashraf Ghani came to power as a result of a compromise brokered between him and Dr Abdullah Abdullah, now his chief executive, by the US which broke the deadlock caused by the inconclusive elections marred by allegations of large scale irregularities. In fact, Secretary John Kerry had to fly down to Kabul twice over two months to ensure that the agreement was reached and went through. Once the agreement was reached, the Election Commission declared Dr Ghani the winner but till date final voting figures have not been released. The circumstances leading to, and the actual formation of this unusual governing arrangement, which goes beyond Constitutional provisions are factors responsible for the political quagmire looming over Afghanistan. The government has not had a smooth sailing, and had great difficulty first in agreeing on names of ministers, and then getting Parliament to ratify its nominations. In fact, the crucial post of defence minister has been vacant for over a year-and-a-half with two 'failed' nominees. Other key posts are similarly unfilled and held by caretakers/acting ministers who lack real authority.

President Ghani's unexpected approach to Pakistan, through China and directly, was recognised as a high-risk strategy. Ghani's correct assumption was that there can be no peace in Afghanistan unless the Pakistan army was on board, but whether it can be won over is the question. The Pakistan army is seen alternatively as controlling the Taliban, using them as their 'strategic asset', or having leverage over them. And Ghani rightly assessed that only the Chinese have leverage over the Pakistan army. The Afghan government handed over anti-Pakistan army elements it had earlier given shelter to. Army-to-army links at the Corp commanders' level, coordinated patrols and operations, deputing Afghan military cadets for training in Pakistan, etc. have been operationalised. Finally, the ISI and the Afghan intelligence agency, National Directorate of Security (NDS) signed an agreement to conduct joint counterterrorism operations and for the training of NDS personnel in Pakistan though the NDS chief opposed the agreement. Perhaps few believed that the ISI will keep its end of the bargain. In fact, subsequently, the Afghan intelligence, its Interior Ministry, its Foreign Ministry and even the President has held the ISI and Pakistan, guilty of facilitating Taliban's horrific attacks on civilians.

Despite such unilateral concessions by Afghanistan, the expected peace dividend is yet to be seen. Far from the Taliban ceasing attacks and coming over-ground to engage with the Afghan government, it has in fact stepped up its attacks. The Taliban has made a show of consulting with foreign governments and Afghan civil society. In fact it has singularly refused to respond to the Afghan government's offer for talks. Instead, it has become more brazen and had even seized the important northern city of Kunduz till they were driven out. They are also in command of many districts in the south and south-east besides stray areas in the north-west.

Side by side, there are also reports of the emergence of the ISIS in Afghanistan. The first reports that emerged in mid-2014 from Ghazni turned out to be false, but subsequently there have been a number of reports that disaffected Afghan insurgents have aligned with the IS, along with a number of Pakistani Taliban. Reportedly there have been numerous clashes between the Taliban and IS, though there could be a tendency to overestimate the latter's strength. Many local government security chiefs cite the IS threat to be able to garner more resources, and small time 'warlords' claim allegiance to the IS in order to increase their profile. Overall, the predominance of the Taliban has been too pervasive to allow the IS much space. However, the spate of suicide attacks in Nangrahar in January this year (2016) demonstrated that the rise of the Wilayat Khurasan, IS' local affiliate, was not something that could be totally ignored.

As part of his outreach to Pakistan, President Ghani had also kept on hold his predecessor's request for security assistance from India. The resultant Pakistan-led peace process came to nought once it was clear that the Taliban negotiators had no locus standi with Mullah Omar who has been dead for two years. Pakistan's perfidy stood exposed and became worse with the stepped up violence in Afghanistan that cost many civilian lives.

At this juncture Ghani approached India for security assistance. Modi, to his credit, responded positively though many analysts had raised doubts about Ghani's motivations. Was he approaching India out of conviction or in desperation? India rightly ignored this question since it was immaterial. In any case unknown to the public, the Modi government had reviewed in detail the pace of progress of India's development projects in Afghanistan, irrespective of India's perceived loss of political space. The Parliament building and the reconstruction/expansion of the Salma Dam came up short. Bureaucratic snafus were sorted out, updated project reports were prepared and adequate financial sources were provided for. But for these steps, both the projects would have continued to drag on, as they had over the past decade, to the utter embarrassment of those Afghans who see India as a reliable friend.

Detailed inter-government talks were held between India and Afghanistan in November-December 2015 with the visits of the Afghan National Security Advisor (Hanif Atmar) and the Deputy Foreign Minister (Hekmat Karzai), and India's positive response led to the Afghan invitation to Prime Minister Modi to inaugurate their Parliament building. The significance of this was not lost on the Afghans and their neighbours—for a democratic country, its Parliament is not just a building but is an institution that embodies the spirit of the nations as it is here that its elected representatives decide the course of the nation. To invite a foreigner to jointly inaugurate it with their President is the highest honour that a country can bestow.

On the occasion of the visit, India also handed over to Afghanistan three of the promised four Mi-25 helicopter gunships, known as 'flying tank' that would give the Afghan National Security Forces much-needed firepower to confront the Taliban.

India also demonstrated that it was a reliable friend of Afghanistan when it deputed External Affairs Minister, Sushma Swaraj, to attend the Heart of Asia Summit in Islamabad, the Afghanistan-centred Istanbul Process where India has the lead on capacity development and building synergies between national chambers of commerce. This had the 'bonus' advantage of allowing leaders of India and Pakistan to meet on the sidelines of this multilateral summit. This was nimble-footed diplomacy that was as much substantial as it was optics—both essential components of international affairs.

One must also understand the current peace initiative, or Quad. Afghanistan is heavily dependent on the US for its security and financial requirements, and cannot afford to go against express American advice. Unfortunately for Afghanistan, the United States' default option is to outsource its Afghan policy to Pakistan, which represents to them a systemically far more important country. The priorities of the US are clear—roll-back ISIS and manage China's rise. The developing Saudi–Iran spat could spiral out of control, leaving US policy in the region in tatters. Afghanistan is a distraction it can do without. Hence, they leaned on Ghani, not directly but through David Cameron, to resume the peace process though Pakistan's deception was by then public. For Ghani, it was an offer he could not refuse.

For the region, China is the dark horse whose attitude and actions could be decisive, in addition to that of the US. It remains committed to Pakistan, despite occasional doubts that it fears the latter's jihadi infection could drag down Xinjiang. This hope that China would rein in Pakistan is overemphasised. China's response to the Pathankot attack is instructive; initially it condemned the attack but hoped that it would not derail the India–Pakistan dialogue. Pointedly, it did not ask Pakistan to take action against the groups behind the attack or to act on India's handing over evidence. Subsequently, it put a technical hold at the UNSC on India's efforts to list Maulana Masood Azhar, the head of the ISI-backed Jaish-e-Mohammad that had carried out the attack—so much for the expectation that China would 'restrain' Pakistan from its jihadi adventurism!

Looking forward, one must understand that India has very substantial goodwill in Afghanistan and along with the USA, India remains the most popular country while Pakistan's ratings are rock-bottom. Public pressure in western Afghanistan led to the government renaming the Salma Dam as the India–Afghanistan Friendship Dam. This project is seen as hugely liberating western Afghanistan from dependence on foreign supply, and will ensure reliable and consistent electric supply and has the potential to economically transform the region. Similarly, the naming of one of the blocks of the new Parliament building as Atal Block, in honour of the former Indian Prime Minister, is symbolic in a country where symbols are very important. A photo tweet showing the Parliament building as India's gift and another photo showing the destroyed Dar-ul-Aman Palace in Kabul as Pakistan's gift went viral in the Afghan social media. Over 10,000 Afghan youths have come to India on scholarship for higher education, and around the same number have also done so using their own money. More than 7,000 have returned to their country after studying in India. It must be remembered that India is the largest regional development partner; by contrast China's support till date has been only US$125 million.

The present writer can speak from personal experience that quite often India is seen as a role model in Afghanistan, both for firmly establishing democracy and for its economic achievements.

Soft power is important but it has its limitations. It cannot substitute for hard power, and is most effective in conjunction with the latter, not in lieu of it. However, it must be remembered that fundamentally, Afghan goals and that of Pakistan are irreconcilable. The Pakistan army, which calls the shots insofar as that country's policies on India, Afghanistan and nuclear weapons are concerned, cannot settle for anything less than a client state in Afghanistan. Its professed fear of an India–Afghanistan axis is a smokescreen for that. Worse a plural, democratic Afghanistan at peace with itself is an existential threat for the garrison state that Pakistan has become. With two plural, peace-loving democracies on its eastern and western borders, the rationale for the Pakistani army's hegemony over domestic policies is questionable. Pakistan's willingness, and ability, to rein in its jihadis who carry out terrorists attacks in India and destabilise Afghanistan is highly suspect, as was made clear in the attack on Pathankot and subsequent cover-up by Pakistan despite India providing hard evidence and unprecedented access to Indian defence installations.

Throughout this period, especially when President Ghani seemed to have relied excessively on the Pakistan army to deliver, even given up almost all his cards, India acted with model restraint, as it did not want to be made a scapegoat in case things went wrong, which it had to. And in case, Pakistan could deliver peace in Afghanistan, this was to be welcomed.

Looking ahead, India must continue to display such mature reactions, not get carried away by unnecessary fears of being marginalised, and continue to support the legitimate Afghan government's efforts to bring peace, stability and development to its people.

CHAPTER 11

FRAMEWORK FOR SUSTAINABLE RELATIONSHIP BETWEEN BANGLADESH AND INDIA

SHAHAB KHAN

On 6 June 2015, Bangladesh Prime Minister Sheikh Hasina and India's Prime Minister Narendra Modi issued a joint statement in Dhaka. It proclaimed their shared commitment to facilitate a 'pragmatic, mature and practical approach' in India–Bangladesh relationship. Since then, the two governments have set about implementing the commitments expressed in the joint statement. Senior officials from both the countries have exchanged visits and institutionalised their exchanges on major strategic and economic issues. At the unofficial level, the so-called track-two groups have explored possible evolutions of the India–Bangladesh relations. Yet as cooperation has increased, doubts are being expressed about the sustainability of the relationship given Bangladesh's domestic politics and concerns over some anti-Indian sentiment.

Prime Minister Modi, in his hour-long speech to a gathering of nearly 2,000 at the Bangabandhu International Centre in Dhaka, spoke on terrorism, fake currency, connectivity and India's track record on peace. Referring to Pakistan several times, he said, 'What has the world got from this? Terrorism is the enemy of humanity. All forces of humanity should unite and isolate terrorism. Tourism unites the world, terrorism divides.' He further lauded Sheikh Hasina and her government for showing 'zero-tolerance' to terrorism. Importantly, he mentioned that a solution on Teesta will be found and that water cannot be used for politics. He spoke about how rivers unite and that he wished the same future for Bangladesh as he wished for India.

India–Bangladesh relationship has strong historical and cultural consonance. However, only recently have both sides practically realised the immense benefits of trust and cooperation. Undoubtedly, Modi's 'Neighbourhood First' approach and his visit to Dhaka has ignited optimism across the entire political spectrum. Bangladesh feels that Modi's stewardship and attention towards Bangladesh can help resolve long-standing issues against India. This, however, is not to say that Bangladesh has defined its national identity merely in terms of being anti-India, nor has it neglected historical and cultural commonalities. Historically, Bangladesh maintained a degree of autonomy in its foreign policy. However, it is seen to be inimitably closer to India since the accession of Prime Minister Sheikh Hasina in 2009. Bangladesh has a vibrant middle class and private sector that would like to reap the dividends of a stronger tie with India, which has been enjoying steady economic growth of around 6 per cent.

The Awami League government has also granted India's long-pending request for transit rights through Bangladesh to India's North East, which would contribute to boosting the Indian economy, particularly that of the 'seven sisters' states. This transit facility, that includes roads, rails, rivers, sea, transmission lines, petroleum pipelines and digital links will also allow Delhi's access to Southeast Asia through Bangladesh. This would, in turn, enable India to pursue an effective Act East Policy, too.

Despite all this positivity and confidence-building measures, the sustainability of this relationship is often questioned. Why so?

PUBLIC PERCEPTION

Public perception is crucially important in the relationship between Bangladesh and India. A common perception is that India gives more weight to fulfilling its interest in Bangladesh than to addressing Bangladeshi causes. Furthermore, it is widely believed that India is 'obsessed' with Pakistan and consequently issues concerning Bangladesh get marginalised.

Both the leadership in Dhaka and New Delhi will have to manage the gap in the political and security perceptions. The Awami League government, on its part, has cracked down on extremists with ties to Pakistan or India's home-grown terrorist groups. The government has also come down hard on Islamist parties or groups which are professedly anti-Indian. At the risk of alienating a segment of the populace, the Bangladeshi government has boldly established a secular polity. It would thus need the sustained support of the Modi-led NDA government.

India must understand that no mainstream political party in Bangladesh will pursue an anti-India policy since the economic dependency between these two countries has become stronger than ever. A functional multi-party democracy in Bangladesh, in the eyes of the people, is important for political stability in that country, as well as for India's interests and standing in Bangladesh.[1]

There is a likelihood that the non-functional democracy may lead to the rise of radical Islamic outfits and organisations and even spill over into the east and north-east India. The Modi government, in its wider national interests, is wise not to follow the partisan approach of the earlier UPA government. A sustained even-handed policy in turn may encourage and facilitate a move towards a meaningful, substantive, multiparty democracy in Bangladesh that would usher in political stability and policy continuity.[2]

TRADE DYNAMICS

Over the past four decades, Bangladesh and India have recognised the importance of cooperation in the areas of trade and investment. The volume of trade has increased phenomenally over the past two decades as Bangladesh presents itself as a liberal economy and has opened up its market for investment to the world with least possible protectionism and trade bottlenecks. Nonetheless, Bangladesh's trade deficit with India has swelled in recent years with import continuously rising while export hitting rock bottom. The gap amounted to US$5.579 billion in 2015. According to Bangladesh Bank statistics, the country imported goods worth about US$6.036 billion from India in 2015, as against total exports worth US$456.633 million. It leaves an import-export gap amounting to US$5.579 billion in favour of India. On the other hand, import from India increased by 27.34 per cent over the previous fiscal.

---

[1] Bhattacharjee, Rupak, 'The future of India–Bangladesh ties', *IDSA Comment*. Institute for Defence Studies and Analysis, (2014), Available at http://www.idsa.in/idsacomments/ThefutureofIndiaBangladeshTies_rbhattacharjee_060514 (Accessed on 29 March 2016).

[2] Khan, Shahab Enam and Abbasi, Parvez Karim, 'Will Modi realise his superpower aspirations?', available at: http://www.dhakatribune.com/long-form/2015/feb/19/will-modi-realise-his-superpower-aspirations.

India emerged as one of the largest sources of raw materials for Bangladeshi manufacturing industries, resulting in the import surge. At the same time, Bangladeshi exports hit various non-tariff barriers (NTB) to enter the Indian market. Even after allowing duty-free access of Bangladeshi-made apparels to India, Bangladeshi merchants could not make any significant growth in export. Business leaders and experts are continuously demanding that India remove non-tariff and para-tariff barriers to help Bangladesh increase exports to the country and thereby reduce the galloping trade gap between the two countries.[3] A major NTB to increasing Bangladeshi exports to India is the non-acceptance of Bangladeshi standard certification by the Indian authority. Although Bangladesh Standard and Testing Institution (BSTI) and Bureau of Indian Standards (BIS) signed a bilateral agreement in 2015, initiatives are yet to be implemented.

After Prime Minister Modi's visit, to further boost the trade relations, Bangladesh has offered to establish two Special Economic Zones for Indian companies besides allowing Life Insurance Corporation to start operations in the country. It may also be noted that Bangladesh has shown interest to invest in Bhutanese and Nepalese hydropower markets to meet its ever-increasing demand for generating electricity, which is critical to sustain its growth rate.

Moreover, Bhutan is keen to export hydropower to Bangladesh at 'the cheapest possible rate' that would be of economic benefit for the subregional growth quadrangle that includes Bangladesh, India, Nepal and Bhutan. The major problem in developing this particular energy market lies with transmission lines and grids, which would require usage of Indian territory. A major breakthrough in this regard is yet to materialise. Bangladesh agreed to allow India a transmission of 7,000MW of power from Rangia Raota of Assam to Borakpur in Bihar through Barapukuria in Dinajpur. For the transmission, India will pay 'wheeling charge'.

Bangladesh, along with the Indian states of Meghalaya, Tripura and Assam, has been stressing on the need of establishing border *haat*s along the borders to curtail informal trade, improve people-to-people confidence along the border, and increase trade in the bordering towns which are generally poorer compared to the main towns and cities. On a positive note, an MoU was signed

---

[3] Ibid.

between the governments of Bangladesh and India which came into effect in 2015. What remains to be seen is how fast and extensively this MoU will be implemented.

FRAMEWORK FOR SUSTAINABLE RELATIONSHIP

Despite economic, political and security trammels and a historical record of mistrust, Bangladesh and India are looking at each other beyond the myopia of realpolitik. Both the countries are emerging as economic power hubs which need to be complimented by each other. In fact, both countries have the economic and strategic advantages to promote growth and prosperity in South Asia as a whole. India needs to attach measurable importance to regional development issues so that benefits can be reaped from regional arrangements already in place under the framework of regional cooperation. South Asia's intra-regional trade accounts for just 5 per cent of total trade with India as its major stakeholder.[4] Greater regional multilateral cooperation will enhance prospects for growth and shared prosperity in South Asia, home to 44 per cent of the world's poor.

The more Bangladesh and India keep straining their relations, at least at the perception level, the process of intra-regional cooperation will incur more dents and smaller neighbours will look around for other suitable alternatives. However, the current state of India–Bangladesh relations will depend on how India addresses the stress dynamics. And as said earlier, one senses that Modi is willing to walk the extra mile on certain issues with Bangladesh.

Sheikh Hasina has her limitations. While she is central in making foreign policy within the government, it does not mean that she will have complete freedom of action in the long term. After all, foreign policy is neither formulated in a vacuum, nor will it remain constant. Internal dynamics and external environment constantly put limits and constraints on the foreign policy of a state. Hasina government's positive policy towards India needs to be viewed as a product of competing forces and pressures. As a result her foreign policy may not operate in a way that India envisages.

There is also a strong perception in India that Bangladesh uses the China card to supplement its bargaining capacity, and the growing relationship

---

[4]The World Bank, 'Regional Integration in South Asia', (2015), available at: http://www.worldbank.org/en/region/sar/brief/south-asia-regional-integration. Accessed on 9 April 2016.

between China and Bangladesh is often visualised by India as potentially problematic.[5] Bangladesh does not seek good relations with China at the cost of its relations with India, or any other country; rather it is important for Bangladesh to maintain functional and economically-benefitting relations with all the countries in the region and beyond. Over the period of time, given the trade gaps with India, Bangladesh will need to simultaneously pursue its relationship with both India and China on the basis of tripartite collaboration and cooperation to achieve a win-win situation where neither China nor India could lose anything from the same trusted relationship with Bangladesh.

India–Bangladesh relations should be able to address four interrelated arrangements to make their mutual cooperation sustainable:

- Translate the political and bureaucratic commitments into reality and compliance of major treaty provisions by India.
- Develop bilateral mechanisms to build positive perceptions at the state-state, government-government, public-government and public-public levels. This will require political trust, political respect and political understanding among the politicians in both the countries.
- India–Bangladesh relationship should not be seen only through the prism of bilateral cooperation and connectivity. This relationship should have components to facilitate regional trade and investment, connectivity and strategic cooperation with the regional neighbours including China, Myanmar and other ASEAN countries.
- A strong security and strategic coordination is in place between Dhaka and New Delhi to combat terrorism and insurgencies. These transnational threats in the region cannot be dealt without reaching a regional solution. This is also applicable in dealing against poverty, environmental threats and different types of trafficking. Therefore, both the countries should act as conduits to strengthen the institutions (or initiatives) such as SAARC, Bangladesh, China, India, Myanmar Forum for Regional Cooperation (BCIM) and Bay of Bengal Initiative for Multi-Sectoral Technical and Economic Cooperation (BIMSTEC)

[5] Haq, Emdadul, 'Indo-Bangladesh Relations Revisited', *International Policy Digest*, (2014), available at: http://intpolicydigest.org/2014/08/30/indo-bangladesh-relations-revisited/. Accessed on 22 March 2016.

to mobilise collective strengths to counter set of factors that hinder peace and stability.

CONCLUSION

Despite the ups and downs in the bilateral relationship, Bangladesh considers India as a great neighbour due to its eminent role during the Great Liberation War in 1971. Bangladesh has posthumously conferred the Freedom Honour on Indira Gandhi. During the visit of Prime Minister Narendra Modi, Bangladesh conferred 'Friends of Bangladesh Liberation War Award' on former Prime Minister Atal Bihari Vajpayee for his 'active role' in its independence struggle and consolidating friendship with India. The 'Bangladesh Liberation War Honour' was also conferred on former Indian president Fakhruddin Ali Ahmed and former Indian Prime Minister Gulzarilal Nanda. Modi's visit to Dhaka in 2015 was regarded as a milestone in the history of India–Bangladesh relationship. The public in general welcomed him wholeheartedly and his views were embraced very positively by the public as well as the politicians from different blocs. Modi has given Bangladesh hope for future negotiations and settlement of long-standing issues. The Bangladesh government is willing to keep the faith in Modi.

However, one must understand the distinction between pro-Modi and pro-India perceptions in Bangladesh. Modi's visit to Dhaka emphasised the fact that under his leadership, India's relations with Dhaka will no longer be left in the cold storage or completely in the hands of the bureaucracy and the intelligence. While indeed a new era in India–Bangladesh relationship is unfolding, the facts on the ground still remain challenging.

To make the relationship sustainable, India needs to deliver what it has promised over the past decades. At the economic and security level, the best strategy is to deliver the aspirations that the Bangladeshis in general hold without prejudice or over-hyped security dilemmas.

One is positive, however challenging it may be, that Prime Minister Modi will balance the two cornerstones of his vision of Indian foreign policy—*Shanti* and *Shakti*. The key actors in Modi's regime—Sushma Swaraj, Ajit Doval and Subrahmanyam Jaishankar would be the cardinal characters in ensuring implementation of Hasina and Modi's shared commitment to facilitate a 'pragmatic, mature and practical' relationship which would be essential in facilitating sustainable and even-handed relationship between these two 'organic' neighbours. A lot rests on Prime Minister Modi's policies towards Bangladesh which may very well decide the future course of South Asian politics and international relations in the coming decades.

CHAPTER 12

INDIA–JAPAN RELATIONS ON A NEW HIGH

Takenori Horimoto

Introduction

India–Japan relations are today at an all-time high. The two countries' overall perceptions, interests and concerns dovetail. The current period can be categorised as the second stage of their bilateral relations.

What then has been the first phase? That phase roughly included the years between the 1950s and 1980s. The two countries enjoyed a brief honeymoon period after mutual relations were established in 1952. It did not last, however, because efforts to foster the relationship were thwarted by the unfolding Cold War. The two countries pursued incompatible policy orientations in both the foreign and economic sphere.

Such inconsistency has been mulled over in their infrequent interactions. At the head of governmental levels, Prime Minister Yasuhiro Nakasone visited India in 1984, two decades after Prime Minister Hayato Ikeda visited in 1961. Similarly, Prime Minister Indira Gandhi visited in 1982 more than a decade after her visit in 1969.

With the end of the Cold War in the early 1990s, bilateral relations entered the second phase, which continues till today. This phase has been marked by numerous visits of Prime Ministers, cabinet ministers and other high officials of both countries. There were twenty-seven such visits in the 1990s. In the 2000s, the number had trebled to eighty-four.

This rapprochement is the result of growing convergence between the two countries' world views, interests and goals. In other words, they have become partners of convenience and mutually indispensable in both economic issues and their respective China policies. The present bilateral relationship can be designated as the second honeymoon period of greater depth and width than the first, which occurred shortly after World War II.

The major contributing factors to the contemporary relations are the liberalisation of India's economic policy and the two countries' search for a true partner against the backdrop of the disintegration of the Soviet Union, the rapid advance of China and the shift of US policy to Asia.

To dig into the two countries' rapprochement since 1990s, I would like to explain briefly the growth of bilateral relations from 1990s onwards, then India's foreign policy mandala, Prime Minister Modi's foreign policy and finally the future perspectives of bilateral relations.

TRIPLE JUMP OF INDIA–JAPAN RELATIONS

Bilateral relations have soared in the second phase since the 1990s. However, when looking back, one must note that the relationship has been a gradual, step-by-step process that can best be described as the triple jump of hop, step and jump—from the 1990s, 2000s and 2010s onwards.

The 1990s

During this decade, India initiated several foreign policy orientations. The past two policies of Non-Alignment (1940s-1960s) and the quasi-alliance with the Soviet Union (1970s-1980s) have been only applicable during the Cold War period. They have lost their utility as mainstays of foreign policy in the post-Cold War period.

Prime Minister PV Narasimha Rao initiated his new foreign policy orientation by visiting China in 1993 and concluding an Agreement on the Maintenance of Peace and Tranquility along the LAC.[1] The Look East Policy

---

[1] Horimoto, Takenori, 'Ambivalent Relations of India and China: Cooperation and Caution', *Journal of Contemporary China Studies* (October 2014), Vol. 3, No. 2.

has been in motion since 1993.[2] In 1994, Rao visited the US to improve bilateral relations. It was not very successful. Thereon, India established its first strategic partnership with South Africa in 1997, followed by the Pokhran nuclear tests in 1998. Although these policy initiatives have been outstanding and have presented a new India to the world, they have often lacked clarity and the objectives have not been defined.

Japan started to warm up to India with Prime Minister Toshiki Kaifu's visit in 1990. But it failed to get the necessary traction. There was limited interest both in Japan and India. It is said that very few Members of Parliament attended PM Kaifu's address to the Indian Parliament and the secretariat employees apparently had to be rallied to fill the vacant seats.[3] India's limited interest in Japan could be attributed to the fact that the fulcrum of India's diplomacy since the early 1960s had shifted from Asia to West Asia (the Middle East), where many NRIs were living.

It might be necessary to add a noteworthy event that led India to develop a more positive image of Japan. It occurred in April 1991, when Japan provided an emergency foreign exchange loan to India. Partly because of the Gulf Crisis, India's foreign exchange reserves plummeted to US$1.1 billion. To meet its financial obligations, the Government of India was considering selling its Embassy office property in Tokyo.[4] Of all the countries that India sought help for emergency assistance, only Japan responded. Even today this support is well appreciated in India.[5]

The momentum for closer bilateral relations ebbed as a result of the diplomatic fallout from India's nuclear tests conducted in 1998. Japan has maintained non-proliferation as a basic foreign policy tenet and responded to India's nuclear tests by immediately suspending any new Official Development Assistance (ODA). Japan had been India's largest ODA donor from 1986–

---

[2] Haidar, Salman, 'Look East', in Ram, Amar Nath (ed.), *Two Decades of India's Look East Policy* (New Delhi: Manohar, 2012), p. 53.

[3] *India Today*, 15 June 1990.

[4] Asrani, Arjun, 'India–Japan Relating: Looking Back, Looking Ahead', Gendai Indo Forum [Contemporary India Forum], Winter Issue, (2012) No. 12.

[5] Choudhry, Srabani Roy, 'India–Japan Economic Partnership: Scope and Prospect', in Horimoto, Takenori and Varma, Lalima (eds.), *India–Japan Relations in Emerging Asia*, (New Delhi: Manohar Publishers & Distributors, 2013), p. 223.

onward, but the Yen loans that formed the core of that assistance were slashed in 1998 and no new loans were issued.

For its part, India was puzzled that Japan, as a nation protected by the US nuclear umbrella, could criticise India for undertaking nuclear tests with the aim of achieving an autonomous defence capability while remaining silent about China's nuclear testing.[6]

2000s

India's aspiration of becoming a major power gradually came to focus. One might say that 1998 was the latent starting point of such an ambition. Ironically it was not the nuclear achievement that gave it a power status but the economic grouping BRIC that came into popular use in 2002.

The Bharatiya Janata Party (BJP) manifesto of the 2004 general election presented a 'Shining India' reflecting the confident mood of the people at large. Consequently, there emerged arguments such as those by C Raja Mohan, who said, 'After disappointing itself for decades, India is now on the verge of becoming a great power.'[7] In fact, India achieved a 7.4 per cent annual GDP growth rate throughout the 2000s. The favourable improvement in India–Japan relations, which began quite modestly in the 1990s, gained momentum by 2005 and is now one of strategic engagement.

What are the major factors contributing to closer ties between the two countries? China is a common factor. Dealing with China's remarkable economic growth and its new status as a major global power has become the top priority for both India and Japan. So much so that it overrides their mutual difficulties.

In 2004, Japan's trade with China (including Hong Kong) reached 22 trillion Yen, which was more than the trade between the US (20 trillion Yen). China thus became Japan's largest trading partner. Ironically that year anti-Japanese behaviour was displayed by Chinese spectators at the AFC Asian Cup football match in Chongqing. Furthermore, between March-April 2005, large-

---

[6] Responding to nuclear testing by China in May and August 1995, the Japanese government 'decided to freeze grant aid to China with the exception of emergency and humanitarian assistance until the cessation of Chinese nuclear testing' (*Diplomatic Bluebook 1996*). (http://www.mofa.go.jp/mofaj/gaiko/bluebook/96/seisho_1.html#2 (Accessed 27 November 2013).

[7] Mohan, C Raja, 'India and the Balance of Power', *Foreign Affairs*, July/August 2006.

scale riots targeting Japanese stores broke out in Chengdu, Beijing, Shanghai and other cities. This turn of events raised grave concern about China and as a consequence many companies began increasing their direct investment in Vietnam and India 'to take advantage of the high growth and significant market scale expected in these countries, as well as to defuse the risk of investment concentration in China.'[8]

Economic circumstances were certainly a factor in the India–Japan rapprochement. An even more important factor was security policy designed to cope with rising China. Rather than being based on policy direction, the rapprochement were instead the result of fortuitous timing and the convergences since 2000. Viewed from the perspective of their China policies, both India–Japan engagement in economic areas and hedging in terms of security has drawn them closer. This same double-sided policy of engagement and hedging is pursued by the US vis-à-vis China with its 'rebalancing' Asia policy.

2010s

By 2010, India as an emerging major power was commonly expressed worldwide. When India launched its Agni missile in December 2011, even the *China Daily* remarked on India's great power status.[9] In 2013, *The Economist* published a special issue announcing India as a great power.

In the 2014 general election, the BJP won its largest victory ever. With its election slogan of *Shreshtha Bharat* (Great India) and high economic growth, Narendra Modi and his party BJP captured the people's imagination of a strong and prosperous India.

INDIA'S FOREIGN POLICY MANDALA

Under Prime Minister Modi's leadership, it would be safe to assume that India's foreign policy has a vision and a clear strategic objective. This can be represented in the mandala (matrix) of foreign policy.

India has many attributes and a geopolitical position sufficient to be a major power. During the Cold War period, India, still in its early period of nation-building, did not have the structural power as measured by its economy

---

[8] Tsutsumi, Hidetaka, 'Choryu: Look West', [Trends: Look West] in *Kinyu Shijo* [Financial Markets], October issue, (2005).

[9] *The Times of India*, 18 December 2011.

and defence. In 2014, India ranked ninth in terms of national GDP[10] and seventh in terms of defence expenditures.[11] It is interesting to note that in 2013, Japan was seventh in defence expenditures and India ninth. The position has been reversed.

To achieve such an objective, India is unfolding various external measures at the global, regional and subregional levels. Each level has its specific role with different objectives and corresponding measures. Perhaps such differences make the world sit up and marvel at the proactive foreign policy that India has undertaken, unlike during the Cold War period.

At the global level, India actively cooperates with other major actors like China, Russia and the US to establish a multi-polar international system. Such an orientation connotes India's revisionist thinking. India's ultimate objective, and possibly China's also, is to acquire the capability of influencing and shaping the international order. The US after the end of the Second World War, with its extraordinary national power, led the process of founding global institutions such as UN, World Bank and IMF.

At the regional level (Asia, Western Pacific, Middle East, Africa and the Indian Ocean), India is striving to attain a dominant position and relative presence by joining hands with the US, Japan and others while facing China.

At a subregional level (South Asia), India has become a de facto major power in consolidating its dominant position. It does not hesitate to cooperate with the US and others in matters directly or indirectly related to China, but it would fundamentally prefer to act independently, particularly in the Indian Ocean.

As presented in the above mandala, India's foreign policy has been difficult for foreign watchers and scholars to understand. At times it leans to the US and Japan and at other times befriends China and Russia. One can have various views on this but there can be little doubt that India's foreign policy is dynamic and responds to circumstances and timing. In the coming years, India's foreign policy will undergo transformation with China, US and Japan as major contributing factor.

---

[10] World Development Indicators database, World Bank, 22 September 2014, available at: http://databank.worldbank.org/data/download/GDP.pdf (Accessed on 8 March 2016).

[11] SIPRI fact sheet, April 2015, available at: http://books.sipri.org/files/FS/SIPRIFS1504.pdf (Accessed on 8 March 2016).

FROM INDIA'S TAOGUANG YANGHUI TO LEADING POWER

India's foreign policy is attributable to two primary factors. First, there is no official document or white paper that outlines or explains its foreign policy. Nevertheless, three documents were compiled between 2000 and 2012 to indicate the objectives and goals.

The first such document was the 'Report of GOM on National Security' (2001). The report suggested that India has no reasonable alternative but to opt for closer relations with the US.[12] Thereafter a task force report headed by K Subrahmanyam titled, 'The Challenge: India and the New American Global Strategy' (2006) was submitted to Prime Minister Manmohan Singh. Though not in the public domain, Sanjaya Baru, the then Prime Minister's media adviser, disclosed the gist of it in his book. He writes, 'the time has come for India to advance its interests through greater integration with the global economy, making the best use of economic opportunities provided by developed economies, especially the US.'[13] It carries an almost identical tone to that of the 2001 report. Then in 2012, a semi-official report 'NonAlignment 2.0'[14] was published. Subsequently, it aroused severe criticism particularly from the Indian strategic community. Its main argument can be summarised as emphasising strategic autonomy and how to realise it.

As the world now eagerly looks at India, these three documents provide excellent materials and data elucidating India's current foreign policy. Apart from these documents, various arguments have been put forth to characterise India's foreign policy as a diversified, multi-level, multilateral and swing-state policy.[15] However, they remain incomplete, failing to provide a comprehensive outlook, particularly the main objectives of India's foreign policy.

The second factor of the illegibility of India's foreign policy would be

---

[12] Group of Ministers (Government of India), *Report of the Group of Ministers on National Security*, (New Delhi, 2001).

[13] Baru, Sanjaya, *The Accidental Prime Minister: The Making and Unmaking of Manmohan Singh*, (Viking, 2014), p.168. New Delhi, India

[14] Centre for Policy Research, *NonAlignment 2.0: A Foreign and Strategic Policy for India in the Twenty First Century*, (2012). http://www.cprindia.org/workingpapers/3844-nonalignment-20-foreign-and-strategic-policy-india-twenty-first-century (Accessed on 8 March).

[15] Kliman, Daniel M and Fontaine, Richard, *Global Swing States Brazil, India Indonesia, Turkey and the Future of International Order*, The German Marshall Fund of the United States & Center for a New American Security, 2012.

that various opinions have arisen to deny India's emergence as a major power. For example, Miller pointed out that India's diplomatic elites tend to resist to its rise.[16] Former National Security Advisor, MK Narayanan characterised India as a 'reluctant power'.[17] His successor, Shiv Shankar Menon, considers India's strategic thoughts to have been imported from overseas but have strategic autonomy. One might read *Arthashastra*.[18] The foreign policy debate will assume high attention as India's emergence as a major power is a recent phenomenon.

At times, India seems likely to adopt the Chinese-style external policy of 'Taoguang Yanghui', 'biding one's time while strengthening one's power', as propounded by Deng Xiaoping and observed by Hu Jintao, but not Xi Jinping now. In short, India aspires to be a major power, but it continues to conceal its true objective. Presuming that India sets out its aspiration of becoming a major power, it might cause unfavourable situations.

The Modi government, however, with a greater degree of clarity looks to cast aside India's wary posture. Expressing a confident view, Foreign Secretary S Jaishankar said in a lecture that India's foreign policy dimension is 'to aspire to be a leading power, rather than just a balancing power.'[19]

MODI'S FOREIGN POLICY AND INDIA–JAPAN RELATIONS

The Modi government can be characterised as conducting its foreign policy objectives along the lines of the mandala. The BJP alone commands a parliamentary majority not witnessed since the 1984 general election. With a commanding majority Prime Minister Modi is truly at the helm of the government. Furthermore, he brings in a unique style that is unprecedented in Indian diplomatic history. He is hardly a follower of Nehruvian diplomacy, unlike his predecessors, including Prime Minister Vajpayee.[20]

Early glimpses of Modi's world view can be seen in his remarks at a gathering

---

[16] Miller, Manjari Chatterjee, 'India's Feeble Foreign Policy: A Would-Be Great Power Resists Its Own Rise', *Foreign Affairs*, May/June 2013.

[17] Narayanan, MK, *Keynote Address at the 16th Asian Security Conference* on 19 February 2014, available at: http://www.idsa.in/asc/keySPeeches.html (Accessed on 16 March 2104).

[18] Press Trust of India, 18 October 2012.

[19] https://www.iiss.org/en/events/events/archive/2015-f463/july-636f/fullerton-lecture-jaishankar-f64e (Accessed on 8 March 2016).

[20] Goel, Vijay, Minister of State in the Prime Minister's Office, has known Vajpayee for about 30 years, available at: http://muraleedharan.tripod.com/legends_vajpayee.html (Accessed on 24 December 2015).

in Chennai on 18 October 2013. He said, 'India's foreign policy should be built on the foundation of our culture, tradition, strength, economy, trade, strategy and security.'

The BJP's election manifesto, a reflection of Modi's thinking, included the slogan of 'Ek Bharat' and 'Shreshtha Bharat'. Furthermore, President Pranab Mukherjee's Parliamentary address on 9 June 2014 revealed Modi's policy framework. The President said, 'We will pursue our international engagement based on enlightened national interest, *combining the strength of our values with pragmatism*.' (emphasis added).

Modi's foreign policy balances economic growth with defence capabilities, what can be described as prosperity and power. For Modi, a strong economy means not only the economy per se, but also the foundation of his diplomacy. A 'strong economy is a base of effective foreign policy.'[21] In short, he appears to be implementing his foreign policy through the lens of geoeconomics than geopolitics.

He is compelled, however, to confront the dilemma of domestic politics and foreign policy. This is best demonstrated over the issue of Trade Facilitation Agreement, with an economic benefit of US$1 trillion. India agreed to join the TFA on December 2013 at Bali with the grace period of four years with regard to its agricultural procurements. However, in July 2014, India backpedalled taking into consideration the concerns of the farmers. Similarly, the Regional Comprehensive Economic Partnership (RCEP) initiated in 2013, to be concluded by 2016, and 'Make in India' will be subjected to domestic concerns. It will be a challenge for Modi to balance the political dichotomy of localism versus globalism.

Against the backdrop of Modi's foreign policy, how will India–Japan relations proceed? While the present equations can be interpreted as a relationship of convenience, it needs to be maximised keeping their respective national interests.

Sandy Gordon of the Australian National University has observed that 'India would possibly seek the best deal it can from China, both economically and in terms of a border settlement, while attempting to maintain its hedge against a rise of China by cooperating with the US and Japan'.[22] Former India

---

[21] *Business Standard*, 19 October 2014.

[22] Gordon, Sandy, 'Will China "Wedge" India and the US', *South Asia Masala*, 5 June 2014.

Foreign Secretary Kanwal Sibal shared identical views.[23] Similarly, Japan would entertain its close relations with India vis-à-vis China. Eventually, the bilateral relations can be located mainly at the regional level of India's foreign policy mandala and not at the global or subregional levels.

The rise of China is a critical driver of India–Japan rapprochement. And since the China factor seems unlikely to disappear, India–Japan relations will continue to grow. In other words, the bilateral relations will transcend the personal equation between the two leaders, Abe and Modi.[24]

Additionally, the possibility of continued tension with Pakistan will nudge India to opt for maintaining closer relations with Japan given Pakistan's strategic proximity to China. For China, its all-weather diplomatic relations with Pakistan is largely framed to limit India's influence in South Asia and to obstruct India's reach in Asia. China's support of Pakistan can be expected to keep India–Pakistan tensions intensified or at least tension by proxy. To circumvent the situation, India's strengthening relations with Japan is an important countermeasure. For Japan too, close cooperation with India is quite desirable.

CONCLUSION

Modi's ascent to power constitutes a historic confluence of interests and opportunities. After the end of the Cold War, various models such as the Washington Consensus, the Beijing Consensus and the Arab Spring have been attempted without much success. India's economic growth and inclusive development under the liberal democratic set-up carries historic meaning.

China will be observing India's future with great curiosity. India's success in achieving its goals would be a blow to China, which increasingly confronts domestic demands for economic equality and democratic rights.

Modi's greatest challenge will be to successfully coordinate and accommodate domestic concerns with foreign policies. Upon overcoming these challenges, India will be poised to take a great leap forward to become a major global power.

---

[23] Sibal, Kanwal, 'It is cherry blossom time in India–Japan relations', 23 January 2014, *The Hindustan Times*. He remarked, 'Japan's economic stakes in China are huge; our own political and economic stakes in China are high, given China's contiguity with us and our direct exposure to its power. Neither Japan nor India seek a confrontation with China, but both have a responsibility to build lines of defence against any disruptive exercise of power by a rising China.'

[24] Horimoto, Takenori, 'Between Friends', *India Today*, 9 June 2014.

CHAPTER 13

INDIA–GERMANY RELATIONSHIP: STRENGTHENING THE STRATEGIC PARTNERSHIP

CHRISTIAN WAGNER AND GAURAV SHARMA

INTRODUCTION

India and Germany share a long and amicable relationship. India was one of the first countries to recognise the Federal Republic of Germany on 7 March 1951. A new momentum of engagement started after the fall of the Berlin Wall and the opening up of the Indian economy in 1989 and 1991, respectively. With Asia's rising economic, political and military importance, Germany has also intensified its relations with the emerging powers in the region. The vigour of engagement between India and Germany has always been primarily driven by the economic engagement and business communities in both countries. The 1990s saw both India and Germany taking special interest and enhancing cooperation in multiple fields of engagement and expanding the fields of cooperation. India was the first rising power in Asia with whom Germany agreed on a Strategic Partnership Agreement in May 2000. In 2011, both sides agreed on 'Inter-Governmental Consultations' (IGC)[1] which are undertaken on a bi-annual basis at the cabinet level. This has established comprehensive interaction between India and Germany with a special set of institutionalised agreements of bilateral talks such as Strategic Dialogue, Foreign Office Consultations,

---

[1]The IGC on cabinet level are chaired by the German Chancellor and the Prime Minister of India.

Joint Commission on Industrial and Economic Cooperation, High Technology Partnership Group, High Defence Committee and Joint Working Group on Counterterrorism, India–German Consultative Group between India and Germany.

COMPLEMENTARITIES

The partnership between India and Germany has many complimentary topics. Germany is a key provider of high-end technology, has surplus capital and suffers a demographic deficit. India offers a growing middle class, a stable political system, is looking for more technology and capital investment and hopes to yield a demographic dividend. This will be most critical in the next decade, when in 2020 India will be poised to become the youngest country in the world with an average age of twenty-nine years.[2] India's vast population requires education and skills development (both semi-skill and vocational training) for which Germany, with the lowest rate of youth employment in the EU, has been accredited as one of the learning models in the world.[3] In addition, both Germany and India have a common perspective on United Nations reforms. Moreover, they aim for a resolution of current global conflicts through 'political solutions and not military ones', as stated by Prime Minister Modi during the third IGC joint press conference.[4] His current government has adopted a new approach to federalism emphasising Centre-state cooperation and heightened interstate competition.[5] This is evident in the fact that his government scrapped the decades-old Planning Commission and increased the share of central revenue devolved directly to the states. This approach is attractive to the German government as it opens up direct channels of communication with Indian states and presents a more likeable ideological interface to extending partnership with India. This also facilitates more direct subnational cooperation between the Indian and German states (Laender) and provides opportunities

---

[2] 'State of the Urban Youth, India 2012', UN Habitat, April 2013, p. 123.

[3] 'In Global Demand – Vocational training in Germany', available at: https://www.deutschland.de/en/topic/knowledge/education-learning/in-global-demand-vocational-training-in-germany.

[4] Merkel puts her weight behind Modi's Make in India drive, available at: http://www.dw.com/en/merkel-puts-her-weight-behind-modis-make-in-india-drive/a-18761965.

[5] 'Modi stresses cooperative, competitive federalism to take development agenda forward', available at: http://netindian.in/news/2015/02/08/00032520/modi-stresses-cooperative-competitive-federalism-take-development-agenda-fo.

towards collective development and learning with regard to the furtherance of decentralisation of authority at the Indian states.[6]

DIVERGENCES

The divergences erupt from two fundamental facts. One, Germany as member state of the EU puts strong emphasis on European approaches in many foreign policy issues. In contrast, India pursues a more traditional foreign policy approach with a strong focus on national interests. Second, Germany puts significant diplomatic effort to promote international binding agreements, for instance the Non-Proliferation Treaty (NPT), the ICC and international climate agreements. India however, follows a more traditional approach and is critical of any foreign interference that seems to restrict its national sovereignty. The different foreign policy approaches often bring India and Germany to opposite camps, for instance in global governance issues. Both countries also have different foreign policy instruments at their disposal. India has only around 900 diplomats, whereas Germany has around 2,000 diplomats to pursue its national interests and international commitments.

The India–Germany relationship should be viewed through the prism of the following five dimensions. A keen outlook into the existing strategic framework between India and Germany under these dimensions presents a more realistic and optimistic outlook into the relationship.

1. Security Policy Interface
2. Economic Engagement
3. Scientific and Cultural Exchange
4. Energy Cooperation (Renewable and Climate Change) and
5. Human Development Partners

SECURITY POLICY INTERFACE

India and Germany share a strong commitment for a peaceful international order. Both countries are supporting the United Nations (UN) Peacekeeping operations for many years. India is the third largest troop[7] contributing country

---

[6]Johnson, N, *State & Government in the Federal Republic of Germany: The Executive at Work*, Amsterdam: Elsevier, 1983, pp. 155-6.

[7]'Ranking of Military and Police Contributions to UN Operations', available at: http://www.un.org/en/peacekeeping/contributors/2015/dec15_2.pdf.

to UN operations and Germany the fourth largest financing[8] peacekeeping partner to the UN operations. India and Germany are part of the G4 together with Brazil and Japan which advocate UN reforms and an expansion of the permanent members of the Security Council (UNSC).

In 2006, India and Germany signed a Defence Cooperation Agreement and established annual talks at the Defence Secretary level. But both countries still have only a limited military technological interface, although firms like Atlas Elektronik, Krauss-Maffei Wegmann and Diehl Defence have branches based in India.[9] There are indirect contributions to the Indian defence sector by German arms manufacturers, for example Messerschmitt-Boelkow-Blohm, which is now part of European Aeronautic and Defence Space Company (EADS), assisted India in building its Light Combat Aircraft (LCA) and Advanced Light (Dhruv) Helicopter[10], and ThyssenKrupp Marine Systems (TKMS—manufactures of Type 214 conventional submarine) has worked with local Indian manufactures and shipyards.[11] The transfer of technology through the Make in India initiative would open up enormous avenues of investment and training for the German defence manufacturers and also help in fulfilling India's ambition to be a self-sustained defence market.

ECONOMIC ENGAGEMENT

The Indian economy was the fastest growing economy in 2015[12] and had a gross domestic product growth of 7.5 per cent. This was the best GDP growth percentage in Asia in 2015 with China dipping to 6.8 per cent and the average 'emerging and developing Asia' as a whole to 6.5 per cent[13]. Germany is one of India's largest trade and investment partners and in 2014 India–German trade stood at sixteen billion Euros.[14] Germany ranked seventh with regard to the investment volume inflows into India in the financial year 2014-15.

---

[8] 'Financing Peacekeeping', available at: http://www.un.org/en/peacekeeping/operations/financing.shtml

[9] 'Germany's Deals With India: A Major Arms Sale?', available at: http://www.indianlink.com.au/germanys-deals-with-india-a-major-arms-sale/.

[10] Ibid.

[11] Ibid.

[12] World Economic Outlook, September 2015.

[13] Ibid.

[14] 'Indo-German Trade: Steady improvement in 2014', available at: http://indien.ahk.de/fileadmin/ahk_indien/Bilder/2015_News_and_Info/economic_news/Trade_-_2014.pdf.

From April 2014 to March 2015, German investment inflows to India amounted to US\$1,125 million.[15] In 2016, the Indo-German Chamber of Commerce (IGCC) celebrates its sixtieth anniversary in India and represents the largest foreign chamber of business in India and by far the largest German bi-national chamber worldwide.[16] India hosts almost 1600 German companies[17] and was the partner country at the Hannover trade fair 2015, the world's largest and most important technology fair for the second time in less than ten years (first time in 2006). German luxury car brands Audi, BMW, Mercedes and Volkswagen present the nature of desire and engagement in an ever-growing supply and demand market economy between India and Germany.

The third IGC consisted of signing eighteen agreements[18] between India and Germany in all possible areas, including education, energy, 'Smart Cities' and cleaning of polluted rivers. The question has never been whether India and Germany would benefit from this strategic partnership, but how both countries can further expand their economic relationship. The signing of the 'fast track'[19] agreement to speed up license mechanism process for German companies as part of the third IGC indicates India's genuine interest in attracting German enterprises in order for them to contribute to the Indian economy. The 'fast track' system for the German companies, now operational, is opening up new horizons of 'single window' clearances for businesses looking to make capital investment in India.

SCIENTIFIC AND CULTURAL EXCHANGE

Science and technology has always played an important role in this bilateral relationship. Previously in 1959, Germany supported the creation of the Indian

---

[15] 'German Investments in India', available at: http://indien.ahk.de/fileadmin/ahk_indien/Bilder/2015_News_and_Info/economic_news/collab_-gernan_fdi.pdf.

[16] Pande, Shamni, 'Why Germany is interested in India', Rediff News, 10 February 2006, available at: http://www.rediff.com//money/2006/feb/10spec.htm.

[17] 'German Investments in India Survey 2015', available at: http://indien.ahk.de/fileadmin/ahk_indien/Bilder/2015_Business_survey/Business_Survey_15.pdf.

[18] 'Why India and Germany need each other', available at: http://www.dw.com/en/why-india-and-germany-need-each-other/a-18764386.

[19] 'Germany our natural partner, says PM Modi after meeting Chancellor Merkel', available at: http://indianexpress.com/article/india/india-news-india/modi-merkel-talks-germany-offers-euro-2-bln-to-india-for-solar-clean-energy/.

Institute of Technology (IIT) in Madras (now Chennai). With the expansion of economic relations, the area of scientific cooperation gained new momentum in the 1990s. Key driving examples have been the Max Planck Centre in New Delhi, the Indo-German Science and Technology working group, the research fellowships in Germany to Indian scholars and the increased engagement and interest in Space Technology. The focal points lie in the areas of biotechnology, health research, information technology, environmental research, sustainability research, materials research and production technology.

Setting up of the Indo-German Max Planck Center for Computer Science in New Delhi and the Indo-German Max Planck-NCBS Center for Research on Lipids at the National Center for Biological Sciences in Bengaluru has made India one of the largest partner countries of the Max Planck Society. India represents one of the most scientific and technical youth heartlands in Asia. Max Planck institutes in India are a testimony of India–German scientific partnership taking shape and building ideas for the mutual growth of the scientific community. Outside Europe, India is second only to China as the most important partner of the Max Planck Society (MPS)[20] and which showcases the benefits of the engagement structure between the Indian and German scientific communities. In addition, all major German research institutions like the Helmholtz Association, the Leibniz Association and the Fraunhofer Gesellschaft have their own representative offices or research and development programmes represented in India. India has always held a special place in the hearts of German scholars. The famous names of Goethe and Max Mueller are deeply engrained and evident in everyday conversation of Indian scholars and students alike. German Indology has contributed to the development of Indian languages and still enjoys a high international reputation. This is a testimony of Germany's continuing interest in India's cultural and linguistic interface. The rapid increase in academic collaboration has also led to increased student exchange. The year 2014-15 saw a rise of 23 per cent compared to 2013-14 in the number of Indian students enrolled in German universities with a total of 11,860 students currently studying in Germany.[21]

---

[20] See https://www.mpg.de/1346919/S006_Max-Planck-Community_107-110.pdf.

[21] 'Germany scores high for students; record growth in Indians studying in Germany for 2014-15', available at: http://blogs.economictimes.indiatimes.com/globalindian/germany-scores-high-for-students-record-growth-in-indians-studying-in-germany-for-2014-15/.

The film industry in Mumbai, popularly referred to as Bollywood, has always symbolised India's soft power dynamics globally and benefitted India in projecting the diversity of its culture, colour and people. Indian classical music and dance are becoming increasingly popular in Europe. Germany provides an opening into Europe of India's soft power projection through films. One of India's largest TV networks, Zee TV, launched a channel in Germany in July 2016 (free via satellite).[22] Consecutive success of many Indian film productions as part of the Berlinale (The Berlin Film Festival) has happened recently. For example, this year (2016), the movie *Ottaal* won the Crystal Bear Award in the Generation Kplus section. Similarly, the movie *Killa*[23] won the Crystal Bear award at Berlinale 2014 and *Lunchbox* (2013) was co-produced with French-German collaboration.[24] And most importantly, Shah Rukh Khan[25] is the most popular film actor in Germany. This showcases the interest and spread of a new age Indian film community within the German audience. It is also important to mention that Ranga Yogeshwar who has Indian roots, is Germany's most famous TV scientist.[26] Indian food, music, yoga and meditation have become increasingly popular in Germany.[27]

ENERGY COOPERATION (RENEWABLE AND CLIMATE CHANGE)

As India's need for energy increases in line with its economic growth and also its responsibility set grows in line with the United Nations Framework Convention on Climate Change (UNFCCC), Germany presents a natural partnership in the field of renewable energy. India has pledged to expand the share of non-fossil fuel energy to 40 per cent by 2030.[28] This pledge got a push when India

---

[22] 'India's Zee TV chief: "We believe we will succeed in the German market"', available at: http://www.dw.com/en/indias-zee-tv-chief-we-believe-we-will-succeed-in-the-german-market/a-19009303.

[23] India Berlinale 2014, http://mib.nic.in/writereaddata/documents/India_at_Berlinale_2014_Report.pdf.

[24] 'Cannes: *The Lunchbox* Director Ritesh Batra (Q&A)', available at: http://www.hollywoodreporter.com/news/cannes-lunchbox-director-ritesh-batra-524943.

[25] 'Shah Rukh Khan: The face of Bollywood', available at: http://www.dw.com/en/shah-rukh-khan-the-face-of-bollywood/a-16747028.

[26] 'Deutschland's Bollywood affair', available at: http://forbesindia.com/printcontent/39181.

[27] 'Germans and their love for freedom', available at: http://www.dw.com/en/germans-and-their-love-of-freedom/a-18918840.

[28] 'India's Intended Nationally Determined Contribution', available at: http://www4.unfccc.int/submissions/INDC/Published%20Documents/India/1/INDIA%20INDC%20TO%20UNFCCC.pdf.

and Germany formed the Climate and Renewable Energy Alliance[29] with a portfolio investment of two billion Euros for clean energy and to foster climate change mitigation efforts. In addition, the memorandum of understanding on Indo-German Solar Energy Partnership allows concessional loans in the range of one billion Euros over the next five years (2015-20) (until 2020).[30] Germany's engagement with India within the framework of the Indo-German Energy Programme (2003-14)[31] represented Germany's eagerness in developing energy efficiency measures and renewable energy sources towards more sustainable measurement of energy and contributing to climate protection.

HUMAN DEVELOPMENT PARTNERS

Germany has always supported the cause of uplifting humanity from the shackles of poverty, bringing about better health access to people and contributing to better management of natural resources in the form of waste management, air pollution and water management. In 2014, India became the largest recipient of German ODA. Germany has consistently increased the bilateral assistance to India in the last three years (from 517.7 million Euros in 2011[32] to 1.2 billion Euros in 2014)[33], has backed India's efforts in poverty reduction, and is contributing to areas of sustainable economic development with contribution to cooperative banks and the improvement of the microcredit system. With the government's internal efforts in public welfare schemes in the form of Jan Dhan Yojana (Peoples Money Scheme)[34] which includes opening up of accounts for the poor (more than 220 million accounts opened till June 2016), accessibility of basic medicines to villages and electrification of off-grid villages, and emphasis on girl child education (Beti Bachao, Beti Padhao campaign)[35], India–Germany

[29]'India, Germany launch tie-up for clean energy', available at: http://www.thehindu.com/news/national/india-germany-launch-tieup-for-clean-energy/article7727601.ece.

[30]'Indo-German Joint Statement on Climate Change and Energy Technology Cooperation', available at: https://www.bundesregierung.de/Content/EN/Pressemitteilungen/BPA/2015/2015-10-05-erklaerung-klima-und-energie-indien_en.html.

[31]'Indo-German Energy Programme (IGEN)', available at: https://www.giz.de/en/worldwide/15767.html.

[32]'Leading Donors to India', available at: https://www.devex.com/news/leading-donors-to-india-80663.

[33]India; https://www.bmz.de/en/what_we_do/countries_regions/asien/indien/index.html.

[34]Pradhan Mantri Jan Dhan Yojana; http://www.pmjdy.gov.in/home.

[35]http://timesofindia.indiatimes.com/india/PM-Modi-launches-Beti-Bachao-Beti-Padhao-campaign-says-female-foeticide-is-a-sign-of-mental-illness/articleshow/45985741.cms.

partnership will contribute to the vision of *Sabka Saath, Sabka Vikas*. India and Germany are also partnering in developing the social security system for India.[36] Moreover, India is Germany's biggest partner in NGO cooperation[37] in the area of poverty reduction, health, social and institutional structures as well as rural development.

PROSPECTS: LOOKING INTO THE CRYSTAL BOWL

The strategic partnership between India and Germany is strongly rooted in their common values of democracy and pluralism. The bilateral relationship offers excellent perspectives. Germany as Europe's economic powerhouse and India as the fastest growing democracy share a broad agenda of mutual interests that range from infrastructure development to technology transfer and skill development. India's reform agenda and Germany technological capabilities make them a perfect match for a broadening of their bilateral relationship. Both countries will continue their collaboration on the international level as well. Strengthening the multilateral system by the efforts of the G4 and a reform of the United Nations is a part of their international agenda as their joint endeavour to ensure freedom of navigation and sea lanes of communication.

The Indo-German Strategic Partnership celebrated its fifteen years of signatory in the year 2015. 2015 also marked the third IGC talks between India and Germany in October 2015 in New Delhi. The general impression with regards to India–Germany IGC talks is sometimes with scepticism of being slow and not being able to reach its true objectivity in terms of deliverables and promises. There are multiple examples depicting that the bilateral relationship is still in a state of maturing, but carries great potential and promise if taken more seriously and understood more clearly by both India and Germany. There are many promising developments in the field of research and development. Germany is a premium destination for Indian firms which have consistently acquired local firms, seeking access to technology and patent portfolios in order to augment their house R&D capabilities.[38] In contrast to this, cooperation

---

[36] India; http://www.auswaertiges-amt.de/EN/Aussenpolitik/Laender/Laenderinfos/01-Nodes/Indien_node.html.

[37] http://www.india.diplo.de/contentblob/3476630/Daten/2148968/EZ_Brochure.pdf.

[38] 'Indian Firms in Germany: Recent Developments and the Road Ahead', available at: http://indien.ahk.de/fileadmin/ahk_indien/Bilder/2013_News_and_Info/economic_news/Indian_Firms_in_Germany.pdf.

in the defence sector remains low and has not met the expectations from both sides.

Both countries face similar constraints in their international cooperation because they have to concentrate on their regional challenges in the foreseeable future. Germany and Europe will have to deal with Russia's new assertive policy in Eastern Europe, with the refugee crisis and with the situation in the Middle East. India will have to concentrate its foreign policy resources on the political and economic implications of China's rise in South and Southeast Asia by strengthening its ties with Japan, Australia and the ASEAN countries.

In order to deepen their international cooperation, India and Germany may also have to explore the possibilities of collaboration in Third World countries. Afghanistan was a missed opportunity for both sides despite their common interests in promoting peace, stability and democracy in that country. The Indian Ocean may be a better, less contentious region where India and Germany can look for common opportunities for closer cooperation, for instance in areas like maritime governance, anti-piracy and strengthening of regional institutions. Exploring these opportunities will also open a new area of cooperation that will make the partnership more robust and strategic.

CHAPTER 14

MODI IN CENTRAL ASIA: WIDENING STRATEGIC PERIMETER

P STOBDAN

One of the key features of Prime Minister Narendra Modi's foreign policy outlook has been to rebuild India on its glorious past but with a modern content. Reconnecting with Central Asia formed a critical part of this approach. A six-day integrated tour of Central Asia by Prime Minister Modi in June 2015 covering all the five states—Uzbekistan, Kazakhstan, Turkmenistan, Kyrgyzstan and Tajikistan—proved not only a symbolic feat for Indian diplomacy but also a smart strategic move that paved the way for overcoming predicaments that have so far stymied India's outreach to an important region lying in its strategic vicinity.

In fact, reconnecting with the land of *Sakas* (Kushans) was long overdue. India's historical links with this region go back to more than 2,500 years—since the days of *Sakas* many facets of history linked India with Central Asia. The ancient Indian texts referred to nations lying beyond the Himalayas or Hindu Kush as *Uttara-kuru*. The *Mahabharata* and ancient Pali literatures mentioned the ancient trade route of *Uttarapatha* that connected the Indo-Gangetic with Central Asia through Takshashila and Gandhara. It joined the fabled Silk Route through which Indian religion, philosophy, commerce, trade and science spread across Asia. Central Asia played the bridge role for Buddhism to spread to the rest of Asia.

In the sixteenth century Zahir-ud-Din Babur came from the Ferghana Valley to establish the Mughal Dynasty in India. However, the events of contemporary history, especially after the eighteenth-nineteenth century, Anglo-Russian 'Great Game' led to total snapping of India's age-old cultural and trade ties with the region. The partition of India and subsequent Pakistani occupation of parts of Jammu & Kashmir finally led to direct physical cut-off that sounded the death knell for India's northern outreach. In fact, this snapping of ties is still reflected from the fact that the sum total of two-way trade with the whole region is a paltry US$1.2 billion.

Central Asia has been rapidly changing since its re-emergence following the Soviet collapse two-and-a-half decades back. The world has started taking notice of its geopolitical importance and energy resource potentials. Already, investment flow, infrastructure development and trade expansion are triggering a wave of transformation that was earlier witnessed in Europe and Southeast Asia. In fact, a major power rivalry is afoot in Central Asia.

India had so far lacked a cogent Central Asia policy; reconnecting with Eurasia should have been an important national strategic endeavour, for India's stakes here go beyond accessing energy and economic interests. The region forms the outermost circle of India's strategic perimeter having geographical proximity to Pakistan, Afghanistan, Iran and China. For India, to maintain a strategic foothold in Central Asia, therefore, becomes vital.

A focused attention to Central Asia was needed for several reasons, and Prime Minister Modi's visit took place against the backdrop of major trends. Two major noticeable trends should draw our attention:

First, the region has been speedily getting swamped by the Chinese. China has pushed for an interlocking of economic and security interests to break a century-and-a-half of Russian monopoly in Central Asia. China now controls the flow of goods and services to and from the region. China has come to enjoy an air of respectability in the region. The states are seeking to benefit from China's aspirations pushed under the US$40 billion 'Silk Road Economic Belt' initiative. For them, the One Road-One Belt (OBOR) would revive the legendary Silk Route marvel. Interestingly, China's growing presence in the region invoked neither resistance from Russia nor has it stirred any challenge from the US and India. The West questions Russia's economic agenda, but remains silent on China's drive in the region.

Second, Central Asia along with Russia's Caucasus area and China's Xinjiang province is emerging as the next frontier of the Islamic world resembling the Middle East. The fear is that this region comprising about seventy million Salafi Muslims, could form a new arc of instability.

In fact, behind the current secular settings, a major shift is underway towards political Islam. The fundamentalist wave has been growing with a variant of local outfits like the Islamic Movement of Uzbekistan (IMU), Islamic Movement of Turkistan (IMT), Hizb ut-Tahrir (HuT), Jund al-Khilafah and Takfir wal-Hijra who have emerged to challenge the local regimes. Their desire is to establish Caliphate-i-Rashida (The Rightly Guided Caliphs) in the entire Central Asian space. They have carried out a spate of terrorist attacks.

Central Asia is also located next to the world's most unstable AfPak (Afghanistan–Pakistan) region. The states here continue to live under the constant and pervasive shadow of threat posed by the Taliban and al-Qaida trained terrorists. Borders with Afghanistan are extremely porous for those engaged in drug trafficking and weapons proliferation.

The emergence of ISIS in eastern Afghanistan, purportedly to recreate Wilayat Khurasan poses additional security threat. Worst, the appearance of ISIS' footprints in Central Asia had sent shock waves across the region. It has heavily recruited Kazakhs, Uzbeks, Tajiks and Kyrgyz to fight in its ranks. Western media quoted some 7,000 recruits from Russia and the former Soviet Union joined the ISIS. Additionally, 1,500 ethnic Uzbeks (500 from Uzbekistan and 1,000 from Southern Kyrgyzstan) are fighting alongside Jabhat al Nusra in Syria and Iraq.

In fact, ever since ISIS' Chief Abu Bakr al-Baghdadi appointed Tajik and Uzbek jihadists as *Amir* of fighting brigades, the recruits from Central Asia have increased by at least 300 per cent. In 2015, the Collective Security Treaty Organization (CSTO) special services had identified (and blocked) more than fifty-seven websites created to recruit from local Tabliqi cadres, home-grown outfits, schools, universities, madrasas, and from migrant worker communities in Russia into the ISIS' ranks.

Clearly, for the ISIS, the heart of Asia offers greater geopolitical stakes than the Middle East. Central Asia provides an ideal geopolitical environment, socio-cultural conditions and the requisite economic parameters for ISIS' growth. The authoritarian political backdrop apart, the oil/gas revenue as well as the rising ethno-religious nationalism heavily influence the power play here. There is also the drug factor that could add to complexity due to the region's proximity to Afghanistan.

The prospects of these jihadists returning home to fan out the ISIS cause, therefore, become alarming. After having learned ISIS' strategies and tactics, the returnees would be inspired to establish a Khurasan state in Central Asia. Clearly, they would be waiting, in the wings, to strike possibly as and when a power vacuum arises out of the looming succession crises in the region. In fact, appointing Central Asian jihadists as *Amir* was meant to inspire and reignite the regional Islamic cadres including Islamic Renaissance Party (IRP), IMU and others. This may have prompted Russia's intervention in Syria. Reports suggested as many as 2,000 Russian-speaking jihadists may have been eliminated during the air raids.

The idea behind situating Wilayat Khurasan in AfPak region as its pivot baseline could be to broaden its expansion to other parts of Asia. Any scenario of ISIS gaining a toehold in Central Asia would have grave implications for the region and beyond including for India. Even though it may not be able to trigger a massive campaign, the Khurasan idea will inspire new radical elements that may pose a formidable security irritant to countries like India.

The fragility of Central Asia is a source of concern for India. Clearly, both the trends of rising extremism as well as China's deep penetration in Central Asia do not augur well for India. Together they could spell the death knell for India's northern outreach. Ideally, Russia's benign presence in Central Asia all along was a preferable option for India. But Russia's influence and capacity to be a potential bulwark for Central Asia is waning. Instead, Russia seeks convergence with China in the face of its worsening standoff with the West.

It was against this geopolitical backdrop that the importance of Prime Minister Modi touching base with Central Asia assumed significance.

India for the first time seemed to have understood the deeper underpinnings of India's need for pursuing its overarching interests. Prime Minister Modi must have realised the need for imparting critical momentum to India's ties with these countries. Uzbekistan is the nerve centre of Central Asia and India cannot wish away the deep cultural contacts with the land of Babur. The energy-rich Kazakhstan and Turkmenistan deserved India's immediate attention. Kyrgyzstan has huge hydropower potential and, like Mongolia, it is a democracy.

India enjoys historical affinity with Tajikistan, besides the country is strategically critical in the context of the AfPak region.

IMPORTANT TAKEAWAYS

The recurring themes in the Prime Minister's discussions with the leaders of five Central Asian countries included the need for enhancing connectivity, strengthening economic and energy ties, cooperating on combating terrorism, cementing defence and security relationship and promoting the traditional cultural bonds. In all, twenty-one bilateral agreements were signed with the five countries.

Improving connectivity with Central Asia remains a formidable challenge. The reasons are numerous and intrinsic. Routing through Iran and Afghanistan or via the International North-South Transport Corridor (INSTC) are important pursuits, but even the best pursued connectivity and pipelines projects like the TAPI have not seen the light of day. The delays involved in actualising them went against India's economic interests.

Prime Minister Modi during his visit stressed on harnessing transport corridors and ports via Iran and Turkmenistan. In February 2016, the Government approved a US$150 million credit line for the development of Chabahar Port in Iran. This plus the completion of the Kazakh-Turkmen-Iran rail link should help to realise India's untapped economic potential with Central Asian states. Chabahar is the key to India's efforts to circumvent Pakistan to access the Central Asia through a route to Afghanistan. The Prime Minister also mooted the idea of bypassing Afghanistan to link with Central Asia through surface, digital and air connectivity. This is in line with India's desire to further its economic interest. Today, China's trade with the region is over US$50 billion compared to India's paltry US$1.2 billion.

Central Asian energy reserves offered alluring possibilities for India. However, thus far, pursuits of energy interest with Kazakhstan had been anything but simple as the Kazakh authorities repeatedly cold-shouldered India's bidding efforts. But, Prime Minister Modi's visit helped impart new momentum for furthering these interests. Four path-breaking developments in this regard deserve attention:

First, in Kazakhstan, after a prolonged delay, India's ONGC-Videsh Ltd (OVL) has finally made its first breakthrough when Prime Minister Modi launched the drilling operations in the Satpayev oil block on 7 July 2015. Hopefully, it should pave the way for India winning more contracts in Kazakh oil exploration business. It could also lead to India exploring the possibility, if any, of transportation of hydrocarbons through long-distance pipeline route with Kazakhstan.

Second, the Kazakh President also took a daring decision to sign a major contract for a renewed long-term supply of 5,000 metric tonnes (MT) of uranium to India during the next five years. It was the most significant takeaway of the Prime Minister's visit. In fact, the deal on nuclear fuel supply with Kazakhstan has proved more promising than achievements on the hydrocarbons side.

Third, in Uzbekistan, Modi sought to operationalise the deal for supplying 2,000 MT of uranium signed between the two countries in 2014. The contract with Uzbekistan is highly significant as Tashkent has put the least number of riders in allowing the access to its nuclear material. However, it needs to be seen how it gets implemented finally.

Fourth, in Turkmenistan, Prime Minister Modi's visit had shown the way finally for the TAPI pipeline to see the light of day. In Ashgabat, the Prime Minister called the TAPI project a 'key pillar' and pushed for its realisation 'quickly'.

No major deal was signed with Kyrgyzstan, although India could have explored the possibility of benefitting from Kyrgyz hydropower, agriculture, health and education potentials. India and Kyrgyzstan reinforced each other's commitment to work together once the India–Eurasian Economic Union (EEU) Free Trade Agreement came into effect. Inking the MoU for cooperation between the Indian and Kyrgyz Election Commissions is significant, though the Kyrgyz have been looking to Western countries for democratic experience.

The flurry of agreements on defence and security were signed, but they remain largely symbolic. They have been there for quite some time without much significance. India has deployed a defence attaché in each of the Indian Embassies of the five Central Asian Republics. Military training and joint exercises have been conducted with some of them. The defence agreements signed with these states are significant but one should note that Kazakhstan, Kyrgyzstan and Tajikistan are members of the Russian-led security alliance, the CSTO and thus they are obliged to follow its direction.

Take the case of Ayni airbase in Tajikistan that India acquired post-Kargil and IC-814 hijacking. India refurbished the base at a cost of US$70 million in 2007, yet we do not know whether it is really using the base or Tajikistan is allowed to permit India to use the base under the CSTO obligation. There was no mention in this regard in the official statements. However, Prime Minister Modi's visit to the newly-built military hospital at Farkhor was widely tweeted.

Combating terrorism, especially the threat posed by the ISIS, gained prominence with Prime Minister Modi suggesting that it is a 'threat without borders'. Central Asia is not a hotbed of terrorism. But, the Prime Minister rightly touched on the shared Islamic heritage and Sufi traditions of Central Asia and India. Like in the Indian subcontinent, Sufism is also rooted in Central Asia's local culture. The region's major Sufi orders include Kubrawiya, Naqshbandi (Uzbekistan), Qadriya (Ferghana), Yassavi (Kazakhstan), Hamdani (Tajikistan) and many others. Sufism rejects extremist ideology. It would be wise for New Delhi to focus on regenerating the traditional Sufi schools of Central Asia that may serve to work as a de-radicalisation process for preventing the birth of radicalism and terrorism in Central Asia.

The Prime Minister's visit had a strong cultural connotation though the past links with Central Asia have not yet given the desired results. Prime Minister Modi gifted a reproduction of *Khamsa-i-Khusrau* to President Islam Karimov. Similarly, he invoked the linguistic and literary links with the Tajiks. Clearly, the visit entailed a strong joint socio-cultural rhetoric—references to Yoga, Hindi, Sufism, IT, among others, added substance to India's soft power.

Prime Minister Modi's visit has certainly aroused expectations for a closer outlook towards Central Asia in an imaginative way. He has infused new energy into India's relationship with the region that had lost momentum in the past decades. Of course, there were no big ticket items to turn the spotlight, but the Prime Minister's own strong presence seems to have created a huge excitement, perhaps no less than the imprints that Raj Kapoor, Indira Gandhi, Mithun Chakraborty and a few others had earlier made on the people's imaginations. Modi has become a factor in Central Asia and this is important. In fact, it has been decades since any popular Indian leader visited these countries. Such a visit was long desired; as one friend of this author put it, 'we needed such a thing because Indian leaders have always appealed to everyone in Central Asia'.

Also, it was imperative for India to widen its strategic perimeter towards the region lying beyond Pakistan and China. Prime Minister Modi's visit helped realise this goal. In fact, he has proved to be the most historically conscious Indian leader after Jawaharlal Nehru. Sadly, the Indian media failed to highlight this. Barring the state-owned channels, mainstream media remained muted simply because the visit lacked the scintillating 'rock-star' image and the diaspora patriotic fervour.

CHALLENGES AHEAD

Surely, India's ties with Central Asia remain strong, but it is yet to capitalise on various opportunities and potentials. Modi has seized the opportunity to set the agenda for India's future engagement in Central Asia.

Looking ahead and if India is keen to up its game in Central Asia, it will have to first solve the connectivity problems and this cannot be overcome without improving ties with India's immediate neighbours like Pakistan—the reason why Prime Minister Modi was perhaps trying to broaden the scope of India's geopolitical engagement. His visit to the Central Asian states followed by a visit to Russia, Afghanistan and even his brief stopover in Pakistan wouldn't have been planned without a well thought-out strategy. Clearly, as India's energy demands increase, it will find itself in the centre of important geopolitical and energy relationships in Eurasia.

Second, Russia is and will remain an important factor for India's ability to do business in Central Asia. India's premature discounting of Russia was a mistake. In fact, such a policy line not only delayed India's success but also made its diplomacy in Central Asia a more arduous exercise. India's energy requirements in Central Asia suggest a continuing positive relationship with Russia.

Third, India faces financial limitations and the current engagement policy does not have vitality for spurring economic interdependence. Geography is not the only factor. Even the private sector with deep pockets has been hesitant to make a foray into the region. They too have tended to take shelter under the government patronised schemes abroad.

Fourth, the lack of scholarship and knowledge to deal with the region is another handicap. Indians have avoided understanding the intricate socio-tribal structural underpinnings that regulate the decision-making process in Central Asia. As a result, relying on official and diplomatic channels has not yielded the desired results. Not surprising, the approach has led to a distortion in overall relations—the reason why the depth of India–Central Asia ties has always remained in question.

Fifth, India certainly enjoys a huge cultural edge not only in historical affinities but also in terms of goodwill in all the five countries. The adulation for Indian culture, Indology, dance, music, Bollywood, Hindi TV soaps, etc. is palpable among people, yet nothing much has been done to transform it to the next level of partnership.

Sixth, India has been helping these countries with half-baked skill development and capacity-building programmes. India needs to explore smart projects that will push direct development processes and people-to-people contacts through increased air traffic and promotion of tourism with these countries.

Seventh, Central Asia is a region of immense resources. The region's agro-farming and mining are important sectors for venture. Indian companies should be investing in pharmaceuticals, textiles, engineering, construction and small and medium enterprises. They should also invest in refineries, petrochemicals and fertiliser plants in the region.

Eighth, the opportunity seems to be opening up now that India is ready to join the regional mechanisms like the Shanghai Cooperation Organisation (SCO) as a full member and where the Central Asian republics have wanted India to play a larger strategic role. Last year, China too has finally welcomed India into the SCO.

Certainly, India stands to benefit from SCO's Regional Anti-Terrorist Structure (RATS) and also learn from its counterterror exercises. Being part of the SCO means that opportunity would also open for India to cooperate in soft-political areas of the region that it knows little about.

However, the SCO is likely to come at odds with India's vision and world views. The SCO is essentially a counterweight to the West and for India to play an ancillary role of offsetting the US is tricky.

New Delhi remains less than enthusiastic over China's OBOR initiative and strongly resents China's plans for building an economic corridor through Pakistan-occupied Kashmir. Herein lies a potential problem for India as a member of the SCO.

Besides, the SCO could also become a forum for inimical forces to drum up anti-India voices. Thus, staying outside cannot be to India's advantage.

Already, on countering terrorism, the SCO's key anchor, China, has decided to block India's bid at the UN to ban Jaish-e-Mohammad chief Masood Azhar, the mastermind of the Pathankot terror attack. Earlier, China blocked India's demand for taking action against Pakistan for freeing the 26/11 mastermind Zakiur Rehman Lakhvi of the LeT. To India's shock and disbelief, its good friend Russia took a stand at a Brisbane meet on anti-terror financing against India's demand for censuring Pakistan for its inaction against the Jamaat-ud-Dawa and Lashkar-e-Taiba.

The key issue, therefore, is whether SCO could help India get out of the current geopolitical quandary of being wedged between a wall of Pakistani hostility and the fear of cooperating with China. Pakistan seems already gearing up to fully operate in Eurasia with its acceptance growing in the SCO and that too with Russia's support.

It needs to be underscored that Central Asian countries' terror threat perceptions are linked to tightening their domestic control. India should take their concerns on radicalisation seriously and assist them in counterterror technology and training. However, India should be mindful that the Central Asian countries' position on key security issues will ultimately be guided by China and Russia.

The SCO sees itself becoming a pivoting point for a possible India–Pakistan thaw. Russia has been dreaming about it for a long time. In 2015 in Ufa, Chinese Vice Foreign Minister Cheng Guoping reportedly said that 'SCO will play a constructive role in pushing for the improvement of their (India–Pakistan) bilateral relations.'

Finally, Central Asians undeniably consider India to be a reliable, trustworthy and predictable partner. But at the same time they do not consider India to be a good performer. Many have argued that New Delhi's indecisiveness always influenced Nursultan Nazarbayev against energy deals with India. Even though these states realise the importance of engaging India, they also know well that it is only China that can fit the bill ultimately. Hopefully, the SCO can help resolve at least some of these problems.

Prime Minister Modi's Central Asia foray has undeniably added a new momentum and energy to the web of relationships between India and Central Asian republics. It opens up further possibilities for a dynamic and strategic partnership between India and the region.

CHAPTER 15

INDIA–MONGOLIA: SPIRITUAL NEIGHBOURS AND STRATEGIC PARTNERS

GONCHIG GANBOLD

Mongolia and India are ancient nations. The Mongolians' acquaintance with India first came through the teachings of Lord Buddha. The thirteenth-century manuscript, *The Sacred History of Mongols* (chapters 261-264) referred to India as Hindu or Hindustan and the Indus River as Sinegol or a 'New River'. The two countries have nurtured deep-rooted ties with shared cultural, religious and spiritual legacies.

The Mughal dynasty, a pivotal part in India's history, had established many areas and places in Delhi and other parts of India with names such as Mangolpuri, Mangolbad and Mangolore. While Buddhism was spread to Mongolia by Ashoka and his disciples, Babur who established the Mughal Empire in India, was a descendant of Chingiz Khan. A large number of manuscripts and literature on our historical ties are being preserved and restored in archives, museums, libraries and research institutions.

Narendra Modi, the Prime Minister of India, during his official visit to Mongolia in May 2015 presented saplings of the Bodhi Tree to the main Buddhist (Gandantegchiling) monastery, as an illustration of our common spiritual legacy and close feelings. The teachings of Buddha are inseparably intertwined with the way of life, mindset and philosophy of the Mongolian people.

In one of his parables, the Buddha noted that man should seek the middle path between self-indulgence and self-mortification. This middle way, known as the Noble Eightfold Path, consisted of right view, right thought, right speech, right action, right mode of living, right endeavour, right mindfulness and right consciousness. The teachings of Buddha helped not only to form our thoughts but also transformed into a philosophy of permanent neutrality, a core feature of our foreign policy.

India's freedom struggle against the British Raj saw the emergence of leaders from diverse ethnicities and faiths like Mahatma Gandhi, Jawaharlal Nehru, Netaji Subhash Chandra Bose, Baba Saheb Ambedkar, Sardar Vallabhbhai Patel, Maulana Abul Kalam Azad, Sarojini Naidu. The freedom struggle was based on ahimsa (non-violence)—a way of thought that existed for over two centuries. The same philosophy was applied by leaders like Jayaprakash Narayan who had stood for political freedom and human liberty in the 1970s. Likewise, the Mongolians by the early 1990s got rid of the authoritarian regime and embarked on a path of twin transformation, namely, parliamentary democracy and market economy, without a single window-pane broken. The shared experiences of independence and sovereignty have evolved into formal state-to-state relations.

Mongolia and India are spiritual neighbours sitting on the northern and southern edges of Buddhist Asia. Despite geographical barriers, we have been connected with ancient bonds of history, culture and religion which formed the bedrock of our official diplomatic relations.

Mongolians respect India as a sacred land of Lord Buddha and a source of wisdom and knowledge. Travellers of ancient past used to note that Mongolian monks studied at Nalanda University. Moreover, in my childhood, I used to hear from elders that acharyas from Hindustan were living in Khentii Aimag of Mongolia. These spiritual ties are an important foundation of our close bonds.

I am pleased that India has announced its willingness to accept Mongolian students at Nalanda University. Mongolia and India have contributed in the fields of arts, literature and poetry as well as research on oriental culture. This needs to be carried forward by our young generation.

Chingiz Khan, founder of the unified Mongolian state, touted that winning of heart and mind is the best way to govern. Even in the thirteenth century, the Mongols appreciated and respected the diverse cultures and civilisations. Marco Polo, Plano Carpini and others have noted that instead of discriminating or contradicting, the Mongols used to co-exist and debate with all the major faiths in their respective temples, monasteries, mosques and ashrams.

This year Mongolia marks the twenty-fifth anniversary of the first free and fair elections which ushered the country into political democracy and market economy. Following the great Indian tradition of ahimsa, we peacefully brought democratic changes in Mongolia in the early 1990s. India supported these sweeping transformations and the Parliament of India along with some other Asian legislative bodies made its valuable contributions in inserting democratic values and principles in our Constitution in 1992.

Mongolia and India have defined the core principles of their relations and cooperation in a Joint Declaration of 1973. Since then we have concluded the Treaty on Friendship and Cooperation in 1994, the Treaty on Comprehensive Partnership in 2008 and the Treaty on Strategic Partnership in 2015 and have agreed to collaborate in all available fields. At present over fifty treaties and agreements are being implemented between our countries. Deep-rooted historical ties have grown into strategic partnership with promising outcomes.

Agriculture and animal husbandry play a critical role in both the countries' economies and it is crucial that Mongolia and India pay greater attention to and collaborate on climate change and environmental protection. India has rendered assistance to Mongolia in training its personnel and promoting Small and Medium Enterprises under the Indian Technical and Economic Cooperation (ITEC) programme since 1987. A large number of our students have been enrolled in India's universities on government and private sector stipends. I am in utmost hope that they will become a bridge connecting the two countries closer in the coming years.

Mongolia and India, both peace-loving nations and being averse to any military alliances, are constructively collaborating within the Non-Aligned Movement, the United Nations, World Trade Organization, Shanghai Cooperation Organization and the UNFCCC in order to avoid conflicts and facilitate understanding and cooperation for global peace and security. We unanimously denounce all forms of extremism and have expressed our firm determination to strive against religious fundamentalism and violent terrorism.

A Land afar but closer to the heart

When Prime Minister Narendra Modi visited Mongolia in May 2015, Ch Saikhanbileg the Prime Minister of Mongolia introduced me to Modi, who said, 'India welcomes you, Mr Ambassador'. Soon after this encouraging moment and having received the Letter of Credence as Ambassador of Mongolia to India on 2 September 2015, Pranab Mukherjee, the President of India, vividly underlined the ancient cultural and spiritual ties between India and Mongolia.

The following day as the newly appointed Ambassador, I had the opportunity to attend the international symposium on 'Global Hindu-Buddhist Initiative on Conflict Avoidance and Environmental Consciousness' co-hosted by the Vivekananda International Foundation of India and the Tokyo Foundation of Japan. This international symposium held in New Delhi and Bodh Gaya in Bihar, more than anything, helped me to recall what the President of India had highlighted in his remarks on the age-old ties between our two nations.

We in Mongolia often recall the teachings of Swami Vivekananda, such as 'We are what our thoughts have made us; so take care about what you think. Words are secondary. Thoughts live; they travel far' and 'You have to grow from the inside out. None can teach you, none can make you spiritual. There is no teacher but your own soul'. Another of Vivekananda's thoughts with which we are familiar is, 'Neither money pays, nor name, nor fame, nor learning; it is character that can cleave through adamantine walls of difficulties'.

We like to pass these pearls of wisdom on to our new generation saying that, 'You ought to know thoughts in order to know the men' and 'Check yourself being amidst the people and check your thoughts while being alone'. Some other thoughts that we inculcate in our youth are: 'Sight is blind where as thoughts are not blind' and 'The best form of wealth is knowledge which is better than material wealth'.

Representing my country in an amazing land like India, with a fascinating blend of colourful traditions and a rapid pace of transformations, I am compelled to look at the changes in terms of gains and avenues for Mongolia and India's bilateral relations, which to say the least is brimming with promising prospects. Despite our centuries' old ties, Mongolia and India are marking the sixtieth year of their diplomatic relations that was established on 24 December 1955 as a year-long event.

As the first Prime Minister of India to visit Mongolia, Narendra Modi emphasised the ancient but reinvigorating ties between India and Mongolia.

He expressed the hope that these ties would have a positive impact on regional and international peace, stability and progress. During his visit, India announced US$1 billion Line of Credit to encourage India's export of goods and services and to assist Mongolia in its infrastructure development and capacity-building. Various projects and programmes are to be financed through this Line of Credit and are being processed.

Another important engagement has been on the economic front with an investment agreement of US$4.4 billion signed between Oyu Tolgoi, one of the world's largest new copper-gold mines in south Gobi region and Turquoise Hill Resources (THR) and Rio Tinto in Ulaanbaatar. The agreement confirmed the financing package for Oyu Tolgoi's underground mine, which represents 80 per cent of the project's total value.

This agreement, one of the largest ever in the mining industry in Mongolia, is provided by a syndicate of international financial institutions and export credit agencies representing the governments of Canada, the United States of America and Australia, along with fifteen commercial banks. Canada is the source of over 21 per cent of the financing. Other international lenders include the International Finance Corporation and the European Bank for Reconstruction and Development (each at US$400 million), as well as the US Export-Import Bank (US$367 million) and Australia's Export Finance and Insurance Corporation (US$150 million). The remaining funds are from fifteen commercial banks. The Multilateral Investment Guarantee Agency (MIGA) provides political risk insurance for the commercial banks.

Another encouraging forward movement is that the Mongolian Parliament has formally abolished capital punishment through its recent amendment to the Criminal Law which had been frozen by Presidential decree since 2009. It also justifies the country's election to the United Nations Human Rights Council for the period of 2016-17. Mongolia also successfully led the young but vibrant international movement, the Freedom Online Coalition and hosted its fifth Ministerial Conference in Ulaanbaatar in 2015 followed by assumption of the Chairmanship of the International Institute for Democracy and Elections Assistance for 2016. Ulaanbaatar will also be the venue for the eleventh Asia–Europe Meeting (ASEM) in July 2016. These series of activities clearly go to demonstrate Mongolia's increasing participation and contribution to regional and international understanding and stability.

With no access to the sea and surrounded by two big neighbours, Mongolia aspires for further consolidation of its freedom, independence and sovereignty. This sparsely populated, small country opted to stay away from conflicts and contradictions while making its contributions in promoting dialogues and cooperation at regional and international levels. Judging from our previous experience of being non-aligned we view the status of neutrality as serving well our interest. Neutrality though not proclaimed has always been a pillar in the years when the Mongolians fought for restoration of freedom and independence, and during the tense days of democratic revolution too. Mongolia officially announced the country as neutral at the UN General Assembly's seventieth session in October 2015.

Nowadays, we are required to study neutrality in depth and objectively espouse it to our friends and partners far and near. International law views the neutrality status in two main categories. This classification entirely depends on the decisions and proclamations a neutral state undertakes. The first category is a neutrality status quo in wartime. The second category is active and inactive neutrality in peace time. There are also certain treaties and agreements in international relations that identify the policy essence and principles of neutrality.

Mongolia's foreign policy in substance, form and action is fully coherent with the principles of neutrality. We, in a certain sense, take pride that our national laws and the international treaties/agreements that Mongolia is party to, are coherent with the neutrality principles. More specifically, Mongolia's neutrality is delicately reflected in the very letter and spirit of the treaties/agreements which we have concluded with our neighbouring and other friendly states.

The following factors have contributed to Mongolia's neutrality policy.
- First, the Constitution of 1992 and its principles led Mongolia to actively pursue neutral policies. While we did not officially declare it, in form, the neutral direction was guided by the spirit of the new Constitution.
- Second, the history of Mongolia, its geographic location and development are congruent with the spirit and principles of neutrality. It enables us to maintain equal and balanced international relations. Our neighbours, friends and partners respect status quo of a neutral state.

- Third, while international order and strategic equation change over time, neutral policies and actions sustain over a longer period of time. Also importantly, the state which upholds neutrality reserves full authority to amend, renew or abandon its neutral approach.

Permanent neutrality is a policy whereby a sovereign state declares itself to be aloft of the belligerents during wartime and maintain neutrality at peace time. In the event that a neutral state is subjected to external aggression, it has full right for defence. At the same time, it voluntarily assumes a duty not to wage or join wars. A permanent neutral state reserves a right to have its own armed forces and troops. And this very right serves as the assurance of immunity of its neutrality. The fundamentals of Mongolia's defence and foreign policy are consonant with neutralism.

The territorial immunity of a neutral state is reassured by international law. This includes both air space and coastal borders. It is prohibited to conduct war on the territories of a neutral state. Also a neutral state has the right to not allow passage or transit of belligerent countries' soldiers, arms and war materials across its territory. Permanent neutrality also has certain implications for nuclear weapons and the country's membership in any military alliance. Mongolia proclaimed its territory as a Nuclear Weapon Free Zone and this has been acknowledged by the UN and the nuclear powers.

Judging from other neutral countries' experiences, like Austria, Sweden and Switzerland, it is not necessary for a state to seek support from any particular country or international organisation to validate its status quo. Internationally a country's neutrality is acknowledged. Our forefathers always maintained dignity and temperance which has helped to frame and guide our Constitution. We equally hold high and respect the UN Charter.

Unity, continuity and clarity in foreign policy are at the core of Mongolia's interests. Neutrality is a tool to harness and build upon our existing potentials and to pursue active, flexible relations with other nations. This may also be seen as a pragmatic approach resulting in opportunities. But what is of greater significance is a foreign policy that is persistent and consistent. Inarguably, neutrality will help invigorate many policies, initiatives and actions at a time when the world is coming to terms with wide-ranging unconventional challenges like climate change, organised crime and terrorism that require consolidated endeavour.

BETTER TO SEE THAN TO HEAR

The CNN has included Mongolia in the list of most ethical travel destinations for 2016. In fact Mongolians have a saying, 'It is always better to see once through own eyes than to hear other's saying many times.' Mongolia has much to offer to travellers who dare to visit one of the oldest but relatively unchartered lands in Asia.

Mongolia is the most sparsely populated landlocked country. Altai-Khanghai mountain ranges with eternally snow-capped peaks and glaciers comprise two-third of its land, which is nearly half of India.

The mountainous areas include wet meadow pastures and seemingly endless steppe. It has thousands of lakes and rivers and with an elevation of about 4,500 ft there is sufficient sunshine for almost 300 days a year. Across centuries, Mongolians have engaged with pastoral animal husbandry, which is interwoven with their nomadic lifestyle.

The vast expanse makes Mongolia conducive for horse riding. Ever since the horse named 'Mongolian Saturday' trained by the Mongolian Enebish Ganbat won the Breeders' Cup Sprint in 2015, equine sports is on the rise. In recent years auto rallies through Mongolia's landscape are becoming very popular amongst Europeans.

Different religious faiths add their respective shades to the present-day spiritual tapestry in Mongolia. Shamanism had prevailed in Mongolia which left its mark on native culture and traditional rituals and gradually gave way to Buddhism while Kazakhs residing in western Mongolia traditionally adhere to Islam.

Mongolian cities and towns have historical significance. The ancient Mongolian capital Kharkhorim founded in 1220 in the Orkhon Valley was a bustling area. Chingiz Khan had set up a supply base here and his son made it into a capital, drawing traders and skilled workers from across Asia and Europe. Kharkhorim was at the crossroads of the Silk Road and was the centre of the Mongol Empire until Kublai Khan moved it to Beijing.

The strictly protected area of Khan Khentii is covered with taiga and mountain forest steppe. As the birthplace of Chingiz Khan, it is described vividly in the thirteenth-century manuscript *The Secret History of Mongols*. This sacred land in the north-east of Ulaanbaatar has become a popular route for soul searchers. Khuvsgul known as Dark Blue Pearl is Mongolia's largest and deepest lake in the northern part of the country. The name of this lake is derived from the Sanskrit word 'Khuvsurut' meaning beautiful. Ulaanbaatar, the capital of Mongolia, is a pulsating urban centre that brings together an exciting blend of traditional and modern lifestyles.

CONCLUSION

India's relationship with Mongolia has significantly progressed since 1973, when it signed an eight-point joint declaration. In fact, Mongolia often looks upon India as its 'spiritual neighbour', given its deep-rooted cultural links with Buddhism. India, to recall, played a critical role in getting Mongolia admitted to the United Nations in 1961, despite strong opposition from China and Taiwan. In 1972, Mongolia co-sponsored a UN resolution with India and Bhutan for the recognition of the newly-liberated Bangladesh. The cultural connect, the historical trust and the subsequent joint declarations of 2001, 2004 and 2009 provide a solid platform to take the relationship further and to greater heights. Defence and security has been a core area of cooperation between the two countries, which includes joint defence exercises. Mongolia is a mineral-rich country with vast coal, petroleum and uranium resources and in 2009 it was among the first to sign a uranium deal with India. On the economy front, bilateral trade of US$60.2 million in 2012 had fallen to US$35 million in 2013. This needs to be bolstered as there is vast scope for greater economic interaction and Mongolia is more than keen to extend the third neighbour policy to India.

Thematically
Tied to the World

CHAPTER 16

ENHANCING ECONOMIC AND STRATEGIC SPACE: KEY GOALS OF PRIME MINISTER MODI'S DIPLOMACY

MUKUL ASHER

INTRODUCTION

The Prime Minister Narendra Modi-led government, which was entrusted with governance responsibilities as a result of winning the 2014 General Elections, has significantly energised India's diplomacy and engagement with the rest of the world, with a coherent and sustained focus on enhancing India's economic and strategic space. India's former ambassador to the United States, Nirupama Rao has termed India's recent diplomacy as a 'new, strong and clear outreach'.[1]

This is, however, being pursued in the context of a subdued global macroeconomic environment and a less vibrant world trade outlook.[2] There is also a downward phase in the oil and metals cycles, which leads to further reassessment and restructuring of domestic economic and political priorities in resource-rich countries.[3] This downward cycle however has been positive

---

[1] 'New, strong and clear outreach', *The Hindu*, 4 March 2016, available at: http://www.thehindu.com/opinion/op-ed/narendra-modi-new-strong-and-clear-outreach/article8310200.ece.
[2] The World Trade Organization (WTO) estimates that world trade over the 2012-16 period is likely to grow at approximately the same rate as global GDP, rather than twice as previously reported, available at: https://www.wto.org/english/news_e/pres16_e/pr768_e.htm.
[3] IMF World Economic Outlook, available at: http://www.imf.org/external/pubs/ft/weo/2016/01/.

for India, as on balance the country is a net importer of oil and other energy products and metals.

There is a gradual global realignment of economic, strategic, and to some extent of 'soft' power, away from the United States and Europe towards Asia and the Pacific. Such realignment however will be neither automatic nor likely to proceed in a linear fashion.

The global strategic environment, therefore, is likely to continue to exhibit considerable uncertainty and complexity. Managing relationships with confidence and agility, particularly with the US and China, both bilaterally and multilaterally would be crucial for India (Srinivasan, 2016).[4] Deepening and broadening strategic partnership with Japan, a country with which India shares complementarities in factor endowments and strategic interests, will be high among India's priorities.[5]

Thus, substantially-enhanced competence and allocation of resources in pursuing diplomacy will be needed to manage the current and emerging global environment by Indian policymakers.

The rest of the essay is organised as follows. The section 'The Rationale for Expanding Economic and Strategic Space' provides the rationale for focusing on expanding India's economic and strategic space. In 'Recent Initiatives', selected diplomatic initiatives of the Prime Minister Modi-led government are briefly reviewed. The final section concludes with several observations.

THE RATIONALE FOR EXPANDING ECONOMIC AND STRATEGIC SPACE

The rationale for expanding India's economic and strategic space arises from several factors. First, Indian policymakers have realised that the distinction between domestic and international spheres in policymaking has not only become much less sharp, but requires integrated approaches which appropriately take into account the impact of domestic policies on the external position of the country and vice versa.

---

[4] Srinivasan, R, 'Narendra Modi and foreign policy', in Ganguly, Anirban (ed.), *Redefining Governance* (New Delhi: Prabhat Prakashan India, 2015), pp. 163-73.

[5] It is noteworthy that a strategic partnership is already being developed as expressed in a joint statement by the Ministry of External Affairs on 12 December 2015, available at: http://www.mea.gov.in/bilateral-documents.htm?dtl/26176/Joint_Statement_on_India_and_Japan_Vision_2025_Special_Strategic_and_Global_Partnership_Working_Together_for_Peace_and_Prosperity_of_the_IndoPacific_R).

In India's case, many of its key growth constraints, particularly in technology, energy, infrastructure, the need for markets for India's goods and services, and better utilisation of its 30 to 35 million strong diaspora can be more fully addressed only by synchronising internal initiatives and external diplomacy that is designed to expand its economic and strategic space. The diaspora could also gain economic, political and social leverage in their respective countries if India exhibits robust and resilient growth, and is perceived to be addressing its development challenges. Thus there is a commonality of interest between India on the one hand and its diaspora on the other.

As India's businesses expand abroad, they become a source of livelihoods and support to households and businesses in the respective countries, while also contributing to government revenue. Thus, the systematic collection of data on India's outward investment flows deserves serious consideration.

The strategic importance of the Indian diaspora is expected to increase significantly as China has an active policy to widen and deepen the engagement of the Chinese diaspora with all parts of the world, particularly in the US, Africa, Latin America and the rest of Asia and the Pacific. Competition from other countries in Asia such as the Philippines and Vietnam, and from Eastern Europe is also increasing for the export of professional services and skills. This, in conjunction with the diminished growth prospects of the resource-rich countries, could impact considerably on India's remittances and livelihood opportunities which have been an important method of handling India's international trade deficit as will be noted later in this section.

It is, therefore, erroneous to infer that foreign visits by India's leaders for bilateral or multilateral forums necessarily distract from attention on domestic issues. This also applies to the events which are focused on the Indian diaspora abroad as is evidenced by Prime Minister Modi's addresses to the diaspora in Brussels, Kuala Lumpur, London, New York, Riyadh,[6] Silicon Valley, Singapore, Sydney and elsewhere. India needs to utilise its people-to-people diplomacy, knowledge, enterprise and capital to address its own development challenges.

---

[6] Prime Minister Modi's lunch with the Indian workers in Riyadh illustrates that his conception of the importance of the Indian diaspora extends to all levels of skills and occupations. Saudi Arabia hosts nearly 3 million Indian workers, besides being the largest supplier of crude oil. Available at: http://www.thenewsminute.com/article/pm-modi-touches-hearts-indian-migrants-shares-meal-them-riyadh-41116.

The above discussion suggests that, for India, its diaspora, if appropriately broadened, deepened, as well as motivated, could become a major asset in improving the country's growth prospects and in addressing its domestic and external challenges.[7] The above is a significant implication of the globalised era, which does not appear to have received due recognition by the political commentators, the media and even by scholars and researchers in various academic and research institutions.

The second rationale is that India has been steadily expanding integration with the global economy. And this trend is expected to accelerate in the current phase of India's economic management and growth dynamics. Several indicators reinforce this point.

In 2015, India's merchandise exports were valued at US$267 billion and at US$158 billion for services. This corresponds to approximately 1.6 per cent and 3.3 per cent of global exports respectively. Merchandise imports totalled US$392 billion, or 2.3 per cent of world imports, and services were US$126 billion (2.7 per cent of world services imports). Respectively, total exports (of merchandise and services) were 20.7 per cent of nominal (2014) GDP and imports were 25.2 per cent of GDP. Thus, India's total trade was 46 per cent of GDP, suggesting a moderate degree of integration with the rest of the world. According to the Ministry of Commerce and Industry, India's overall trade deficit in 2015-16 was approximately US$118.5 billion.

Foreign direct investment (FDI) inflows totalled US$28.78 in 2014, according to the Department of Industrial Policy and Promotion. This increased to US$39.32 billion in 2015. More importantly, it is necessary to highlight that total inward remittance flows to India, according to World Bank, totalled US$72 billion in 2015, making it the largest remittances receiving country. Alternatively, this indirectly implies that official remittances from India's diaspora contributed to approximately half of the financing of India's imports. This further underscores the importance of the diaspora, and how a win-win cultivation of the diaspora can make considerable contribution to not just India's external macroeconomic management, but also to India's domestic economic and other policy objectives.

---

[7] This appears to be a deserving area of research, particularly on the roles the Indian diaspora has played in the USA, the UK, and in the African continent.

The key sustainable benefit of the diaspora, however, is not remittances, but in their energies, skills, entrepreneurship and new ideas which they could potentially bring to India. The responsibility is particularly to key diaspora-sending states such as Andhra Pradesh, Gujarat, Kerala, West Bengal, Maharashtra and others to create conducive environments by which to induce the diaspora to make more critical and sustainable contributions.

Third, Prime Minister Modi's government has based its diplomacy with the explicit recognition that the country's leverage is dependent primarily on the size of the Indian economy, its growth trajectory and the country's ability to address challenges both competently and in a sustainable manner that does not compromise or endanger the country's future growth and development prospects.

India aims to become a US$10 trillion economy by 2032 (from US$2.05 trillion in 2014) and to create 175 million jobs by 2032.[8] India's immediate official targets for 2019 are striving to become the top start-up destination in the world, achieving a top-30 ranking in the global ease of doing business, achieving 60 per cent digital penetration and increasing the share of manufacturing from 16 per cent of GDP in 2014 to 25 per cent by 2022. Each ministry will be given targets with dates by which they need to be achieved, and monitoring will be done by an online dashboard of their progress by NITI Aayog.

Progress in achieving these goals and targets will have an impact on how India is perceived externally as a partner. But, crucially, it will depend on the internal reforms and initiatives which the country undertakes. This, again, underlines the close links between the domestic and external spheres of policymaking, which may be highlighted as follows.

India plans to double its aggregate global trade over the next decade. This is a huge challenge given the current global macroeconomic environment and will require considerable investments in infrastructure, particularly in transport, power and water management. Despite India's large overall merchandise trade deficit, it is noteworthy that the agricultural sector generates a moderately large trade surplus. Thus in 2014, the share of agricultural products was 13.5 per cent of the exports but only 5.9 per cent of imports. Conversely, in services,

---

[8] As reported in the *Economic Times* on 22 April 2016, 'India to become $10 trillion economy by 2032: Amitabh Kant', available at: http://articles.economictimes.indiatimes.com/2016-04-22/news/72536372_1_growth-rate-amitabh-kant-gdp.

transport services accounted for only 12 per cent of India's total services exports; yet its share in services imports was 52.6 per cent. Policy imperatives, thus, appear to be how the trade surplus generated by the agricultural sector may be increased, which in turn would increase India's external economic and strategic space. India needs to develop greater competitiveness and competence in the transport sector to reduce the share of imports in this sector.

Another area deserving urgent attention is the imbalance in the service transactions of financial services. As India increases its investments in projects around the country, financial package engineering services in all phases becomes an important expenditure. Currently, complex project financing services are, to a large extent, undertaken abroad. To develop capacity to perform international financial services domestically, through appropriate policy and regulatory changes, and through investment is essential. The Gujarat International Financial Tec-City (GIFT) project (http://giftgujarat.in/) is designed to be a small step in this direction and initiatives to develop other such centres, especially in Mumbai, India's commercial capital, merit much greater urgency.

India's share in 2015 in global tourist arrivals was less than 1 per cent, though domestic tourist flows are large (but inadequately documented).[9] This share is negligible given India's size, history and civilisational imprints. This is an area that holds potential to not only improve India's trade balance, but also to provide livelihoods. India has introduced e-visa and visa-on-arrival facilities. The initiative to establish National Medical and Wellness Tourism Board is also a step in the right direction. The key however is to modernise India's tourism infrastructure and organisations, backed up by result-oriented promotion methods.

Besides identifying key sectors of the economy, what is equally important, and often overlooked, is that analyses of external trade has often focused on its gross value share of gross national income, but there needs to be emphasis also on the value a country obtains from production networks and supply chains, the types of commodities that are traded, and the geographical distribution of trade, particularly in the east and north-east regions of India which currently exhibit lower external (and internal) trade in both absolute and in per capita terms. The government's emphasis on the development of these regions is,[10]

---

[9] Available at: http://pib.nic.in/newsite/PrintRelease.aspx?relid=144794.

[10] Available at: http://www.thehindu.com/news/national/govt-to-work-for-all-round-development-of-northeast-says-pm-modi/article8119490.ece.

therefore, appropriate as this will enhance India's capacity to engage globally while narrowing regional imbalances.

The importance of integrating both domestic and external spheres of policy making is clear in this case as investment decisions, particularly in enhancing infrastructure and communication links between and across regions will have considerable impact on trade flows, economic growth, and also impacting India's overall trade balance.

As the next section discusses further, there are clear signs which suggest that the initiatives undertaken by the Modi government are aimed at enhancing both of India's economic and security space.

RECENT INITIATIVES

This section discusses how India's recent diplomatic initiatives have attempted to address the key constraints which are serving to restrain India's future growth prospects, and how India can use the external sector as an important node in its growth strategy, an avenue which it has so far not utilised to its full potential. These initiatives are integrated with improving India's defence capabilities and security cooperation and partnerships.

The key initiatives may be classified as enhancing energy security, improving domestic and international connectivity and strengthening the organisational and institutional foundations for broader and deeper engagement with the rest of the world.

Enhancing Energy Security

India, in partnership with France, has established the International Solar Alliance (ISA) which currently has a membership of about 120 countries.[11] The objective of the ISA is to facilitate global investment and knowledge sharing to better harness the potential of solar power (India aims to have a renewable energy capacity of 175GW by 2022) for socio-economic development and to diversify its reliance on fossil fuels for energy. The headquarters of the organisation will be based in Gurgaon in Haryana, India.

India has since contributed US$30 million as the initial financial capital and the Alliance aims to raise US$400 million from membership fees and

---

[11] Available at: http://www.theguardian.com/environment/2015/nov/30/india-set-to-unveil-global-solar-alliance-of-120-countries-at-paris-climate-summit.

international agencies. This will subsequently be leveraged to generate investments in solar industry globally from many sources.

The ISA not only provides another energy forum option to the world (besides OPEC, Organization of Petroleum Exporting Countries) but also provides a forum to share knowledge and ideas on energy issues. For India, knowledge and understanding of technology dynamics in this area is critical for its energy security.

Besides the ISA, India's diplomacy has further enhanced energy security with success in obtaining a supply of uranium from countries such as Australia, Canada and Kazakhstan, countries which had previously expressed reservations on the provision and supply of uranium. India and Japan's agreement on civilian nuclear cooperation, which allows India access to both material and expertise for the nuclear power plants, also illustrates the potential improvements in India's energy security.

The focus on the shift to cleaner energy sources was concurrently undertaken with successful diplomatic advances to Iran during Prime Minister Modi's visit on 21 May 2016. This follows from earlier visits to both the United Arab Emirates and Saudi Arabia, both of whom are major oil and gas exporting countries,[12] necessary to safeguard India's short-to-medium-term energy needs.

Domestically, recent initiatives to reform the coal mining sector, and allowing foreign investors will further enhance energy security, with the introduction of new technology and knowledge, and raising the overall efficiency of the coal mining industry.[13]

Improving Domestic and International Connectivity

Connectivity is a key element for India's engagement and economic development with the rest of the world. There is physical connectivity, digital connectivity and connectivity in terms of sharing of ideas, knowledge and information. The Modi government has undertaken a considerable number of initiatives in all these aspects of connectivity.

---

[12] Available at: http://www.thehindu.com/news/national/modi-likely-to-travel-to-iran-on-may-21/article8542436.ece.

[13] Available at: http://articles.economictimes.indiatimes.com/2015-03-21/news/60346501_1_coal-mining-coal-india-minister-for-coal.

In physical connectivity, an important initiative is illustrated by the joint statement of India and Japan Vision 2025. To quote,

> The two Prime Ministers decided to develop and strengthen reliable, sustainable and resilient infrastructures that augment connectivity within India and between India and other countries in the region. The two Prime Ministers pledged to advance industrial networks and regional value chains with open, fair and transparent business environment in the region. They recognised the importance of enhancing their cooperation and coordination bilaterally and with other stakeholders to realise this strategic initiative.
>
> They also welcomed the progress in the flagship projects such as the Western Dedicated Freight Corridor (DFC), and reaffirmed the determination to expedite the Delhi-Mumbai Industrial Corridor (DMIC) projects. The two Prime Ministers further concurred to take the Chennai Bengaluru Industrial Corridor (CBIC) project to the next stage of concrete implementation including by utilizing ODA loan schemes and other facility measures. Indian side expressed a hope to attract US$5.5 billion of investment and other support.

The above also illustrates how domestic and international initiatives need to be integrated to expand India's economic and strategic space.

Another illustration concerns India's ambitious port development programme and the development of inland waterways as economic arteries for connectivity between the coast and the interior regions of the country. Externally, India is considering setting up a port in Bangladesh to deepen economic engagement between the two countries.[14]

India is also participating in the Asian road connectivity programmes so that it will be feasible to travel by road from New Delhi to Bangkok and beyond. This will provide an economic boost to, particularly, India's north-east regions, which can become a growth node for the country.

India needs to deepen its knowledge connectivity by encouraging partnerships between its domestic and international academic and research institutions. Several leading universities such as Harvard University and several leading

---

[14] Available at: http://articles.economictimes.indiatimes.com/2016-04-11/news/72238118_1_chabahar-port-union-minister-nitin-gadkari-bangladesh.

think tanks have set up India centres.[15] More exchanges of students, faculty and research personnel would be desirable, as will be greater encouragement for foreign universities to begin educational and research activities in India.

On the information front, India has joined the initiative of the Group of 20 (G20), of which it is a member, for exchange of information on taxation[16] and to address the practice of shifting of tax bases when there is no real economic activity there. The exchange of tax information will accelerate between India and other countries. It hopes thereby to reduce the flow of the shifting of its tax base to other countries.

Strengthening Institutional Structure

India has been strengthening the institutional structure for both commercial and strategic engagement with the rest of the world, as well as participating in initiatives which would broaden the number of multilateral institutions and create a degree of contestability between these new organisations and the more traditional Bretton-Woods institutions, the United Nations and regional development banks such as the Asian Development Bank, African Development Bank and the Inter-American Development Bank.

As India seeks greater voice and participation in the existing multilateral institutions, it has also been a founding member of the New Development Bank (NDB) (formerly called the BRICS Development Bank) in 2014.[17] The NDB is located in Shanghai, but its first president is from India. India is also a founding member of the China-led AIIB headquartered in Beijing in 2014.

India is also actively participating in the ongoing negotiations for the Regional Comprehensive Economic Partnership (RCEP) which comprises the ten members of the ASEAN and six other sovereign states, including India. India, however, is anxious that any trade or economic partnerships and agreements do not unduly disadvantage it from pursuing livelihoods creation, particularly access to services and manpower flows to its trading partners, and supports, in a dynamic sense, its goal of increasing the share of manufacturing in GDP, under the 'Made in India' initiative.

---

[15] For example, http://www.brookings.edu/about/centers/india/about.

[16] Available at: http://www.oecd.org/tax/transparency/automaticexchangeofinformation.htm.

[17] The acronym BRICS stands for Brazil, Russia, India, China and South Africa. See: http://ndbbrics.org/.

India is also bilaterally expanding its economic and strategic partnerships, in some cases such as with Japan and Australia towards strategic partnership and is also keen to upgrade its relationship with the USA from being 'natural' partners to 'best' partners as suggested by Nirupama Rao, India's former ambassador to the USA.[18] In March 2006, India had instituted Raisina Dialogue Forum in New Delhi, with the theme of 'Asian Connectivity' inaugurated by India's then External Affairs Minister.[19] Today the Prime Minister and the External Affairs Minister have, as a team, provided policy coherence and energy to the institutional dimensions of India's diplomacy.

On the domestic front, India has recognised that the country requires the expertise in coordinating the roles of the Commerce Ministry and the MEA in undertaking external diplomacy, particularly in trade negotiations. Thus, it is merging two bodies that handle anti-dumping and import safeguard actions into the Director General of Trade Remedies (DGTR), which is similar to the US International Trade Commission (USITC).[20] The capacity to negotiate trade and economic agreements, and to create institutional memory for such negotiations are also being strengthened. The lateral entry of relevant experts in these areas is becoming more acceptable, thus professionalising the trade and economic diplomacy.

Other Initiatives

India has also taken other initiatives which could help expand its soft power, and economic and strategic space. A good illustration is Prime Minister Modi's leadership on the United Nations in declaring 21 June as the International Yoga Day. This illustrates how specific soft power initiatives can be combined with preventive health care and with material opportunities globally for many individuals and businesses spread around the world.

India has also been selectively and cautiously encouraging internationalisation of its currency. Thus, there are 12 'masala bonds' (bonds denominated in INR but listed on the foreign exchanges, with the exchange rate risk being borne by

---

[18] Available at: http://www.thehindu.com/opinion/op-ed/narendra-modi-new-strong-and-clear-outreach/article 8310200.ece.

[19] Available at: http://mea.gov.in/Speeches-Statements.htm?dtl/26432.

[20] Available at: http://www.livemint.com/Politics/zqbxOwcgkjYqvpXbIOEnvO/Govt-plans-merger-of-antidumping-import-safeguard-bodies.html.

the purchaser of the bond, rather than the Indian issuer) which are listed on the London Stock Exchange for terms ranging from 2 years to 15 years.[21]

CONCLUDING REMARKS

The diplomatic strategy and initiatives pursued by Prime Minister Narendra Modi's government since assuming governance responsibilities in May 2014 have the overarching objective of enhancing India's economic and strategic space globally. This aim has been pursued with unusual energy and a high degree of competence in an uncertain, fragile and complex global economic and geopolitical environment.

The policymakers recognise that in the era of globalisation and technological developments, including, in some areas, the introduction of disruptive technologies which will need to be managed, domestic and foreign policies and initiatives cannot be sharply distinguished. This is a crucial recognition. The corollary is that when policymakers and leaders participate in bilateral and multilateral forums abroad, this does not necessarily imply that domestic issues are not being addressed.

The essay has explained the rationale for pursuing the objective of expanding India's economic and strategic space for overcoming India's internal growth constraints. These include technology, knowledge and management capabilities in order to obtain greater growth-leverage from the external sector, and to ensure that India sustains high broad-based growth and is perceived to be addressing its challenges to enhance its value to its global partners.

This essay has focused on selected, specific initiatives involving energy security, connectivity, strengthening of institutional structure and soft power. The discussion underscores the need to integrate domestic and international initiatives in a coherent and coordinated manner; and India's need to extend its engagement in all parts of the world such that its external options and risks are diversified.

The first two years of Prime Minister Narendra Modi's government have vastly improved the perceptions of India's usefulness as a global partner. This is an impressive achievement, but even a successful strategy and initiatives need continued focus and adaptation to changing contexts and requirements,

[21] Available at: http://www.londonstockexchange.com/specialist-issuers/debts-bonds/masala/masala-factsheet.pdf.

with particular emphasis on institutional development and capacity building. Both process competence and the ability to manage the environment will be increasingly needed in pursuing India's diplomacy in an increasingly complex environment if India's global rise is to be managed relatively smoothly.

CHAPTER 17

CLEANING RIVERS IN INDIA: EXPERIENCES FROM BAVARIA/ GERMANY

MARTIN GRAMBOW, UTTAM KUMAR SINHA AND HANS-DIETRICH UHL

We are still learning that water is the source of all life. The availability of water as the foremost natural resource is limited, yet human activities involve a high demand for water. Significantly, water is a 'gravimetric resource'—it connects every life on earth in a fateful upstream–downstream relation. This makes water the most political resource and water policy, a crucial issue for any society.

As early as the 1970s (first Report to the Club of Rome), it became widely recognised that man–nature relationships will eventually come to a tipping point, a point where natural systems may lose balance and change their state towards a new equilibrium that most likely is not in favour of humankind. Will that happen?

We have recognised since the seventies two parallel cultural processes. One, it still seems that most humans conquer, plunder and mutilate their environment. At the same time humans can be distinguished from all living matter through their distinctive power to reflect, to articulate and to be wise. An increasing number of politicians and scientists are trying to protect the environment and searching for new ways for a better, peaceful life. Which behaviour will predominate? Which story will be told about us in the next hundred years? A story of continuing decline or of changes to a sustainable way of life?

Is India under Prime Minister Narendra Modi on the way to the latter by its Clean Ganga programme? It would seem so. Possibly one of the most modernising policy approaches of the current BJP-led national government has been to raise the profile of rivers. Water is indispensable to governance and development plans, livelihood and healthy life, expressed as *sujalam sufalam* (water for prosperity) and Swachh Bharat Abhiyan. It is also a key instrument of regional prosperity and integration.

This essay will highlight some of the key situations that rivers in Germany have gone through on their way from once being heavily polluted, abused and close to collapse to today's good balance in water management. It took Germany more than a century and several serious setbacks to learn how to treat water and environment in an appropriate way. Maybe Germany's experience can help India in that respect.

RELATION BETWEEN ECONOMIC DEVELOPMENT AND ECOLOGICALLY SOUND PROSPERITY

Prosperous and secure living conditions rely on thriving economy, productive agriculture, urban sprawl and efficient infrastructure. On the other hand, healthy and comfortable living conditions depend very much on clean water, soil and air. At first sight, there seems to be a contradiction between economic growth and a clean environment, e.g. between urbanisation and clean rivers. Economists often claim that investments in good environment conditions are costly and contra-productive. Quite simply, this is not true. Despite an impressive economic development over decades, today's state of the environment in Germany is fairly good. This is the result of a long-term development and ongoing efforts. To tell the truth, there were and still are many obstacles and struggles to regain and preserve good conditions for aquatic habitats. In the history of pollution control, management of waters in Germany is a good evidence for these interrelations.

We learned step by step: Water protection and an environmentally sound water infrastructure is not a privilege, but rather a precondition for wealth and prosperity.

NEED FOR HYGIENE TRIGGERS FIRST STEPS FOR WASTE WATER COLLECTION

As soon as the connection between contaminated drinking water and outbreaks of cholera and typhus was detected by Max Joseph von Pettenkofer, known as the founder of the discipline of hygiene in Germany, health conditions and life expectancy in cities sharply increased around 1880 through collection and controlled disposal of sewage and waste. Pathways and parks in the cities soon became cleaner and lost their bad odour. The number of parasites dropped significantly.

There were two important developments that made waste water collection systems work.

First, the motivation: The number of people sick from waterborne diseases rose in several epidemics to an extent that it led to an economic downturn. Hospitals were overcrowded and health costs soared. Apart from humanity approaches, calculations showed that sewers as a measure of hygiene, together with safe drinking water supply, would lead to less financial burden than the high numbers of sick did. That understanding formed a strong political determination to change the situation.

Today, we have also learned about the tremendous positive impact gained from measures related to the question of dignity, especially for the poorer section of the population. This was a contribution to the social contract and therefore one of the reasons for Germany's successful economic development.

Second, the implementation: This introduced, in turn, the actual change driver. The administration structure underwent a reform. For the first time all water-related topics were brought together in interlinked structures. In 1878, a new state agency for water quality analysis and drinking water supply control was set up, the eldest ancestor of today's Bavarian State Office for the Environment.

Today, we have also learned that a transparent administrative structure and responsibility is a precondition for implementation of measures and with that for successful politics.

Around 1900, the story went nationwide. In the beginning, waste water was simply collected and transferred onto arable land or directly into surface waters. However, population growth and rapid industrialisation made the growing discharges into groundwater and rivers increasingly problematic. Soon after World War II, the ecology of surface waters was close to a collapse in

156 | THE MODI DOCTRINE

many places. The disease had been transferred from the health of the people to the resilience of the environment—and thus became dangerous again for the people! Hence waste water treatment capacities were improved significantly. The degree of treatment was now determined by the susceptibility of the receiving water. For example, further treatment and especially transport of waste water away from lakes and standing waters soon brought visible success. The first ring-sewer to collect and derivate waste water was built as early as 1957 at Lake Tegernsee, a picturesque lake at the foot of the Alps. The first treatment plant with advanced phosphorus removal was built close to Lake Chiemsee in 1965. Subsequently the fisheries recovered and living conditions for the local population as well as attractiveness for tourists soared.

We learned that taking action really can do both: Rejuvenate the environment and strengthen the society.

INITIATIVES IN THE END COMING FROM THE PEOPLE, NOT FROM THE REGULATOR
Building infrastructures for waste water treatment is expensive. With the 'polluter pays' principle, applicable in all of Germany, the costs had to be covered by the waste water producers—households and industries connected to the sewers. Although state subsidies eased the financial burden for households, it still is remarkable that strengthening waste water treatment was a demand from the people. What led to this acceptance and support from the population? In the first place it was the visibility of deterioration in terms of disappearing life, even killing of fish, and increasing alterations of the rivers such as colouring, foaming or bad odour. A turning point was reached when a white whale swam upstream in the river Rhine in May 1966. For the people the fact that this special animal came from the sea into the heavily polluted river and accompanied ships travelling upstream for almost a week, was like a miracle and at the same time a signal. Very similar to mythical figures in India such as crocodiles, tortoises or swans, the white whale had a strong meaning to the people. It was taken as an omen signalling for help, for the need to be more careful with the rivers. This popular movement was not driven by a thorough understanding of the complex structure of the ecosystem such as resilience: rather it was an act of instinct, an emotional and empathy-based understanding that the quality of our environment is directly connected to our true living quality, to dignity and culture.

Even more convincing were the prompt successes that were achieved by revitalising rivers. Fish returned to rivers and lakes, together with other aquatic lifelike mussels or crayfish. The people enjoyed the regained possibility to take a bath in the river without immediate threat to their health.

We learned: Investment into protecting the environment adds value and produces growth, especially for the common people.

COOPERATIVE APPROACH

The Rhine River as one of the largest European catchments was a pioneer in international conventions on water management. The Rhine with its tributaries not only travels through several of the German federal states but stretches across six European countries. It also serves as border between countries over some length. Within Germany, an interstate water cooperation organisation (LAWA-Länder-Arbeitsgemeinschaft Wasser) was set up and provided water guidance from as early as 1947 (even before the foundation of the Federal Republic; the first federal water law only came into force in 1960). To discuss border-crossing issues in the immediate post-war period was extremely difficult. However, it was soon recognised that the river was vital for all countries. Pollution and water uses lead to first talks on a sound water management in the international catchment. In 1950, the International Commission for the Rhine against Pollution (ICPR) was founded. Actually, as cooperation requires faith in the partners, ICPR dedicated its first twenty years mainly to creating a positive atmosphere between the participating countries, establishing a common understanding of problems, needs and interdependencies together with trust and confidence.

A major low water level period in 1976 and a vast spill of polluting chemicals during a fire accident in 1986 marked the low point of water quality in the River Rhine. Those disasters, and the resulting pressure by an enraged population, triggered a serious effort to recover rivers and to assess the conditions of rivers in general. The established cooperation was used to initiate active measures. Monitoring networks, research on appropriate quality indicators and on the preconditions for self-cleaning capacities were started.

We learned that protection and rejuvenation of rivers needs coordination and cooperation with the neighbours and that mutual trust is a precondition for coordination.

INTEGRATIVE LEGAL PROVISIONS ON WATER MANAGEMENT

It was only in the early 1970s when binding legal provisions were set at the European level, with water being one of the first areas to be addressed by EU environmental policy. At first, water-related European legislation was concerned with water quality, starting with measures against organic pollution and the first European directive on discharge of toxic substances in 1976 (76/464/EEC). The second wave of European regulations gave more detailed specifications on water quality, including the urban waste water directive from 1991 and, being the most predominant regulation, the nitrates directive. Finally, the holistic and interlinking view helped frame the Water Framework Directive in 2000 and the Marine Strategy Directive. Both do not only limit emissions but define quality goals for the receiving waters (by also limiting emissions) which is called the 'combined approach'. Together with principles set out in the EU Treaty and specified beginning with the first EU Environmental Action Plan in 1973, it included precautionary principle, the polluter pays principle, principle of preventive action, public participation to name but a few. The water legislation in Europe meanwhile has a long history. The directives include intensive monitoring and reporting requirements.

INSTRUMENTS AND CORNERSTONES

Since it took quite some time to build up today's water infrastructure with the chance to gather various experiences, we want to simply highlight some of the aspects (in loose order!) that proved to be helpful in the process of establishing and maintaining clean rivers before going into a deeper analysis.

- Legal minimum requirements for waste water treatment: Standards are set for the most important pollutants, which in case of waste water from households are organic parameters (BOD, COD) and, for 'large' plants starting with 5.000-10.000 population equivalent, nutrient parameters (N, P). For industrial waste water a list with thresholds for typical pollutants is set for some 50 branches. Thresholds are derived by assessing Best Available Techniques (BAT). Some like to emphasise that there might be a need to identify BATNEEC ('best available techniques not entailing excessive costs').

- Prohibitions of and obligations for substances: Mostly for limiting substances hazardous to water. An early example is the Act on Washing and Cleaning Agents.

- Continuous improvement: Voluntary benchmarking projects allow public utilities to compare their efforts with those of similar utilities. The projects are accompanied by the professional water associations and lead to profound management decisions.

- Full cost recovery as a basis for calculating tariffs is applied by law: Tariffs depend on the amount of waste water produced and are multiplied with the metered drinking water consumption. Nowadays the average tariff is approximately two Euros per cubic meter waste water (together with water supply it is approximately 1-2 per cent of the mean annual family income). Each utility is recalculating its tariffs every four years. Public utilities are not targeted at profit. The tariff paid describes the actual costs of waste water disposal including maintenance and financing of the infrastructure.

- State subsidies: Building the infrastructure necessary for sewage disposal particularly in rural areas was supported fundamentally by public funding. With initial funding rates of 60-80 per cent, a more rapid connection of houses was achieved (incentive) at the same time facilitating moderate tariffs for the population.

- Monitoring and enforcement: Continuous control of effluent quality by state bodies and a pollution levy depending on the level of pollution caused in the receiving river, led to high compliance with standards for waste water discharge. Self-monitoring requirements are the basis for dependability and management of plants and machinery.

- Knowledge transfer: Intensive training of all staff, namely, local administration, municipal officers and plant operators. The network of 'neighbourhood meetings' of adjacent utility staff proved to be successful in ensuring a sufficient quality level of knowledge and in exchanging experience. These neighbourhoods comprise regular meetings and further training undertaken by the professional water association. The benefit is manifold: the staff is up to date, the association learns about the local specialities and, maybe most important, for the neighbours there is help at hand, when a problem or an immediate question arises during regular operation.

- Public perception of environmental topics: The unification of the two Germanys in 1990 made clear, how much two approaches towards protecting the environment can differ. On one side decade-long abuse of the natural resources and on the other a well-established ecological consideration. In the 1990s the environmental regulation underwent a renovation with the aim of (1) preventing pollution by monitoring new products and projects; (2) requiring the polluter to pay damages, rather than society at large, together with establishing controlling instances; and (3) relying on cooperation among government, industry and society to protect the environment.
- Sufficient resources: Institutions and bodies, administration and treatment plants need stable funding and (fair-paid) manpower.

FUTURE CHALLENGES IN WATER MANAGEMENT

The climate is changing. There are periods with natural water abundance and periods with draught. We try to recalculate and predict our water system to manage it in a more resilient way.

Additionally we feel the pressure of the anthropogenic over-forming of our environment. Actually, the age of the anthropogenic confronts us with added challenges—micro-pollution and the increasing understanding of the vulnerability of the ecosystem. We are just learning in the environmental quality process, that for the ecosystem sometimes much more stringent standards might be necessary than for human use. Thus, it certainly would be no mistake to claim at least near drinking water quality for all groundwater resources and streams, because these form the big rivers such as Rhine or Ganga. Name it worshipping or respect towards the entity of the rivers, it is wise to call for a zero emission industry (compare the Indian zero liquid approach) and something equal for agriculture. This has to be accompanied by a zero waste or zero littering process, in principle, for any part of nature but at the very least to protect the rivers and water bodies.

Last but not the least, we learn that our world economic system seems not to be ideal to support sustainable life. Intensive use of resources and heavy pollution by various chemicals including those caused by the agricultural sector ruin our environment and nature. Typically those costs are not included in the price of the products. The environment thus becomes the most threatened and scarce good, but in our economic system nobody (except future generations) has to pay the price.

We learn that living in peace with the environment also is a maxim for social equality. We can do this without reducing our overall benefit. Eventually even the economic profiteers will change from ruthless ones to attentive ones.

SYNTHESIS

Rethinking water management is essential before setting up new systems. Coming back to the German and Bavarian experiences, the core tasks in waste water collection and treatment are to setup a system that is acknowledged, transparent, robustly funded to cover running costs and re-investment, broadly accessible, affordable but not for free (appraisal of the service!). And, in the context of water quality, it needs to be accompanied by sound water quantity management.

Key to success is skills. It takes people on location that promote the aspects of waste water collection and treatment—people who support knowledge transfer.

Another key to success is the reflection and cooperation both between centralised and decentralised structures within the riverine neighbourhood. It is a challenge and chance for federal states to be able to train and practise this in both situations, the interior and the external water diplomacy. The adequate platform is joined bodies, the protagonists are the experts and the decision-makers of the water sector and the big picture is the hydro-political security complex. The players should be trained in trust, fairness, responsibility and attentiveness—which is, as we try to understand, very near to the Indian principle of *samarasata*.

Ganga is the fifth most polluted river in the world. While this remains a shameful reality, it is important to continuously reinstate the symbolism of Ganga—as the river of faith, devotion and worship. Rabindranath Tagore made several references to Ganga in his works, particularly *Jiban Smriti* and *Rabindra Rachnabali* by expressing Ganga as the sacred thread of Indian *yajna*—connecting years of wisdom, religion and meditation. There is a Ganga in every part of India and the emblematic interpretations can be a collective force of change.

Like the experiences of the Rhine and many other rivers in Germany, the Ganga and other rivers in India represent numerous difficulties of development and management. For one, cleaning the rivers cannot be separated from rejuvenating the flow. But rivers also need to be harnessed for the wider national need. Economic development and requirement of energy and food cannot be divorced from developing rivers in terms of storage for irrigation and electricity generation. This is critical as India's urban population (419 million) will double by 2050. The 'smart cities' plan in 100 cities across India, cannot be sustainable without more intelligent human-nature symbiosis. The challenge is to balance environmental, human, cultural, pilgrimage and economic interests within the complex system of a major river.

The efforts are worthwhile. A river is a 'mini-cosmos' of history, mythology, spirituality and technological interventions. Each river has a distinct identity and value. Throughout history diverse communities have reinvented themselves on riverbanks with fascinating nuances. Cleaning rivers leads to a more satisfying, more healthy life. Water pollution control helps in protecting the resources of the future and enhances the quality of life—and is a basic step to better social equality.

BIBLIOGRAPHY
1.   BMU/UBA, The German Water Sector Policies and Experiences, 2001, available at: https://www. umweltbundesamt.de/sites/default/files/medien/publikation/long/2752.pdf.
2.   Ganguly, Anirban (ed.), *Redefining Governance* (New Delhi: Prabhat Prakashan, 2015).
3.   Wilderer, Peter, *Treatise on Water Science, Volume 1: Management of Water* Resources (Amsterdam: Elsevier BV, 2011).
4.   Shukla, AC and Asthana, V, *Ganga: A Water Marvel* (New Delhi: Ashish Publishing House, 1995).

CHAPTER 18

ENERGY SECURITY: A PRIORITY CONCERN FOR THE MODI GOVERNMENT

VIRENDRA GUPTA

The broad vision behind India's Integrated Energy Policy is to 'reliably meet the demand for energy services of all sectors including the lifeline energy needs of vulnerable households in all parts of the country with safe, clean and convenient energy at the least cost'. Prime Minister Narendra Modi regards energy security as a key driver of India's long-term and sustained development. He made this clear in a speech at Bhabha Atomic Research Centre, shortly after forming the government, noting that: 'Energy security based on clean and reliable sources is essential for India's future.' Priority attention accorded by the government to securing our energy needs, in fact, flows from the ruling party BJP's policy manifesto which identifies energy as a 'national security issue'.

It has long been agreed that sustained economic growth is a prerequisite for eradication of poverty in India and to meet our 'larger human development goals'. We must grow at a rate of 8-9 per cent and to fuel that growth, primary energy supply has to be augmented by 5-6 per cent per annum. Growth in a country like India, however, cannot be measured solely in terms of macroeconomic indicators. Given our vast and complex socio-economic challenges, it is imperative for us to focus on inclusive growth. It is lamentable that nearly 240 million people in India have no access to electricity. For Modi, provision of energy access to those deprived sections of our population is therefore the foremost concern of our energy security policy and he reiterated his commitment to bring electricity to all the 18,000 villages without electricity within 1,000 days of his term of office while addressing the Indian community in Brussels in March 2016. He informed the gathering that he was personally monitoring the progress and that 7,000 villages had already been electrified.

COAL

Coal is the primary energy source for India, contributing nearly 60 per cent of our energy requirement. India is the world's third-largest producer of coal but we are still heavily dependent on imported coal. Local resistance to mining projects, land acquisition challenges, delays in forest clearances and environment permits and above all displacement issues work as major obstacles. Activities of some international NGOs such as Greenpeace which have sought to spread misinformation and incite public opinion concerning use of coal in India in pursuit of a Western agenda on climate change, in complete disregard of India's national interest, are also under the scrutiny of the government.

In the last decade, coal production managed to grow only by 4.7 per cent, substantially falling behind the growth of thermal power generation capacity in the country thus leading to recurring coal shortages. The government has now set a fairly ambitious target for domestic production raising it from the current 600 million tonnes (mt) per annum to 1.5 billion tonnes (bt) per annum. In 2014-15, we had to import 212 mt of coal, but our import dependence should reduce quite considerably in the coming years and we might need imported coal only for the coastal power plants as indicated by the Minister for Power, Coal and New & Renewable Energy, Piyush Goyal. The coal supply situation is exacerbated by coal transportation issues. In 2015, nearly 50 mt of coal remained stranded at the mines because of limitations of railway infrastructure. The government is attaching priority attention to completion of rail projects in the coal mining areas in Chhattisgarh, Jharkhand and Orissa to tide over that problem.

With the government's Make in India campaign gathering momentum, the power demand in India is set to increase rapidly. While Prime Minister Modi is fully conscious of India's responsibility on the environmental front and has been instrumental in setting ambitious targets in the renewable energy sector, he is only too aware that coal would continue to remain the most important source of electric power in India, at least in the short term. Present overall installed capacity for electricity generation in the country is around 350GW. The government wants to achieve rapid expansion of this capacity with average annual addition of over 100GW installed capacity. Accordingly, the government is moving ahead speedily on all fronts to remove the supply constraints. One of the main impediments in the power sector is the huge financial debts of state power utilities. The government has announced a comprehensive package to restructure these debts and revival of the power utilities with increased tariff and reduced transmission losses.

OIL AND GAS

India is also heavily dependent on imports for meeting its requirements in the key oil and gas sector. Production of crude oil has plateaued at approximately 37 mt per annum because of no major new finds lately leaving a large net gap of around 150 mt to be met through imports (we actually import around 190 mt of crude but export 30 per cent of refined products earning the country valuable foreign exchange). In 2014-15, we spent US$112 billion on import of crude but thankfully in 2015-16 the import bill is expected to have come down to around US$80 billion because of falling crude prices.

Our major supply sources include Saudi Arabia, Iraq, Iran, Kuwait, Nigeria, UAE, Venezuela and Angola. We need to accord priority to our relations with our traditional suppliers while at the same time utilising all available diplomatic leverages to explore and secure new sources. Mindful that a large part of our requirement is met from the Middle East which remains highly volatile in military and political terms, the government has continued to support the initiatives for increasing diversification of our supply sources.

Our imports from Africa have consistently gone up contributing nearly 20 per cent of our overall requirements in 2015. At the India–Africa Hydrocarbon Conference in January 2016, the Indian Petroleum Minister Dharmendra Pradhan reiterated the government's commitment to increasing our imports from Africa even further. Nigeria and Angola have emerged as our major suppliers and we continue to expand our cooperation with those countries. Furthermore, we have added new countries such as Egypt, Algeria, Sudan, Equatorial Guinea and Cameroon to the list of supplier countries providing us a much diversified basket. Alongside that we also attach importance to strengthening our cooperation with African countries in exploration, refining, training and oil infrastructure development.

Latin America has also emerged as an important source of crude oil for India contributing 10-15 per cent of our total requirements. Apart from Venezuela, which remains one of our main suppliers for the last several years, we also import substantial quantities from Brazil, Mexico, Colombia and Ecuador.

In recognition of Saudi Arabia's strategic significance for us not only because of its position as the major oil supplier (meeting 20 per cent of our requirement) but the presence of nearly 3.5 million Indian workers there, Modi has been careful in continuing the momentum created earlier with the visit of the Saudi King to India in 2006 and the return visit of our Prime Minister in 2010. In fact, to take it forward, he visited Saudi Arabia after attending the Nuclear Security Summit in Washington. The visit took place in the backdrop of the Saudi government's desire to raise the relationship beyond the current 'strategic partnership' as articulated by the Saudi Foreign Minister recently.

In overall terms, as is quite evident from a wide range of agreements signed during the visit, it was a highly successful visit. The Prime Minister was warmly received by Saudi King Salman Bin Abdulaziz who conferred the country's highest civilian award on Modi. This obviously signified increasingly converging economic and geopolitical interests of the two countries, which more aptly define international relations today as compared to religion and ideology.

The decision to enhance defence cooperation as well as cooperation in combating terrorism and intelligence sharing on terror financing and money laundering should have the effect of broadening the ties beyond trade and diaspora. Even in the crucial oil sector, the two countries resolved to 'transform the buyer seller relationship to one of deeper partnership focussing on investment and joint ventures'. Reinforcement of Saudi interest in infrastructure development which requires huge overseas investments is also a welcome development. Broader security cooperation with our largest crude supplier should, without doubt, augur well for ensuring our energy security.

West Asia (the Middle East region) is going through an unprecedented crisis. Apart from the conflicts in Yemen and Syria, the Shia–Sunni sectarian divide is threatening to rupture the region. Saudi Arabia is actively involved in all these conflicts and India would have to play a careful balancing role to ensure that it is not accused of taking sides by any party. We will particularly need the Saudis in ensuring that the evolving Sunni coalition where Pakistan could play an important role does not adversely impact on our interests.

Insofar as Iran is concerned, India has had historic relations. It has traditionally been one of the largest crude suppliers to us. Its strategic significance also derives from the consideration that it provides us a potential route to Central Asia, a region which is important from our energy security standpoint. With the finalisation of the Iran nuclear deal and lifting of US-led sanctions against it, the Iranian economy would open up. Our government is cognisant of the new opportunities for Indian companies there and particularly envisages enhanced cooperation in the oil and gas sector including investments in the exploration of oil and gas blocks. Increased opportunities would most certainly imply increased competition from Western and Chinese companies but India seems well poised to succeed.

India is helping to develop Chabahar Port as well as several highway and railway line projects for better connectivity with the port. The Chabahar Port could play an import role in facilitating natural gas imports from Iran. Prime Minister Modi has already had a cordial meeting with President Rouhani at the Shanghai Cooperation Summit in Ufa, Russia in 2015 and seems prepared to provide the requisite political thrust in taking forward our relations with Iran at this critical juncture.

For a longer term solution, India is also exploring the option of a gas pipeline to bring Iranian gas to India. The proposal for an overland pipeline through Pakistan (IPI) has been on the table for quite some time. If that, however, continues to present insurmountable political and security challenges, we could consider the alternative of an undersea pipeline via the Arabian Sea totally bypassing Pakistan.

Overseas equity oil has for long been regarded as one of the most attractive solutions to a country's energy security. At least in public perception this is almost axiomatic. Energy specialist Sudha Mahalingam argues[1] that it is at best 'a misplaced perception' since part or full equity participation in an oil or gas block overseas does not necessarily entitle the country concerned 'to physically access the resources' in the time of critical need. This argument notwithstanding,

---

[1] *The Hindu*, August 2013.

the psychological comfort and a sense of security that equity oil provides cannot be altogether dismissed. It also brings forth investment benefit and provides much-needed cushion against wide fluctuations in crude prices. Keeping this in view the government has encouraged both public and private sector companies to bid for resources overseas resulting in a fairly diversified portfolio covering wide range of countries including Iran, Iraq, Sudan, Libya, Angola, Myanmar, Russia, Vietnam, Syria, Venezuela, Brazil, Egypt, Nigeria, Mozambique, Australia, East Timor, Oman, Indonesia, Gabon, Cuba and Colombia as well as shale acreage in Marcellus, USA.

RENEWABLES

The most noteworthy initiatives by the Modi government have been taken in the field of the renewable energy sector given both its future potential and huge environment benefits. The government has set an ambitious target of additional renewable capacity of 175 GW by 2020 in order to accomplish the declared goal of 40 per cent of our total power capacity being contributed by renewable sources by 2030. Considering that the present renewable energy capacity is less than 40GW, the above target may seem somewhat challenging but the government seems quite determined to remove all impediments and facilitate overseas investment which can be expected to partly meet the required new investments of around US$200 billion given our generally favourable investment climate and growing efforts by the government to make it even more conducive.

The government has initiated conducive land acquisition policies and in July 2014, it took a decision to restore the 'Accelerated Depreciation' programme (allowing 80 per cent depreciation of capital costs in the first year itself) as well as the Generation Based Incentive (GBI) scheme. The decision to shelve these incentives by the previous government had actually resulted in some setback for the establishment of new solar and wind energy projects in the country. The government also allows tax holiday on new projects.

Renewable energy is important for India not so much from the environmental considerations as it is from the standpoint of energy security. This basic difference in our approach from that of the Western nations sometimes becomes a point of friction even though the end result of the government's priority attention to the renewable energy research and development programme would be further reduction in our emission levels taking it far beyond what is required of us equitably. During my days in the Energy Security Division in the MEA, I was frequently lectured by Western diplomats and the International Energy Agency representatives on how India had become a major polluter (!!) and needed to do much more on the renewable energy front to reduce its carbon footprints. I had to strongly counter that by asserting that our record was already far better than those in the developed world and that any further step taken by us was entirely voluntary on our part, out of our concern for the global climate and was not at all obligatory.

Solar Energy

Solar energy is envisaged to be the largest contributor to our renewables basket. The target is to gear up the capacity to 100GW by 2022 comprising 40GW rooftop and 60GW large and medium scale grid connected projects. This would require investment of approximately Rs 5 lakh crores. Most of the funds would have to come from the private sector since it is doubtful whether any funds could be accessed from the elusive 'Climate Fund' envisaged under the ongoing climate change negotiations. The government on its part has committed to doubling investments in R&D and has set aside Rs 15,000 crores partly towards capital subsidy.

Launching the International Solar Alliance at the Climate Summit in Paris along with French President Francois Hollande, Prime Minister Modi invoked our scriptures which regard the Sun as the soul of all beings, noting that 'today when energy sources and excesses of our industrial age have put our planet in peril the world must turn to the Sun to power our future'. The initiative envisages cooperation in training, institution building, regulatory framework exchanges and joint business ventures in solar energy. The world is already witnessing nothing short of a revolution in solar energy with new technologies and steady reduction in costs. Sun Edison, a US firm, recently offered to supply power from a solar project in Andhra Pradesh at less than Rs 5 per unit. The rooftop solar power is already being marketed at a price which is competitive with the average cost of grid supplied and diesel generated power available currently to industrial establishments and large housing complexes. In fact it is already comparable to the cost of power produced from new imported coal-fired projects.

WIND ENERGY

Our installed capacity of wind energy currently is around 25GW, making us the fourth largest player in the world. The advantage lies in the lowest per unit cost of wind energy. The capacity is set to be increased to 75GW by 2022. In September 2015 the government also approved a national offshore wind energy policy which should help promote and streamline wind energy projects in the 'Exclusive Economic Zone' of the country under PPP mode. The potential capacity for such projects is believed to be around 350GW and even if a part of that potential is harnessed it could bring enormous benefit to the country. Suzlon Energy, the largest private sector player in the wind energy sector, is already working on a 600MW offshore project in Gujarat.

NUCLEAR ENERGY

Nuclear energy has a vast potential in addressing our energy security in the long term. The government has drawn up an ambitious programme to raise our capacity from the present 5GW to 20GW by 2020 but safety concerns have slowed down the programme. Domestic uranium reserves are limited and as such efforts are afoot to tie up supplies from diverse sources including Australia which is the third-largest uranium producer. Substantive progress has also been made to resolve the nuclear liability issue and that should help matters.

In conclusion, priority attention to relations with our traditional as well as potential oil and gas suppliers is reflective of the government's utmost concern for ensuring uninterrupted supply of energy resources to fuel our economic growth. While Modi has shown sensitivity for global environmental concerns earning global applause for his bold initiatives for further enhancing our renewable footprints in the coming years, he has remained careful in not abandoning our core interests in the coal sector which is critical for optimum electricity production in the country to support the new thrust for manufacturing activities and for addressing the all-important access issue for the deprived masses.

CHAPTER 19

MODI'S ECONOMIC DIPLOMACY: TURNING CONVENTIONS ON THEIR HEAD

Manoj Ladwa

India was the world's top destination for FDI flows in 2015. According to 'fDi Intelligence', which is part of the *Financial Times*, India attracted US$63 billion in FDI during the year.

Greenfield FDI, which creates the most jobs and contributes the highest to GDP growth, almost tripled during the year. 'Success breeds success and to attract high volumes of FDI, countries need to create the conditions for strong economic growth and development to take place.... FDI is strongly attracted to high growth economies,' the report said.

What a turnaround from two years ago, when global and domestic investors, analysts and even multilateral agencies such as the World Bank, IMF and the Asian Development Bank (ADB) had written India off as a basket case that had missed the growth bus yet again. The consensus opinion in 2012, 2013 and early 2014 was that India was not going to fulfil its potential anytime soon.

The Turning Point

Then came the 2014 Lok Sabha elections, which gave the Narendra Modi-led BJP an absolute majority—the first time any single party had won more than half the seats in the Lower House in three decades.

Even as market and investor euphoria peaked following Modi's victory, he embarked on a series of high profile diplomatic missions, wooing investors in the US, Japan, China and Europe, hard-selling India as a desirable investment destination and highlighting the advantages the country offers compared to others. Modi adopted an audacious strategy by calling on the world to make in India. It was audacious for several reasons. First, no previous Indian Prime Minister had ever been so aggressive in positioning India as the manufacturing hub of choice, and thereby taking on China at its own game. And second, by wooing foreign companies to manufacture in India, it meant trampling over the sensitivities of many Western allies who would see this as a direct threat to their domestic job markets, especially at a time when their own economies were stretched. Modi however has deftly played the saviour, by arguing the case that Make in India is not about job taking but about helping global partners become more competitive.

PM AS THE COUNTRY'S PRIME MARKETEER

Shedding decades of ideological dogma and political consensus in New Delhi that senior government functionaries, especially the Prime Minister, should only speak of lofty ideals and bilateral ties while travelling abroad, Modi turned conventional wisdom on its head when he took it upon himself to become the prime marketeer for the Indian economy.

For the first time ever, India elevated economic diplomacy to the level hitherto occupied by stuffy bilateral ties and pontification.

Ironically, critics and analysts had wondered how Modi, who had no previous experience of handling foreign policy, would conduct India's ties with its allies, friends and rivals. The Prime Minister has answered all these questions convincingly and silenced his critics.

INDIAN DIASPORA

Modi added a new dimension to India's foreign policy matrix by reaching out to the enterprising and increasingly powerful Indian diaspora in many foreign countries. Till he addressed his first gathering of 15,000 NRIs at New York's iconic Madison Square Garden, no Indian leader had bothered to cultivate this constituency.

Yet, Indians make up the US' richest and most educated ethnic group and enjoy significant political clout in the US Congress, Senate as well as the White House.

Their influence in US society is an example of India's soft power. Tragically, this massive reservoir of social power and political heft had never been harnessed by the Indian government. Though the media and sections of civil society took great pride in the achievements of the Indian diaspora, officialdom still laboured under the mistaken and mindless position that these 'Indians' were foreigners because many of them had adopted the citizenship of the countries they lived in.

Modi realised that many NRIs held leadership positions in top US companies, US academia as well as civil society. They would, therefore, be in a far better position to influence US attitudes towards India.

But here again, Modi in galvanising the Indian diaspora, has adopted a winner takes all approach. Madison Square was just the opener, but in every country he has visited, he has knocked up huge responses from Indians living there. In Beijing, which has a population of less than 4,000 Indians, and a regime that is suspicious of outside influences, he attracted a crowd of 5,000. But by far the biggest show of his appeal was at the iconic Wembley Stadium where over 60,000 people gathered and which left David Cameron mentioning in jest that he would barely manage to fill a hall of 500 people. Modi through his diaspora engagements is telling the world that he means business, India has arrived, and its sphere of influence globally, through these 'Lok Doots' (Peoples' Messengers) as he calls them, is almost limitless.

His warm and hugely successful visits to the UAE and Saudi Arabia have also taken the wind out of the sales of his traditional baiters who expected Modi to be viewed as a divisive force on the world stage. Far from it.

AIMING FOR THE TOP

Modi also made sure he included several open and closed door meetings with the top leaders in each of the countries he visited. There, he leveraged the goodwill he had earned with many potential investors as the go-getting chief minister of Gujarat. Only, he was now appealing to them on behalf of all of India and not one state alone. His message was simple: India was the new land of opportunity and countries like the US should invest early for their own benefit.

THE STRATEGIC MEETING GROUND

His foreign policy doctrine has given pride of place to economic diplomacy but he has not lost sight of the old dictum that the flag and the currency always travel hand in hand.

In keeping with the line followed over the last quarter of a century by Prime Ministers PV Narasimha Rao, Atal Bihari Vajpayee and Manmohan Singh, Modi has continued to improve relations with the US government.

Shedding many of the ideological and strategic shibboleths of the past, he has steered India into a closer strategic relationship with the US, based on New Delhi's perception of regional and global geopolitical currents.

Since Independence, India's foreign policy has been marked by its determination to play a balancing role between rival power blocs. This may have worked in an era when India did not have any strategic interests beyond its shores.

But as its economy expanded and its industry developed linkages with the global supply chain, Indian strategic planners slowly became aware of something the British had always known.

KEY LOCATION

That is, India enjoys a key strategic advantage based on its location. Draw an arc with Delhi at the centre—the arc will sweep a large swathe of sea and cover an area from the Persian Gulf, the world's energy basket, to the Malacca Straits, the main shipping channel between the Indian Ocean and the Pacific Ocean, which carries 25 per cent of all global trade.

The British Raj realised this and exercised control over this vast area from New Delhi. Independent India frittered away this strategic legacy. But nature abhors a vacuum.

India's primacy in this region has recently been challenged by China, which is trying to build a so-called Maritime Silk Route to increase its military footprint and strategic influence in this region.

At the same time, there is considerable economic synergy between New Delhi and Beijing. Chinese companies have experience in building large infrastructure projects in record time. Many of these companies are sitting on large idle capacities. India, on the other hand, suffers from a significant infrastructure deficit, which the Chinese companies can help meet.

DANCING WITH THE DRAGON

Modi's outreach to China has a significant economic component. He has made it easier for Chinese companies to invest in India by simplifying security and other clearances. Beijing has committed US$20 billion investments in a wide variety of industries that contribute significantly to India's efforts to lift GDP growth to 9 per cent and higher.

Simultaneously, Modi has stepped into the South China Sea spat and issued a joint statement with the US calling for the right of navigation through that disputed waterway. Strategic analysts say this is a brilliant ploy to nullify the advantage China enjoys along the Line of Actual Control. If China plays hardball on the land border, India can make life difficult for China by cutting off its access to the Indian Ocean. The economic opportunities are the carrots to keep Beijing happy.

It's an approach that is not entirely free of risk and has drawn a fair amount of criticism, especially from those still wedded to India's traditional positions, but many experts have also called it bold and pointed out that Beijing treats New Delhi with most respect when it perceives a warmth in India–US ties.

PERSONAL CHEMISTRY

Modi's foreign policy efforts hinge significantly on his own personality and his ability to strike a rapport with foreign heads of state. He shares excellent personal chemistry with US President Barack Obama, Japanese Prime Minister Shinzo Abe, British Prime Minister David Cameron, Chinese leader Xi Jinping, Russian President Vladimir Putin and his Pakistani counterpart, Nawaz Sharif.

It is this chemistry as well as a coalescing of interests with Japan, the UK, France and Germany that has played a major role in his foreign policy successes.

His efforts, over the last two years, have brought investments or investment commitments of close to US$200 billion from foreign investors, including Foxconn, Softbank, Vedanta, GE, Amazon and the UAE sovereign wealth fund.

OUTREACH TO AFRICA

Africa offers India a massive opportunity to expand its global economic footprint. The continent is an important market for Indian companies; it is a long-term source of raw materials, metals, minerals, uranium and oil.

Deep defence and strategic ties with African nations on the Indian Ocean coastline is critical for India to retain the Indian Ocean as its sphere of influence.

Yet, successive Indian governments have neglected that continent. The fifty-four African states have a combined GDP that is slightly larger than that of India and a population that is slightly smaller. More than half the African states have per capita incomes and human development indicators that are higher or better than India.

A handful of Indian companies, such as the Tatas, Mahindras, Kirloskars and some others have a large presence in the continent but the full potential is nowhere near being realised.

India is belatedly playing a game of catch-up with China. 'India's relationship with Africa is driven by the aim of empowerment, capacity building, human resource development, access to the Indian market and support for Indian investments in Africa,' Modi said at the third India–Africa Summit in New Delhi in November 2015.

THE NEXT STEPS

The jury is still out on the overall success of Modi's foreign policy initiatives. The middle class, by and large, have welcomed the more robust, economy-centric approach. But a section of New Delhi's establishment that has still not reconciled to India's aggressive assertion of its self-interest over its traditional pro-Third World, anti-imperialist approach are waiting for him to falter. Its hard-nosed no-nonsense approach to world trade negotiations is just one point in case.

But with FDI pouring in from across the world and Modi remaining the toast of world capitals, it is clear that his new foreign policy paradigm has struck a chord somewhere. A new beginning has surely been made. The next three years will be crucial in establishing Modi's foreign policy doctrines as the Indian norm.

CHAPTER 20

DEFENCE DIPLOMACY: GOOD, AND NEEDS TO GET BETTER

Nitin A Gokhale

Sometime in mid-2015, top officers of the Ministry of Defence (MoD) and MEA were huddled into a meeting with the deputy National Security Adviser (NSA), trying to come to a common ground on how many more defence attachés (DAs) should India have in its missions abroad. After a couple of hours of intense deliberations, the two ministries agreed to enhance the number of DAs by about forty more to be posted abroad from 2016 onward. The number, the meeting decided would go up to about 110 from the existing seventy.

This was in keeping with Prime Minister Narendra Modi's foreign policy initiatives. Modi began his term in office in the presence of all heads of state of SAARC Nations. His address to the General Assembly of the United Nations was appreciated across the world. Narendra Modi also became the first Indian Prime Minister to embark on a bilateral visit to Nepal after a long period of seventeen years, to Australia after twenty-eight years, to Fiji after thirty-one years and Seychelles after thirty-four years. After taking over, Prime Minister Modi attended the UN, BRICS, SAARC and G20 Summits, where India's interventions and views on a variety of global, economic and political issues were widely appreciated. His visit to Japan marked a momentous chapter to unfold a new era of India–Japan relations. He became the first Prime Minister of India to visit Mongolia and his visits to China and South Korea have been successful in drawing investments to India. His continued engaging with Europe was seen during his visit to France and Germany.

Modi has attached great importance to strong ties with the Arab world. His visit to UAE in August 2015, the first by an Indian PM in thirty-four years, and to Saudi Arabia in April 2016, covered tremendous ground in enhancing India's economic partnership with the Gulf. In July 2015 Modi visited the five Central Asian Nations in a visit that was seen as path-breaking. Vital agreements were signed between India and these nations in spheres like energy, trade, culture and economics.

Several world leaders including the then Prime Minister of Australia Tony Abbott, President Xi Jinping of China, President Maithripala Sirisena of Sri Lanka and President Vladimir Putin of Russia have visited India and these visits have achieved breakthroughs in improving cooperation between India and these nations. The 2015 Republic Day saw President Barack Obama visit India as the Chief Guest, a first in the history of India–USA relations. With this enhanced world profile, India needed to follow up on several fronts not just through traditional diplomacy but also utilise the military as a means of diplomacy. The first steps in defence diplomacy too have been taken and needs to be further worked out.

Till a couple of years ago, New Delhi had been content in posting DAs to countries that were deemed important to India and depended on their limited inputs. So the Soviet Union (now Russia), United States, Pakistan, France, UK, China, Japan and Singapore besides a couple of African countries always topped the Indian defence establishment's priority abroad. For decades, UK used to have representatives of all three armed forces—Indian Army, Air Force and Navy—posted to London. Moscow was another tri-services destination. It still is, given India's dependence on Russia for over 70 per cent of the military hardware it uses across the three services.

But posting DAs is only one facet of New Delhi's growing emphasis on using the goodwill of its military in the diplomatic outreach around the neighbourhood and beyond. India's MOD said in its annual report:

> Defence cooperation with friendly foreign countries is an important tool in strengthening bilateral relations with various countries. It consists of activities undertaken by the Ministry of Defence and the armed forces to avoid hostilities, build and maintain trust and

contribute towards conflict prevention and resolution. Defence diplomacy initiatives with friendly foreign countries have been in the form of high level defence related visits, training exchanges, service to service talks, holding of joint exercises and other forms of cooperation.

The aim as enunciated above is fairly straightforward. The military confines itself to purely professional exchanges and exercises and leaves the political dimension to be handled by the MEA.

But there is much more to defence diplomacy. Several definitions of military diplomacy have been put forward. South African scholar Anton du Plessis defines it thus:

> ...The concept of 'defence diplomacy' fuses two apparently incommensurable extremes, namely violent-coercive (armed force) and pacific-persuasive (diplomatic) means to pursue policy objectives. This 'incommensurability' originates from the traditional distinction between four categories of instruments to implement foreign policy once formulated, namely political, economic, cultural (propaganda) and military techniques.... As a technique of last resort, the military instrument involves the use of military means. Although associated with coercive use of armed forces (offensive, defensive or deterrent) in a situation of war (conventional or unconventional), it also includes military approximations short of war, such as military threats, military interventions, military aid and assistance and the pacific use of the military in peace support operations.

An Indian Army Officer, Brig K Muthanna in his book, *Enabling Military-to-Military Cooperation as a Foreign Policy Tool*, lists out several activities that can be undertaken to further military diplomacy. He opines,

> Defence diplomacy serves specific national, foreign and security policy objectives. In the context of the global and regional strategic engagement, it creates sustainable cooperative relationships, thereby building trust, facilitating conflict prevention, introducing transparency into defence relations; building and reinforcing perceptions of common interests; changing the mindsets of partners and inducing cooperation in other areas. Defence diplomacy can further country specific foreign policy objectives by managing

defence foreign relations and supporting the other diplomatic initiatives of government.

Every year new recruits of the Sri Lankan Army start the young officers (YOs) course at the Indian Army's Mhow-based Infantry School along with hundreds of young Indian infantry officers. They are only a fraction of 800-plus officers from Sri Lanka's three armed forces who travel to India every year to undergo a variety of training courses in various defence establishments.

Apart from attending the YOs course at the Army War College, the Sri Lankans also train at the Military College of Electronics and Mechanical Engineering (MCEME) in southern India's Secunderabad cantonment, at the Counter-Insurgency and Jungle Warfare School (CIJW) located in India's North East, at the Indian Naval Academy based in Kerala or participate in the prestigious National Security and Strategic Studies Course at the National Defence College in New Delhi among many other military training institutions in India.

For years, the islanders formed the largest number of foreign military officers undergoing training in India before being outnumbered by the Afghans over the past four years. Since 2010, India has allotted the largest number of training vacancies to the Afghan National Army at various levels, especially in the National Defence Academy and the Indian Military Academy, meant for training young recruits in the age group of 18 to 25. From a dozen-odd officers who used to train alongside Indian recruits, the number is now in three figures. In 2014 and 2015 itself, more than 100 Afghans have trained at the IMA.

In 2015, India also gifted attack helicopters to the Afghan Army to boost its anti-Taliban capability. Fast Attack Patrol Boats to countries like Sychelles, Maldives and Fiji, Dornier aircraft to other island nations and radars to countries like Sri Lanka and Myanmar have been supplied since 2013.

India's military outreach is however not limited to the immediate neighbourhood. Officials in the Indian Defence Ministry's Planning and International Cooperation (PIC) division have broadly defined the country's neighbourhood in terms of outwardly expanding concentric circles with India at the centre. The engagement is intense in the immediate neighbourhood, followed by relations with nations located in what is called the strategic neighbourhood and finally, the military-diplomatic outreach for nation-states that are categorised as the extended neighbourhood.

So while South Asian neighbours like Afghanistan, Bhutan, Bangladesh, Nepal and Sri Lanka continue to get top priority, countries further afield like Maldives, Vietnam, Philippines, Indonesia, Laos, Thailand, Tajikistan, Kazakhstan, Mongolia, Nigeria, Kenya and Ethiopia, to name a few, are increasingly looking to India for training and expertise for its soldiers in specialist fields apart from seeking bilateral military exercises.

China, in many ways India's biggest adversary, however conducts military or defence diplomacy in a slightly different manner with the all-powerful Peoples Liberation Army (PLA) calling the shots. As a Japanese strategic thinker Yasuhiro Matsuda observed:

> China promotes military diplomacy with other countries to guide its general diplomacy strategy to win benefits for national security and to ensure that the international situation develops in directions beneficial to China. In other words, military diplomacy should probably not be viewed as ordinary diplomatic activity in the political or economic sphere but as diplomacy having strategic and military significance.

India's military on the other hand, has traditionally remained outside the decision-making loop right from early years of India's independence. There are historical reasons for this situation. The Indian military played a stellar role in both World Wars in the twentieth century, albeit under the British Raj. In the first Great War, 1.2 million Indian soldiers fought for the empire in Africa and Europe; In World War II, 2.5 million Indian soldiers were deployed from West and East Africa to South and East Asia, making it the largest all-volunteer force ever. Many Indian nationalist leaders however viewed the pre-independence Indian military as an instrument of British imperialism. India's first Prime Minister Jawaharlal Nehru, made sure that the role of the Indian military under the newly-independent India was severely restricted in the nation's affairs.

There were exceptions though. Indian military training teams were dispatched to the newly-independent African nations and Indian military officers helped set up training institutions in countries such as Ethiopia, Nigeria, Botswana and Uganda, besides countries in the Gulf, like Oman (IDSA 2013). One of the oldest Indian Military Training Team (IMTRAT) is based in Bhutan since the mid-1960s.

Old-timers recall New Delhi even had a training team in Saddam Hussein-ruled Iraq in the 1970s where Indian Army and Indian Air Force Officers trained select officers of Saddam's Baathist forces. But by and large Indian leaders followed the template set by Nehru in keeping the Indian military away from New Delhi's diplomatic outreach except in sending troops as part of UN Missions. New Delhi was an early supporter of UN Peacekeeping when it sent a contingent to India–China during the Korean War in the 1950s.

Today, India's military is among the top two providers to the UN Peacekeeping Force. And yet, the reach and influence of the Indian military was hardly used by the Indian establishment in furthering its national interest till two decades ago. Changing geostrategic equations and growing tension in Asia-Pacific region, triggered in many ways by China's stupendous rise has however led India to do a rethink on many of its old ways of conducting military diplomacy.

Data available from the Indian Navy Headquarters suggests that on an average, India has held a dozen bilateral and multilateral exercises with as diverse countries as US, UK, Japan, Thailand, Indonesia, Russia, Singapore and Myanmar for the past four years. The exercises range from search and rescue to, practising interoperability with diverse navies and even a Special Forces exercise in Guam with the US Navy. More importantly, the Indian Navy plays its role as an extended arm of military diplomacy to the hilt. Between January 2015 and March 2016 for instance Indian ships made over sixty port calls in different parts of the world—from Sydney to Dar es-Salaam and from Da Nang in Vietnam to Port Suez in Egypt These visits, ceremonial in parts, help the Navy to forge ties with forces around the globe. And these come in handy in crises. Yet India's defence diplomacy has to evolve a grand strategic vision.

The Indian military, with its long tradition, professionalism and high standards of training, has won many admirers over the world, especially in UN Peacekeeping Missions. Training stints in Indian military institutions are in huge demand among military professionals across the world. Officers from smaller countries in the neighbourhood who have attended the NDC Course in India have gone on to head their respective armed forces, giving India an unprecedented access.

The MoD has, however, not kept pace with the changing nature of military diplomacy. A group of experts assembled by the New Delhi-based Institute for

Defence Studies and Analyses (IDSA) had an occasion to remark recently in the following manner:

> One of the major shortcomings of the existing arrangement that separates the Armed Forces Headquarters from the civilian bureaucracy of the MoD in so far as interaction between the military and the foreign policy establishments is concerned, is that MoD is interposed between the two almost to the extent of being an adjudicator of the process of consultation and discussion. This is, of course, part of the larger problem of lack of integration. But in terms of optimising foreign policy options by leveraging military capacity, this arrangement imposes serious limitations.

It could not have been put more aptly and needs to be earnestly looked into for an effective and articulate defence diplomacy strategy.

At a tactical level, the Indian military has increased its bilateral engagements substantially, but the Indian government, in the past, failed to build on these gains on a strategic plain mainly because of the UPA government's inability to grasp the big picture.

The Narendra Modi government has displayed a shift from that calcified approach and has a major task ahead to reset India's defence diplomacy especially with the United States and of course the neighbourhood. Even as he goes about pulling India out of the morass that the country finds itself in internally, Narendra Modi along with *Raksha Mantri* Manohar Parrikar will have to reclaim the lost decade by not only involving the military leadership in national security architecture but also by making much more effective use of defence diplomacy in India's outreach to its neighbours, friends and adversaries alike.

CHAPTER 21

INDIA'S NSG MEMBERSHIP QUEST: COMPLETELY JUSTIFIED

Satish Chandra

India's high voltage endeavour for membership of the NSG has attracted some criticism in India consequent upon China's having foiled it at the NSG plenary meeting which concluded at Seoul on 24 June 2016.

The main points made by those critical of India's high level activism in this matter are that this was quite unnecessary as NSG membership is unimportant, particularly as in 2008 we had secured a waiver for import of nuclear fuel and civil nuclear reactors, that India will be a second-class member, and that the setback we have received is an embarrassment.

None of these arguments can sustain serious scrutiny.

India's membership of the NSG as well as other proliferation control regimes such as the MTCR, the Australia Group, and the Wassenaar Arrangement is important for many reasons. Firstly, it will demolish the myth of India being an 'outlier' to the non-proliferation regime and demonstrate that it is an integral and indispensable part of it. Secondly, it will facilitate India's trade, not merely imports but exports as well, of nuclear, missile and other related sensitive materials, equipment and technologies. Thirdly, it will raise India's stature in this critical area as it will no longer only be an adherent but also a rule-maker. Fourthly, it will enable India to ensure that these regimes function strictly as mandated for promoting non-proliferation and not stray into playing political games or hurting its commercial interests. Finally, only India's NSG membership can assure future-proofing of the waiver accorded by it in 2008 for imports of sensitive materials and equipment for our civil nuclear programme. This waiver is not irrevocable as the NSG in 2011 adopted an amendment barring exports to India of enrichment and reprocessing technologies on the ground that it is not an NPT signatory. Had India been an NSG member such an amendment could have been thwarted.

Conscious of the importance of NSG membership, India has been engaged with the NSG since 2004 and has been an adherent to its guidelines since 2008. This engagement intensified following the NSG's India-specific waiver in 2008 and from 2011, India has been discussed within the NSG at every plenary. It is in this backdrop that India formally applied for NSG membership on 12 May 2016. This issue, moreover, acquired immediacy and overriding importance as India's Intended Nationally Determined Contribution set out at Paris envisages a 40 per cent non-fossil power generation capacity by 2030 and without NSG membership this cannot be assured. Hence it was imperative that all stops be pulled out to secure NSG membership.

Though India is ineligible for trade in nuclear reprocessing and enrichment equipment because of an NSG amendment adopted in 2011, this will not diminish India's status. On the contrary, a good case can be made that India will, in fact, be a privileged member as it will be the only non-NPT state admitted on the basis of its record.

India's inability to secure membership of the NSG at the Seoul plenary despite its vigorous efforts cannot be regarded as an embarrassment as the process for admission is still in place. Indeed, some are of the view that India could secure membership by the end of the year. In any case, the question is not if but when India will become an NSG member.

It also needs to be noted that the case for India's admittance to the NSG was viewed positively by an overwhelming majority including heavyweights like USA, Russia, France, UK, Japan, Australia and Canada. If anything, the plenary reflected China's isolation as it was the only country blocking discussion on India's application. If at all others such as Austria, New Zealand and Ireland spoke, it was on the process and not against India.

In these circumstances, India's high-octane diplomacy merits commendation not condemnation. India is fortunate in having in Modi, a Prime Minister who is hands-on, who is prepared to stake his personal reputation when national interests so dictate, and who is not afraid to lead from the front. While such an approach may not necessarily guarantee immediate success, it definitely sets in motion processes that will ultimately lead to it. India's recent admission as a member of the MTCR, for which it had also battled long and hard, is an instance of one such success which can be attributed to the government's activist diplomacy which would not have come our way had we been scared of trying. Indeed, fear of failure has often, in the past, been the bane of our diplomacy and frozen it to inactivity. It is common knowledge that our loss in the 1996 election for a seat in the UN Security Council sent us into such despair that we did not dare to put our hat into the ring again until 2010. The moral of the story is that in life, as in diplomacy, success has to be earned through hard work. It does not come on a platter and accordingly fear of failure should not deter one from striving for success for otherwise it will surely elude us.

The value of the Seoul plenary rests on its having served as a reality check. It once again demonstrated China's inimical mindset *vis-à-vis* India. For openers, China blatantly and in complete disregard of the merits of the case sought to hyphenate Pakistan with India by encouraging the former to also apply for NSG membership despite the fact that unlike India, it has not separated its civil and military nuclear programmes, has not signed the Additional Protocol and has blocked progress on the FMCT negotiations, etc. When such an approach found no traction, China went on to argue that India's admittance to the NSG was problematic as the latter had not signed the NPT. This was clearly a dilatory tactic as there are no mandatory criteria for membership; only a number of factors to be considered such as non-proliferation record, commitment to NSG guidelines and export controls, proliferation benefits that are likely to accrue through accord of membership, etc. On all these counts India's credentials are excellent and in fact much better than those of China which, while enjoying all the privileges of the NPT has been a notorious proliferator. It supplied a tested nuclear weapon design to Pakistan, which found its way to Libya through AQ Khan. Similarly, it has enabled DPRK's missile and nuclear capabilities as also Iran's initial progress in uranium enrichment. While hiding behind principles and rules, China itself is in violation of the NSG's rules with regard to supply of nuclear reactors to Pakistan.

China's role at Seoul will not be without consequences. China's attempted hyphenation of Pakistan with India in blatant disregard of the merits of the case would have raised doubts in the minds of the international community on the maturity of its leadership. Its new-found love for the NPT would not have fooled anyone as it has long violated it and continues to do so to this day. Above all, Seoul showed up China for what it is—notably a hegemonic, unprincipled and ruthless player quite prepared to disregard the common good in order to achieve its narrow ends.

China's inimical approach *vis-à-vis* India at Seoul coming in the wake of its stalling action in the UN on imposition of sanctions on Masood Azhar, will inevitably have an adverse impact on India–China ties. Indian public opinion understandably regards China's obstruction of India's quest for NSG membership coupled with its tilt towards Pakistan as little short of a hostile act, particularly, as such an approach is both unjustified and unfair. If this view festers it cannot but impact negatively on Chinese exports to India as also on the broader initiatives under consideration for upgrading the bilateral relationship. Certainly, when issues of critical import to China come up like those pertaining to the South China Sea, Tibet, Taiwan, etc. the government will be hard put to take up positions supportive of China and will, in fact, be under pressure to impose costs.

CHAPTER 22

MODI AND INDIA'S CIVILISATIONAL QUEST

ANIRBAN GANGULY

SANSKRITI EVAM SABHYATA

Panchamrit has clearly emerged as the new supporting pillar of India's foreign policy under Prime Minister Narendra Modi. '*Samman*—dignity and honour; *Samvad*—greater engagement and dialogue; *Samriddhi*—shared prosperity; *Suraksha*—regional and global security; and *Sanskriti evam Sabhyata*—cultural and civilisational linkages' are the five themes. India's external strategy has discovered a dynamic vehicle to carry forward its future-oriented agenda, a vehicle that can now facilitate and symbolise its global aspirations and potentials.[1]

The last two years have witnessed some of the most dynamic outreach in each of these five areas mentioned above. Prime Minister Modi's global criss-crossing and Foreign Minister Sushma Swaraj's equally determined strategic outreach programmes have inaugurated an era of greater engagement and dialogue while formulating the vision of 'shared prosperity' especially in the context of SAARC. Modi's outreach in the IOR and the Asia-Pacific has also redefined India's approach to global and regional security. His proactive efforts to articulate a civilisational and cultural narrative has introduced a new dimension that has the capacity to remap India's civilisational footprints in Asia

---

[1] Ganguly, Anirban, '*From Panchsheel to Panchamrit*', SPMRF Paper, April 2015: available at: http://spmrf. org/Articles/From%20Panchsheel%20to%20Panchamrit.pdf (April 2016).

and beyond. It would thus be worthwhile to examine in some measure the *Sabhyata-Sanskriti*—civilisational linkages.

One could begin with Modi's engagement with Japan, one of India's pre-eminent civilisational allies in the East. In his message broadcast to the international conference on Asian Values and Democracy in Tokyo on 19 January 2016, Modi made some profound observations reflecting a deeper and sustaining approach to life and living that is essentially based on the Indic approach to the world and the philosophy of creation:

> All Asian civilisations, Indic, Shinto or Dao, had a common value system which could avoid conflicts among humans and between humans and nature. That common value system recognises, accepts and even celebrates diversity among humans. This is what leads to conflict avoidance as it is founded on harmony in diversity. Conflict avoidance based on harmonising the diversity of humans is inherent in Asian democracy as its basic value.[2]

'Asian unity', Modi told his Japanese audience, was envisioned by Indian thinkers like Sri Aurobindo, Swami Vivekananda and Rabindranath Tagore, as reflecting such a higher unity. Prime Minister Shinzo Abe took a keen interest in this conference and in his address articulated the civilisational connect, when he said, recalling his visit to Varanasi:

> I knew that Varanasi was among the most sacred places, and while observing the ceremony, one thought after another struck me...
> I was dazzled at the bottomless depths of history connecting both ends of Asia. Be it loving kindness, benevolence, fraternity or harmony, I believe that in Asia, there extends an underground rootstock of thinking that supports democracy and values freedom and human rights.[3]

In essence, the two civilisations, through a reaching out of minds, philosophies and cultural fundamentals were restating new terms of engagement

---

[2] 'Asia is bustling with energy, enthusiasm & exuberance, driven by dynamism of a youthful population that is constantly innovating: PM Modi', avaialble at: http://www.narendramodi.in/transcription-of-video-message-of-hon-ble-prime-minister-of-india-shri-narendra-modi-for-the-tokyo-meet-on-january-19-2016-400246 (April 2016).

[3] Address by Prime Minister Shinzo Abe at the 'Shared Values and Democracy in Asia' Symposium, available at: http://www.mofa.go.jp/s_sa/sw/page3e_000452.html (April 2016).

and of expression—a new civilisational strategy. Historically, Japan had fascinated Swami Vivekananda, who insisted that the youth of India ought to visit that country at least once in their lifetime in order to imbibe its energy and determination. The Japanese, he had then said, 'seem to have fully awakened themselves to the necessity of the present times.'

The foundation for this civilisational outreach and soft power engagement was initiated in August 2014 when Modi visited Japan on his first ever stand-alone bilateral engagement. While trade, economy and security issues were the dominant themes, the overarching symbolism of the civilisational connect was unmistakably imprinted. The visit was one of the first expressions of how Modi would use the crucial instrument of *Sanskriti evam Sabhyata*. His inaugurating the Vivekananda Cultural Centre in Tokyo was indicative of the importance attached to re-laying the India–Japan civilisational connect.[4]

SAMVAD

It was in September 2015 that Modi initiated a wide and intricate outreach to countries that have been shaped by the ideals and legacy of Buddha. The January 2016 Tokyo conference on Asian Values and Democracy was a sequel to this first outreach. Through an international initiative on the theme of 'Samvad—Hindu-Buddhist Initiative for Conflict Avoidance and Environment Consciousness', hosted by the Vivekananda International Foundation, India stated the aspiration to work for regional stability, prosperity and harmony based on the ancient Indic wisdom to avoid conflict and to re-establish the balance between nature and mankind. As Modi described it, the conference, 'was conceptualised on shifting the paradigm from conflict resolution to conflict avoidance and from environmental regulation to environmental consciousness.'[5]

It was in this conference that Modi first talked of 'climate justice'. He said:

> I want to say that we, the present generation, have the responsibility
> to act as a trustee of the rich natural wealth for the future generations.

---

[4] See Ganguly, Anirban, 'Modi's Japan Visit: Restructuring a Civilisational Agenda', Rediff.com, 30 August 2014.

[5] Text of PM's Address at Mahabodhi Temple at Bodh Gaya, available at: http://pib.nic.in/newsite/PrintRelease.aspx?relid=126653 (April 2016).

The issue is not merely about climate change; it is about climate justice. Again I repeat it is not the issue of climate change, it is about climate justice. In my view, the most adversely affected by climate change are the poor and the downtrodden.[6]

On the need for *Samvad*, Modi argued that the Indic wisdom—Hindu and Buddhist—could evolve a new mechanism of conflict-avoidance,

> Promotion of dialogue calls for a shift from ideological approach to a philosophic one. Without proper dialogue, neither of the two themes of conflict avoidance is possible, or workable. The severe limitations in our conflict resolution mechanisms are becoming more and more obvious. We need significant, collective and strategic efforts to prevent bloodshed and violence. It is, thus, no surprise that the world is taking note of Buddhism... We need to sow the seeds of a conflict-free world, and in this endeavour faiths of Buddhism and Hinduism have a great contribution.[7]

This conference thus ideated the theme and objective of reaching out to the entire Southeast Asian region through the message of Buddha and the Indic philosophical corpus which had attracted this region over millennia and had enhanced its engagement with civilisational India. In fact Prime Minister Modi clearly saw, 'that without embracing the path and ideals shown by Gautam Buddha, this century cannot be an Asian century!'[8]

BODH GAYA: CENTRE OF WORLD BUDDHISM

In order to take the outreach further, Modi joined the entire international assemblage of thinkers, philosophers, monks, diplomats and practitioners in Bodh Gaya, meditated with them under the sacred Bodhi Tree and reiterated India's timeless message of dialogue, harmonious living and reverence for nature. In his valedictory address before the international gathering, Modi made a few significant points which need reiteration because these are closely identified with India's soft power goals or civilisational belief.

---

[6] PM's Address at 'Samvad'–Global Hindu-Buddhist Initiative on Conflict Avoidance & Environment Consciousness, 3 September 2015, available at: http://www.narendramodi.in/text-of-pm-s-address-at-samvad-global-hindu-buddhist-initiative-on-conflict-avoidance-and-environment-consciousness-290614 (April 2016).

[7] Ibid.

[8] Ibid.

On the issue of conflicts—most of which are being driven by religious intolerance—the participants in the conference seem to have agreed that while there is no problem about the freedom to practise one's religion, it is when the radical elements try to force their own ideologies on others, that the potential for conflict arises. On the issue of environment, the conference seems to have agreed that the philosophic underpinning of the Dharma, which stresses the protection of natural heritage, is critical for sustainable development.[9]

But perhaps the most significant aspect of this entire soft exercise was the release of the Bodh Gaya Declaration.[10] Bodh Gaya was declared as the 'seat of enlightenment for the world of Buddhism and Buddhist civilisation that have inspired all religions of the world.' The declaration, with the Prime Minister's sanction, said, 'A Buddhist spiritual and civilisational institution that will bring together and make the entire Buddhist world participate in this momentous task will be built in Bodh Gaya in the coming three years'; that 'Hindu civilisational and spiritual institutions will be invited to work with this new Buddhist institution to share the responsibility for global peace and harmony'; that 'Buddhist spiritual leaders will approach governments of all Buddhist nations to support this monumental and noble task of developing Bodh Gaya as an international centre of Buddhism for the enlightenment of all humankind' and called upon India to provide support for creating such a vibrant centre of civilisational cooperation.

The initiative thus is an expression of the innovation that has permeated India's soft power engagement and diplomacy ever since Modi took over. India's objective in these two intervening years has been to activate its past civilisational linkages and to restate and restructure them to the exigencies of the present where India seeks to pursue a pragmatic foreign policy of multi-alignment, multi-engagement and assertive alliances.

MONGOLIA & THE BODHI TREE SAPLING

Prime Minister Modi's visit to Mongolia in May 2015 was another landmark and demonstrated how India was keen to rekindle and reinvent its

---

[9] Text of PM's Address at Mahabodhi Temple at Bodh Gaya, available at: http://pib.nic.in/newsite/PrintRelease. aspx?relid=126653 (April 2016).

[10] Available at: http://ibcworld.org (April 2016).

civilisational linkages. The Mongolians' reverence and fascination with Buddha's homeland and its representatives has never faded, and one saw its most dynamic and multifaceted expression when the country as a whole geared up to welcome for the first time in six decades, an Indian Prime Minister. Modi, on his part, not only spoke in civilisational terms of the India–Mongolia bond, but also aspired to work out a contemporary dimension that would base itself on that age-old foundation of cultural exchange and assimilation.

While the Mongolian Prime Minister welcomed Modi by terming India a spiritual neighbour, Prime Minister Modi reciprocated by saying that Mongolia was 'integral to India's Act East Policy'. This was an astute expression of purpose and deep civilisational message indicating the shift in India's perception—of actively engaging its civilisational partners in a new paradigm and framework of partnership.

Seen from such a perspective, Modi's Mongolia visit reinforced in the national consciousness, the urge to reinvent India's civilisational linkages. Mongolia, for most Indians was a far-off, inaccessible, arid and cold landlocked country. Modi's visit has changed the perception for good. Visiting the legendary Gandan Monastery and presenting the Bodhi Tree sapling to the venerated Hamba Lama, in fact, symbolised the new direction that the India–Mongolia relations were aspiring to take.

Agreement to cooperate in areas of national security, cyber security, renewable energy, education, culture, etc. and the urge to upgrade the relationship to that of a multidimensional strategic partnership shall emerge as the vital sustaining pillars of this relationship. In the course of a single day, as Modi remarked, 'we have imparted our ancient relations new strength and momentum'.[11]

YOGA IN THE TEMPLE OF HEAVEN

In the same month of May 2015, Prime Minister Modi visited China, beginning his journey in the historic province of Xian which had been home to the Xuanzang, the monk who had travelled to India in the seventh century in search of the light of knowledge. Xuanzang remains the symbol of India's civilisational link with China. Modi's visit to the terracotta warrior's museum, the hosting of the Yoga and Tai Chi show at the Temple of Heaven in Beijing signified India's seriousness in trying to reach out to China. But perhaps what set the

[11] Ganguly, Anirban, *'Modi in Mongolia: Rekindling the Civilisational Link'*, New World India, 18 May 2015.

template of India–China engagement for the next decade and more was Modi's historic speech at the Tsinghua University where he essentially articulated a new framework and contour for engagement that these two Asian powers could look at or experiment with. Modi pointed out how 'the centuries-old story of our relations has been of spiritualism, learning, art and trade. It is a picture of respect for each other's civilisation and of shared prosperity' and how the 'most significant change of this era is the re-emergence of China and India.'[12]

Interestingly Modi spoke of the resurgence of Asia through the rise of many powers and of how in an era of increasing 'inter-dependence', the talk of 'alliance against one another' had no foundation.[13] His emphasis for building a new twenty-first century partnership between the Asian giants was on the civilisational platform, 'we are both ancient civilisations, large and independent nations. Neither of us can be contained or become part of anyone's plans. So, our partnership in international forums should not be determined by the concerns of others, but the interests of our two countries.'[14]

The civilisational dimension thus appears to be the hallmark of India's foreign policy since the summer of 2014.

CENTRAL ASIA: CENTRAL TO CIVILISATIONAL INDIA

Central Asia, which has always been central to civilisational India—central to the spread of its cultural and spiritual ideals and expressions—was at the centre with Modi undertaking a tour of the five countries in the region. Such a multidimensional visit was, in a sense, a reiteration of his vision of evolving and reshaping India's external outreach inspired by, as argued earlier, the pillars of *samvaad, sanskriti* and *sabhyata* (dialogue, culture and civilisation).

Addressing Indologists and a section of the intelligentsia in Tashkent—perhaps the first by an Indian Prime Minister—Modi emphasised the importance of the cultural ideals and values. The joint statement in Uzbekistan recognised that 'shared historical and cultural links between the two countries over the centuries provide a firm basis for the development of the contemporary India–Uzbekistan relations.'

---

[12] Text of the Address by Prime Minister at the Tsinguah University, Beijing, available at: http://www.narendramodi.in/text-of-address-by-prime-minister-at-the-tsinghua-university-beijing-66239 (April 2016).
[13] Ibid.
[14] Ibid.

While the focus was also on trade, energy and security cooperation in the region, the importance of the civilisational linkages cannot be missed. A cultural strategy is being consciously evolved and weaved instead of relegating culture, as it had hitherto been, simply to the realm of entertainment.

While trade has traditionally dominated civilisational India's linkages with the West, its relations and contacts with the countries to its north, east and southeast were mainly cultural. Historian of civilisations, DP Singhal, for example, argues that 'commerce may have initiated contact but it was soon outpaced by culture'. India's finest 'contributions to the human civilisation', observed Singhal, 'lie in Central Asia, East Asia and Southeast Asia and whatever the sum total of the Indian influences on the Western civilisation, there is no doubt that ancient India was the radiating centre of a civilisation which left a deep mark on the greater part of Asia.'[15] The Buddhist influence in Central Asia and beyond has deeply shaped and moulded the region. The spread of Buddhism in the region, in fact, acted as a 'catalyst' helping different societies to bring out their 'dormant strengths and to release their creative energies.'

When Modi, in his address to Indologists in Tashkent, referred in some detail to the similarities of languages from the region to the languages of India, he was drawing attention to the deep penetration and intermingling of civilisational India. The queen was referred to as *devi*, while the prince was addressed as *maharaya-putra*, and the ambassador was designated as *duta* or *dutiya*. Archaeologist Aurel Stein's (1862-1943) discovery of the Kharosthi documents revealed the influence that Hindu social terms had on the people and systems of the region. *Purusa* (male), *pitu* or *pita* for father, *matu* or *madu* for mother, *putra* or *suta* for son, *pitumaha* for grandfather, *bhrata* or *bhratu* for brother were some of the common Hindu words used. The region had remarkable variety and formed a mingling point of civilisations, ideas, languages and expressions. Among these, Buddhism was the 'most popular' and 'Central Asian' cultural life was dominated for about thousand years by the Indian religion, literature, arts and sciences.

In the current evolving geopolitical arrangement where India aspires, and is working hard to emerge as a defining pole in an increasingly multi-polar world, Modi's Central Asia foray has assumed civilisational significance. His visit to

---

[15] Singhal, DP, *India and World Civilisation*, Vols. 1& 2, (1969), 1993.

this region has not only rekindled the past partnership but also seeks to evolve a present cooperative framework that will be not only mutually beneficent in terms of trade, commerce and energy security but also to evolve a determined web that would arrest the growth of extremism in the region.

INDIA'S MESSAGE OF TRUE PARTNERSHIP

India's message and approach to the civilisations of the world has been one of true partnership, of non-exploitation, respect for and enrichment of diversities and the perpetuation of essential civilisational identities and world views.

Prime Minister Modi's thrust through India's soft power and civilisational experience in the past two years, has essentially been a reiteration of that timeless message. It has reinforced and percolated the image of India as a responsible rising power that seeks to lead through the strength of its ageless wisdom that had once radiated across most of the civilised world.

INDEX

EDITORS

Dr Anirban Ganguly is Director of Dr Syama Prasad Mookerjee Research Foundation (SPMRF), a New Delhi based think-tank. He is also a scholar of civilisation, history, politics and culture and a Member of the Central Advisory Board of Education (CABE), MHRD. He is also Member of the National Advisory Committee for setting up the Jaya Prakash Narayan Centre for Excellence in Humanities. Dr Ganguly is also Member of the Indian Council for Cultural Relations' (ICCR) Performance Audit Committee, set up to review the functioning of ICCR's Chairs of Indian Studies in foreign universities and ICCR's Cultural Centres in Indian Missions abroad. He is a Member of the Policy Research Department and Library & Documentation Department of the Bharatiya Janata Party (BJP). Dr Ganguly had his early education at Sri Aurobindo International Centre of Education, Sri Aurobindo Ashram, Puducherry where he spent twenty formative years. He successfully defended his doctoral thesis from the leading Jadavpur University, Kolkata on the early nationalist education movement in India. Between 2010 and 2013, he was Research Fellow at Vivekananda International Foundation, New Delhi, where he focused on studying India's neighbourhood, Indian nationalism, the Indian nationalist movement and civilisational issues. Dr Ganguly regularly lectures in various leading universities and institutions across the country. He has authored/edited *Redefining Governance: Essays on 1 year of Narendra Modi Government* (New Delhi, 2015), *Swami Vivekananda–Buddha & Buddhism: a Mystic Link* (Kolkata, 2014), Debating Culture (New Delhi, 2013), *Education: Philosophy & Practice* (New Delhi, 2011) He has also authored numerous papers, chapters and monographs on civilisational issues, political, educational and cultural issues. He is also a Visiting Faculty at Banaras Hindu University (BHU). Dr Ganguly writes regular columns for the *New Indian Express*, *The Daily Pioneer* and also has a blog with *The Times of India* called, 'The Other View'.

Dr Vijay Chauthaiwale is In-charge, Department of Foreign Affairs, Bharatiya Janata Party (BJP), since November 2014. In this role, he is coordinating with Indian diaspora worldwide through BJP's global outreach platform, Overseas Friends of BJP (OFBJP). OFBJP has chapters in more than forty countries which are comprised of well-wishers of BJP. Interaction with Indian diaspora has been an essential component of overseas visits of Prime Minister Modi. Vijay is actively involved in coordinating community receptions for PM Modi across the globe. Additionally, he interacts with foreign embassies, diplomats and delegates of various countries to put forward party perspective on issues of mutual interests. Before joining active politics, he worked in senior management role in pharmaceutical research and development for eighteen years, his last role being Vice President (Discovery Research) in Torrent Pharmaceuticals Ltd, Ahmedabad, India. His main expertise is new drug discovery and R&D portfolio management. He has attended executive management program at Indian Institute of Management, Bangalore and leadership development program at London Business School. Author of several peer-reviewed scientific papers and inventor of several global patents, he has also served on the Board of Studies of Indian universities.

Dr Uttam Kumar Sinha is a Fellow at Institute for Defence Studies and Analyses (IDSA) and holds an adjunct position at the Malaviya Centre for Peace Research, Benares Hindu University. At IDSA, he is also the Managing Editor of *Strategic Analysis*. His research areas focus on climate change, transboundary water issues and the Arctic region. He was a Chevening Scholar at the LSE in 2008; and in 2015 at the Harvard Kennedy School on a South Asia Leaders Programme. He is actively engaged in Track II dialogue process and was India's representative to the CSCAP Working Group on Water Resources Security. He also chaired the Working Group on Water Dispute Resolution Mechanism of the Strategic Studies Network, National Defense University (NDU) Washington DC. After receiving doctorate from Jawaharlal Nehru University, he worked in the daily *Pioneer* before joining IDSA. He is the author of the book *Riverine Neighbourhood: Hydropolitics in South Asia* (2016). Some of his recent edited volumes include, *Non-Traditional Security Challenges in Asia: Approaches and Responses*; *Arctic: Commerce, Governance and Policy*; *Emerging Strategic Trends in Asia*.

CONTRIBUTORS

Cleo Paskal is Associate Fellow at Chatham House, the Royal Institute of International Affairs, London, UK, Visiting Trudeau Fellow at the Centre d'études et de recherché internationales de l'Université de Montréal, Canada and Adjunct Faculty in the Department of Geopolitics, Manipal University, India. She has given talks at, among many others places, the National Defence College (India), United Services Institute (India), Institute for Defence Studies and Analyses (India), US Army War College, the Royal College of Defence Studies (UK) and the National Defence College (Oman). She has contributed to many academic publications and her book *Global Warring: How Environmental, Economic, and Political Crises Will Redraw the World Map* won multiple awards. Her most recent book is the bestselling *Spielball Erde.*

Ramesh Thakur is Director of the Centre for Nuclear Non-Proliferation and Disarmament and Professor in the Crawford School of Public Policy, Australian National University. He was formerly Senior Vice-Rector of the UN University and Assistant-Secretary General of the United Nations. He has been a Consultant/Advisor to the Australian and New Zealand Governments on international security. He was a commissioner and a principal author of *The Responsibility to Protect* and the principal writer of Secretary-General Kofi Annan's second reform report. The author/editor of fifty books and 400 articles and book chapters, Thakur is also a regular media commentator, serves on the international advisory boards of institutes in Africa, Asia, Europe and North America, and is the Editor-in-Chief of *Global Governance.*

Sreeram Chaulia is Professor and Executive Director of the Centre for Global Governance and Policy (CGGP) at the OP Jindal Global University. Chaulia's areas of specialisation include diplomacy, foreign policy, comparative politics, international political economy, international organisations, armed conflict, humanitarian practices and contemporary world history. He holds a doctorate from Syracuse University, USA and has studied at the LSE, University of Oxford and at St Stephen's College. He is a prolific writer and is the author of a number of books. His latest book is *Politics of the Global Economic Crisis: Regulation, Responsibility and Radicalism* (2013).

Ashok Malik is a Distinguished Fellow and Head of ORF's Neighbourhood Regional Studies Initiative. His work focuses on Indian domestic politics and foreign/trade policy, and their increasing interplay, as well as on the broader process of globalisation and how it is influencing policy choices in not just the economy but in social sector spheres such as health, education and urbanisation. A journalist for twenty years, Malik is a columnist for several leading Indian and international publications (such as *The Times of India, Hindustan Times*, YaleGlobal Online). He is the author of the book *India: Spirit of Enterprise.*

Lisa Curtis is a Senior Research Fellow at the Heritage Foundation. Her research centres on the US–India strategic and defence partnership, US counterterrorism policies in

Afghanistan and Pakistan, and trends in Islamist extremism and has often testified before Congress on these topics. Before joining Heritage in August 2006, Curtis worked for the US government on South Asian issues. She was a member of the professional staff of the Senate Foreign Relations Committee (2003-6) and was the White House-appointed senior Advisor to the Assistant Secretary of State for South Asian affairs (2001-3). Before that, she worked as an analyst for the CIA and, in the mid-1990s, served as a diplomat in the US embassies in Pakistan and India. Curtis regularly travels to the South Asia region and has contributed chapters to books and academic journals.

Tariq A Karim is the immediate past High Commissioner of Bangladesh to India, with the rank and status of a Minister of State of Bangladesh (2009-14). Currently a Distinguished Fellow at the Vivekananda International Foundation in New Delhi, he is concurrently also Advisor to the World Bank on their South Asian Regional Economic Integration programme. As a career diplomat he held numerous key assignments at home and abroad. He was entrusted with a critically important role in finalising the negotiations that resulted in the signing of the landmark Ganges Water Sharing Treaty with India in 1996. Karim was also successful in initiating the process for embarking on subregional cooperation encompassing water management on a basin-wide configuration, joint hydroelectric power generation with Bangladesh, Bhutan, India and Nepal as partners in development, and promoting connectivity and trade.

Karan Bilimoria is an Indian entrepreneur, immigrant to Britain and a life peer. Karan was appointed as a Deputy Lieutenant for Greater London in 2001 and was granted a Commander of the Order of the British Empire (CBE) in the 2004 Birthday Honours for his services to business and entrepreneurship. In 2005 Lord Bilimoria helped to establish the Cobra Foundation, an independent charity that provides health, education and community support for young people in South Asia. In 2006, he was appointed an Independent Life Peer in the House of Lords and in 2014, he was installed as the seventh Chancellor of the University of Birmingham.

Asanga Abeyagoonasekera is a columnist, commentator and author. He is Advisor to the Minister of Finance, Sri Lanka. Asanga has more than a decade of experience in government, serving as the head of several government institutions to positions at the board level. He is the former Advisor to Minister of External Affairs and the Executive Director of the prestigious government think-tank, Lakshman Kadirgamar Institute (LKIIRSS). He was appointed Country Chair by Crown Prince of Norway to conduct the Global Dignity programme in Sri Lanka. He was recognised as a Young Global Leader for the World Economic Forum and was awarded Ambassador of Knowledge accolade along with Dr Edward de Bono in Slovenia. He is the author of *Towards a better world order* (2015).

Hari Bansh Jha is Executive Director of Centre for Economic and Technical Studies (CETS), a research organisation in Kathmandu. Currently he is Visiting Scholar at Indian Council of World Affairs, New Delhi. He was Professor of Economics at Nepal's Tribhuvan University (1976-98). In 2013, he was Visiting Professor at Chengdu American Centre for Study Abroad, Sichuan University. He was also senior ICCR Fellow at IDSA, New Delhi (2011-12). His areas of interest include India–Nepal, China and South Asian affairs. He worked on diverse issues related to strategic, border problems, conflict and peace, international migration, child labour, human trafficking and Madhesh region of Nepal. He has to his credit a number of authored/edited books.

Shakti Sinha is a Director at India Foundation, New Delhi. He was a member of the Indian Administrative Service (1979-2013). He held positions at different levels at the federal, provincial and local, including as Private Secretary/Joint Secretary to Prime Minister (Vajpayee), Head of Delhi's power utility, Finance Secretary in Delhi provincial government, Chief Secretary of the Andaman & Nicobar Administration, Chief Secretary of Goa among others. Internationally, he headed the United Nation's Governance & Development team in Afghanistan (2006-9) coordinating donor support to the Afghan government, and was earlier Senior Advisor to Executive Director on the World Bank board (2000-4). Sinha has worked at think-tanks in India (Observer Research Foundation) and Singapore (Institute of South Asian Studies) and has written extensively on political economy of India, Indian foreign policy and strategic affairs.

Shahab Enam Khan currently serves as the Chairman and Associate Professor at the Department of International Relations, Jahangirnagar University, Bangladesh. He is also a Research Director at the Bangladesh Enterprise Institute. He has drafted several key public policy documents including the 'National Broadcasting Policy 2014' and the 'Counter Terrorism Strategy' paper that was prepared in consultation with various government stakeholders in Bangladesh. He has served as Advisor and/or Senior Consultant to the government of Bangladesh and various international organisations and is also a Member of the International Research Committee of the Regional Center for Strategic Studies, Sri Lanka.

Takenori Horimoto specialises in International Politics of Asia and South Asia. Currently he is Visiting Professor of Open University and Gifu Women's University. His earlier affiliation included the Graduate School of Asian and African Area Studies,

Kyoto University. He was also Professor of Contemporary South Asian Politics and US Asian Policy at Shobi University. He has authored and edited several books including *India: The Big Elephant Globalizes*, Iwanami Shoten (2007) (Japanese); (co-ed) *India as a Rising Military Power*, Askishobo (2010) (Japanese); (co-ed) *Contemporary South Asian Politics* (Japanese); (co-ed) *India-Japan Relations in Emerging Asia* (English).

Christian Wagner is Senior Fellow at the leading German think-tank, Institute for International and Security Affairs (SWP) in Berlin. He was Member of the board of directors of the German Association for Asian Studies until 2012. He studied Political Science, History and Sociology at the University of Freiburg. After various positions at the universities of Freiburg and Mainz he joined the Centre for Modern Oriental Studies in Berlin in 1994/95. From 1996 to 2001 he was Assistant Professor for Political Science at Rostock University where he submitted his habilitation on 'India's quest for Great Power Status'.

Gaurav Sharma is the recipient of the German Chancellor Fellowship for year 2015-16, by the Alexander von-Humboldt Foundation. He is currently a Visiting Fellow at the German Institute for International and Security Affairs (SWP), Asia Division in Berlin. Gaurav was the Political Advisor at the Embassy of the Federal Republic of Germany, New Delhi (2012-15) and earlier worked at the Centre for Land Warfare Studies (CLAWS), New Delhi. He studied at the Geneva Centre for Security Policy (GCSP) and did his Masters in 2011.

P Stobdan is a distinguished academician, diplomat, author and foreign policy expert. He is currently a Senior Fellow at the IDSA, New Delhi. He has been India's Ambassador Extraordinary and Plenipotentiary to the Republic of Kyrgyzstan until recently. Ambassador Stobdan has earlier served in the National Security Council Secretariat (NSCS). He also served as Director of the Centre for Strategic Studies in Jammu & Kashmir. He is the Founding President of Ladakh International Centre, Leh. He is also a leading columnist for *Indian Express* and other national dailies in India.

Gonchig Ganbold is Ambassador of Mongolia in India. He studied in Ulaanbaatar, New Delhi, Moscow, Oxford, Geneva, Hawaii and Munich. Ambassador Ganbold joined the Ministry of Foreign Affairs (MFA) of Mongolia in 1980 and served as Desk officer, Counsellor, Deputy Head and Head of Departments, worked at Mongolia Embassies in New Delhi (1988-91,1996-2000 and since August 2015), Washington DC and London as well as Ministry of Finance and National Security Council, Mongolia. He is well versed in Hindi, English and Russian. He has translated over dozen books.

Mukul Asher is Professorial Fellow at the Lee Kuan Yew School of Public Policy, Singapore. He is also Director, Public Policy, Global Village Foundation and Fellow at Dr Syama Prasad Mookerjee Research Foundation (SPMRF), New Delhi. He specialises in public sector economics and social security issues in Asia. He has published extensively in international journals and has authored and edited several books. He has been a Consultant to the World Bank, International Monetary Fund, World Health Organization, Asian Development Bank, Organization for Economic Cooperation and Development and other institutions. He has interacted with policymakers as a resource person in several Asian countries such as India, Indonesia, Vietnam, People's Republic of China and Sri Lanka. He is on the Editorial Board of *International Social Security Review*, a leading journal in the field. He teaches Applied Public Sector Economics and Economic Reasoning For Public Policy.

Martin Grambow is a water-administrator, living and working in Bavaria. He is Director General, Water and Soil at the Ministry of Environment and Consumer Protection in Munich, Bavaria. Grambow graduated in Civil Engineering and achieved his doctor's degree in 2005. In 1998 he established the governmental project 'Technology Transfer Water'. In this framework, he supports international projects of institutions like the World Bank, the European Union or UNECE. He maintains professional partnerships with water-administisators and scientists globally including in Central Asia and China. Grambow is member of several institutions and foundations, in particular the Institute for Advanced Studies on Sustainability, the International Expert Group on Earth System Preservation (IESP), and the Bavarian Water Foundation. He is author of several books and articles on water management.

Hans-Dietrich Uhl works on water-related topics. He has held different positions within the governmental water administration and currently is Desk Officer for waste water treatment at the Ministry of Environment and Consumer Protection in Bavaria. Uhl studied Civil Engineering and has an additional degree in Environmental Management. Uhl gained a holistic view of water management issues not only from his professional work but also from extensive private watersport activities. He also contributed as an expert to several high-ranking bodies and committee on Water Resource Management, e.g. an EU-COM Expert Advisory Forum or the German Laender-Working group on Waste Water.

Virendra Gupta retired from the Indian Foreign Service recently. During thirty-seven years in the diplomatic career he served as India's Ambassador in many countries including South Africa. In 2007, he set up and headed the new Energy Security

Division in the Ministry of External Affairs. He was the Director General of Indian Council of Cultural Relations (ICCR) and served as Deputy Director General of the IDSA, 2006-7.

Manoj Ladwa is the CEO of India Inc, a media organisation which includes brands such as India Investment Journal and India Investment Conclaves. Ladwa served as Communications Director for the hugely successful 'Narendra Modi for Prime Minister' campaign. He has interests in India-focused advisory services, corporate affairs, online and print publishing, and corporate events. Ladwa is a recognised expert on foreign direct investments into India. In 2003, he established the London office of the Federation of Indian Chambers of Commerce and Industry and has served on various trade promotion committees, including those of UKTI and London Chamber of Commerce. Ladwa is a graduate of the London School of Economics. He is dual qualified as an English solicitor (non-practising) and Indian advocate.

Nitin A Gokhale is a senior journalist and national security analyst. He was NDTV's Security and Strategic Affairs Editor till December 2014. In his reporting career, Gokhale has covered the Kargil, the Eelam War in Sri Lanka and different insurgencies from Kashmir to the North East to the Maoist-inflicted areas. He also focuses on India–China relations and higher defence management issues. He regularly lectures at the National Defence College, The Army War College and the Defence Services Staff College.

Satish Chandra joined the Indian Foreign Service in 1965 and till 1989 was posted in various capacities in Indian missions in Vienna, Karachi, Washington DC, Algiers and Dhaka as well as at headquarters. Subsequently, he served as India's Ambassador to the Philippines (1989-1992), its Permanent Representative to the UN Offices in Geneva (1992-1995) and its High Commissioner to Pakistan (1995-1998). He set up the National Security Council Secretariat (NSCS) in 1999 and headed it as Secretary till demission from office in February 2005 concurrently holding the post of Deputy National Security Advisor from February 2002. Apart from representing India at a variety of multilateral for a such as the IAEA, WHO, ILO, the UN Human Rights Commission, the Disarmament Commission, etc, he served as the President of the Conference on Disarmament during his assignment in Geneva. He was President of the Association of Indian Diplomats in 2010. He is currently Dean, Centre for National Security and Strategic Studies, Vivekananda International Foundation.